Let's Make Some Noise

Let's Make Some Noise

Axé and the African Roots of
Brazilian Popular Music

Clarence Bernard Henry

University Press of Mississippi

Jackson

www.upress.state.ms.us

The University Press of Mississippi is a member of the Association of American University Presses.

First printing 2008
∞
Library of Congress Cataloging-in-Publication Data

Henry, Clarence Bernard.
    Let's make some noise : axé and the African roots of Brazilian popular music / Clarence Bernard Henry.
        p. cm.
    Includes bibliographical references and index.
    ISBN 978-1-60473-082-1 (cloth : alk. paper) 1. Popular music—Brazil—African influences. 2. Candomblé music—History and criticism. I. Title.
    ML3487.B7H46 2008
    781.64089′96981—dc22

                                                    2008004436

British Library Cataloging-in-Publication Data available

To my mother, a woman of great love, faith, and spirituality

Contents

List of Photographs and Music Examples

Photographs

Music Examples

Acknowledgments

In writing this book I have had many different types of experiences. Writing this book was similar to completing a work of art where over different periods of time and experiences the creative process took its course and directions. Many people, places, and experiences inspired the course and directions of this book. I am extremely grateful to all of my black brothers and sisters in Brazil, West Africa, and the African diaspora who gave of their time and shared their talents and experiences to help make the writing of this book such an enriching opportunity. I am also extremely grateful to my entire family, church congregations, peer reviewers, Piers Armstrong, Sanford P. Dumain, and all of my friends at Milberg Weiss, LLP, for the many years of prayers, support, and encouragement.

I believe that every student should have in his/her educational experience a professor such as Maxine Greene who was one of my mentors during my early years of graduate study at Columbia University. Greene inspired my aesthetic imagination beyond the written pages of academic literature to explore the value, philosophy, knowledge, and beauty of people and cultures throughout the world. With this inspiration I was eager to pursue doctoral studies in ethnomusicology at UCLA. On the doctoral level my aesthetic imagination was also inspired by the mentorship of Jacqueline Codgell DjeDje, Steven Joseph Loza, Cheryl L. Keyes, and Randal Johnson that guided my initial research of Afro-Brazilian religion, music, and culture. To these scholars I have much respect and gratitude.

To Chancellor Robert Hemenway and Professors Sherrie Tucker, Anita Herzfeld, Dorthy Pennington, Barbara Ballard, and Daniel Politoske of the University of Kansas I will always consider friends and colleagues who have often encouraged my research and projects in many difficult times and experiences. I deeply acknowledge all of my students and communities at UCLA, Indiana State University, and the University of Kansas that have inspired me to excel at the highest levels of academic teaching and research. Finally, I extend my sincere gratitude to these universities for providing me with the much-needed financial resources for my research in Brazil, West Africa, and the African diaspora. Without such resources I do not believe that the contents of this book would be as rich and informative.

Let's Make Some Noise

Introduction

WHEN I BEGAN my inquiry in 1998, I was interested in conducting multidimensional research to understand the significance of "blackness" and how people of African descent continue to reinvent and reinterpret African religious, musical, and dance traditions in the sociocultural and sociopolitical frameworks of contemporary Brazilian culture. I was fortunate to travel to parts of West Africa and African diaspora areas to experience for myself the variety of African religious and musical traditions. I wanted to explore how Brazil continues to be linked with Africa through the expressions, manifested in Afro-Brazilian culture, of Candomblé religion and musical styles such as samba, samba-reggae, ijexá, and axé. With this experience I believe I have a clearer understanding of how Brazil, West Africa, and other African diasporic areas have responded to remnants of Africanisms and colonialism, resulting in environmental, social, and cultural distinction. In conducting my research I found that what continues to link Brazil with West Africa and other African diasporic areas is a sacred/secular connection and widespread belief in a power/creative energy source that many Brazilians refer to as *axé*.[1]

Axé is an endearing term linked with Afro-Brazilian cultural traditions, black expression, and local identity in Salvador, Bahia, Brazil. This term has a sacred/secular connection that stems from *àsé*, the West African Yoruba concept that was spread to Brazil and throughout the African diaspora. Àsé is imagined as power and creative energy that are bestowed upon human beings by ancestral spirits who act as guardians. This power and creative energy are found within both the sacred and secular realms, which often interact with each other. Àsé is similar to a charge or boost of energy that moves like an electrical current. In the sacred realm àsé is generated in special ceremonies in which participants communicate with the ancestral spirits. During these ceremonies, spirit possession and artistic expressions of music (singing and drumming) and dance are important sources for creating and increasing àsé energy. Many participants believe that àsé creative energy is vital in helping people accomplish their goals in the secular (that is, the real) world. Furthermore, concepts and philosophical principles surrounding the power and creative energy of àsé are embodied in several types of expressions and experiences: spirituality, artistic talent, wisdom and knowledge, perseverance and survival, birth, family, lineage, hope, peace, prosperity, and good health.

In Brazil the Yoruba concept of àsé is known as axé and has been reinvented, spread, and nurtured in Candomblé, an Afro-Brazilian religion that is practiced in Salvador. Candomblé has a sacred/secular connection similar to West African tradition; practitioners often revere axé as a spiritual energy source bestowed upon humans, by a pantheon of ancestral spirits, for success and prosperity in the secular world. Also in Candomblé, spirit possession and artistic expressions of music (singing and drumming) and dance make up an important tripartite that nurtures axé.

In this book I use the term *axé* and African roots to examine how sacred themes, imagery, and symbols from Candomblé religion, music, musicianship, and culture have been appropriated in Brazilian popular music and Afro-Brazilian culture. I also include a discussion of what I believe are sacred/secular connections (or similarities) of black religious and artistic expressions in Brazil with African and other African diasporic areas where West African àsé has spread and been nurtured.

Afro-Brazilian culture brings together different experiences of social, cultural, and historical memory. Since the forced importation of Africans as slaves into the city of Salvador beginning in the mid-sixteenth century, Afro-Brazilian cultural traditions have continued to play a significant role in the development, creativity, and vibrancy of religion, music, dance, and culture in Brazil.

Afro-Brazilians have contributed to popular music by using a palette of old and new traditions—integrating African (the old) and European (the new) musical traditions to produce a lexicon of popular music styles and rhythms in Brazil. Afro-Brazilians introduced an aesthetic that is varied, complex, creative, and involves a substantial amount of communal response and participation. This has included collective and responsorial singing, circle dancing, elaborate choreographic foot, pelvic, and body movements, mock attack and defense stylized movements, stick dancing, syncopated duple and compound meters, the twanging sound of bowed instruments, and ostinato rhythmic patterns often played on drums and bell-type instruments.

Afro-Brazilians have performed popular music successfully as singers, instrumentalists, ensemble musicians, composers, arrangers, and dancers. But within Brazilian society, Afro-Brazilians' cultural traditions have often experienced repression and suppression by local authorities. However, some of these traditions have also been embraced nationally as something "truly Brazilian" (brasilidade) and as local/ethnic identity associated with the true essence of Salvador and the state of Bahia (baianidade), and in contemporary times many styles of Afro-Brazilian music contribute to the globalization and internationalization of Brazilian popular music.

With its extensive history, Salvador offers many local, regional, and national complexities, as exemplified by its many names. Salvador is often referred to as "Bahia," which leads a novice to identify the area more as a state than a city. The popular music, festivities, and annual Carnival celebrations originating from Salvador are in many instances referred to as "Bahian." There is a sacred connotation associated with the area in that it is also called Baía de Todos os Santos (All Saints Bay) because the Portuguese discovered it on November 1. In this book I will refer to the city as simply Salvador. However, there are occasions in discussions when I refer to various artists, popular music, and Carnival as Bahian.

Salvador was the capital of Brazil for approximately 250 years. It has long been the mecca of Afro-Brazilian musical innovation, where the sacred and secular are often connected. Within the city are the Largo do Pelourinho and Terreiro de Jesus, major squares in the city where some of the oldest Catholic churches are located.[2] The Terreiro de Jesus is home to some of Salvador's most famous churches: the seventeenth-century Catedral Basílica, the Ordem Terceira de São Domingos (Dominican Church), and the eighteenth-century São Pedro do Clérigos (Saint Peter's Church). These churches have preserved their ornate European architecture and are filled with beautiful gold-trimmed altars, sculptures, and paintings by famous artisans.

Another important church in Largo do Pelourinho is Nossa Senhora do Rosário dos Pretos (Our Lady of the Rosary of Black People), which was constructed by African slaves. The Rosário dos Pretos in the Pelourinho district of Salvador is unique in that some members are Catholic but also practice Candomblé religion. The church has images of black saints who are celebrated annually. During the many times that I attended services at this congregation the music that was performed was highly rhythmic and incorporated various types of musical instruments—bells, drums, tambourines, and guitars. During regular Sunday services members of the congregation were often encouraged to participate in the musical performances by joining in the singing with the choir.

Salvador is a city where sacred and secular are connected through popular music performances at bars where locals and tourists often participate in dancing and singing. On many Sundays, as the Catholic masses commence, people begin setting up bandstands in both squares for popular music groups that perform samba, reggae, bossa nova, forró, mangue, jazz, blues, funk, soul, and axé music. On many occasions worshippers recite the Lord's Prayer within the sanctums of the Catholic churches while a barrage of polyrhythmic drumming can be heard from outside performed by Carnival organizations such as Filhos de Gandhi (Sons of Gandhi) and Olodum.

On some weekdays it is not unusual to observe students from the local high school, Colégio Estadual Azevedo Fernandes, playing cavaquinhos and tambourines, singing and dancing to samba. It is not uncommon to see people carrying

Rosário dos Pretos Church
in Salvador.

various sizes of drums, guitars, and flutes as they go about their everyday routine. Tuesday nights, after the weekly mass called festa da benção (blessing party) at São Francisco Catholic Church, bandstands for the performance of popular music spring up in the squares where there is dancing, drinking, and excitement. A variety of performers entertain crowds of people—locals and tourists, young and old.

The Afro-Brazilian

What exactly is an Afro-Brazilian? Do all Afro-Brazilians have dark skin and curly hair? In physical appearance, do they have features that are regarded as African or Brazilian? Or can we simply say that Afro-Brazilians are people who identify with their African heritage and background? Do Afro-Brazilians have similar experiences as African Americans in the United States and blacks in other African diasporic areas? These are some of the perplexing questions I had in mind when I began my research in Brazil in 1998.

In a country that has continually denied racism and celebrated miscegenation, issues of racial identity are complex. The complexity of racial identity in Brazil can be seen in national, regional, and local/ethnic affiliation where people have many ways of identifying themselves. An identity often is associated with a regional affiliation: Baiano/Baiana (from Salvador), Cariocas (from Rio de Janeiro), Paulistas (from São Paulo), or Mineros (from Minas Gerias), for example. Several identities are associated with skin color, hair textures, physical features, and racial mixtures such as mestiço, pardo, mulatto, cafuzo, caboclo, mameluco, and Afro-brasileiro (Afro-Brazilian).

Most of the young people that identified themselves to me as black (Negro) and Afro-Brazilian had pronounced African features with dark complexion and curly hair. Some also identified themselves as being part of a community/ neighborhood (e.g., Pelourinho, Liberdade) where they resided in the city of Salvador. Because of my physical features (dark skin and curly hair), while I was in Brazil most people believed that I was Afro-Brazilian. It was only when I began to speak in my American-accented Portuguese that the locals became aware of my African American status and heritage.

Many of the dark-skinned, curly-haired Afro-Brazilians with whom I interacted in Salvador identified themselves as baiano (male), and baiana (female). Some identified themselves as African American (since Brazil is part of the Americas). During my initial research in Salvador I met many young Afro-Brazilians highly influenced by black popular (hip hop) and reggae culture. I must add that I had an opportunity to interact with a few light-skinned, blue-eyed, straight-haired Brazilians who also identified themselves as Afro-Brazilian. They were proud of their heritage that stemmed from what they described as "Mother Africa."

The Historical Makeup of Afro-Brazilian Racial Identity

With European, African, and Native American inhabitants, early in its history Brazil was a multiracial society. Afro-Brazilian racial identity is based on a mixture of historical, social, and cultural experiences: forced importation, colonialism, master/slave relationships, cultural memory, local/ethnic affiliations, miscegenation, religious conversion, and reinvention of ancestral worship.

Afro-Brazilian racial identity is complex partly because of the victimization of Africans that were forced into Brazilian slavery. Between the mid-sixteenth and nineteenth centuries over four million Africans were transported to Brazil. The major ports of entry into Brazil were Salvador and Recife in the northeast and Rio de Janeiro in the south. Afro-Brazilian slaves experienced bondage, shackles and chains, physical abuse, assignment of new identities and name changes, uprisings, and the loss of families and relatives. Afro-Brazilian racial identity is also linked with early struggle and resistance of the *quilombos* (slave communities) and heroism of the legendary Zumbi of the Palmares, a slave community that was formed by Afro-Brazilians in the Brazilian state of Alagoas. In this historic quilombo Afro-Brazilians exhibited courage and a strong sense of pride in their African heritage.[3]

The complexity of Afro-Brazilian racial identity is due not only to colonialism and slavery but also to the constant intimate relations (often forced or coerced) between the members of different ethnic groups. African and Native

American women were often forced into sexual relationships with Portuguese men that produced offspring of mixed heritages. Initially the idea of racial mixing was encouraged, to increase the population and to assimilate Africans into Brazilian society. One of the results is that there is a "fluid system of racial identification."[4] This includes identifying people of mixed heritages in many ways such as mulatto (African and European), caboclo and mameluco (European and Native American), and cafuzo (African and Native American).

Colonialism in Brazil created a two-tiered sociocultural system comprised of a distinct upper class and lower strata where skin color and racial identity influenced one's status in the society. The upper class was mainly comprised of wealthy white (Portuguese) land and slave owners who controlled the economic, political, and social power. African slaves, people of mixed races, and poor whites were relegated to the lower strata of society.

After the abolition of slavery in the nineteenth century, the massive population of Africans was again victimized by Brazilian (Eurocentric) elites of the upper class. Afro-Brazilian identity was often devalued and deemed an inferior status. The elites adopted Darwinian ideologies of categorizing people, cultures, and races in the world as inferior or superior.[5] For the elites, "black" inferiority became a social and cultural "problem" that affected the modernization of Brazilian society. To eliminate blackness and African inferiority, solutions offered by the elites involved scientific theories of "whitening," and mixing of the races through biological processes of miscegenation.

With constant racial mixing, there was no stringent white/black continuum in Brazil. Moreover, slavery and racial relationships did not result in any Jim Crow-type outright segregation laws or ridicule of mixed races, as in the United States. Racial and cultural mixing were societal norms, and people of mixed races could achieve some upward mobility. In some instances it was possible for a mulatto child born of an enslaved African mother and white father to become educated, receive manumission, and achieve a higher status in the society. As opposed to the United States with its stringent white/black segregation, in Brazil financial stability was an important criterion for the acceptance and success of mulattos with lighter skin color, who were often regarded as white.

By the 1930s miscegenation was celebrated as being truly Brazilian and part of the cultural heritage. The flexible system of racial identity that began during colonialism in many ways continues to serve as a means for justifying nonracial discrimination even in contemporary times. Brazil is a country that has promoted ideologies of a racial democracy (*democracia racial*) where people of different colors have equal rights. But in reality, the country has often discouraged the establishment of social organizations that are based on racial identity and that question social inequalities.

The Myth of Racial Democracy (*Democracia Racial*) and the Influence of Gilberto Freyre

Literary sources—books, journals, newspapers—often influence the way that people conceive sociocultural and sociopolitical ideologies and myths about ethnic groups, religious beliefs, racial identity, and artistic creativity. I believe that this is an appropriate theoretical method for beginning a discussion about the influence of Gilberto Freyre and the myth of racial democracy in the Brazilian society. In his most prominent book, *The Masters and the Slaves* (originally published as *Casa Grande e Senzala*, 1933), Freyre set forth a notion that multiracism and multiculturalism were Brazil's greatest strength and miscegenation was something that should be celebrated.[6] Freyre's concepts were centered on a type of racial "solidarity and togetherness," of the cultures that he believed contributed to the uniqueness of Brazil.

In the early part of the twentieth century Freyre studied with Franz Boas at Columbia University.[7] In his notions of multiracism and multiculturalism he moved away from the elitist scientific/biological paradigms to advance a theory that promoted the valuation of cultural/hybrid practices and mixed races that he believed made Brazil a unique nation. Within this concept Afro-Brazilian cultural traditions (e.g., music and dance) were praised as positives that should be celebrated on a national level. But what Freyre actually did was provide a springboard for the upper class to deny racism and perpetuate a myth of racial democracy in Brazil.

In celebrating Afro-Brazilian cultural traditions, Freyre seems to perpetuate an image of a jovial singing and dancing Afro-Brazilian who lives in peace, harmony, and prosperity in Brazilian society. But the notions contained in *The Masters and the Slaves* are geared more to the intellectuals and reading audiences composed of the "masters"—elites, the upper class, local authorities, and educated that even after the abolition of slavery in Brazil continued to control the economic, political, and social power in the society. A book of this magnitude and its implications of a racial democracy may not have been intellectually accessible to less educated populations of the lower strata. In reality, the lower strata continue to struggle for racial equality in a society where, even in contemporary times, a myth of racial democracy persists.

Stereotypical Images of Blackness in the Brazilian Society

Similar to black experiences in other areas, Afro-Brazilians have been confronted with stereotypical images of black identity that relate to such things as customs, physical characteristics, sexual prowess, class status, skin color, and identity. Afro-Brazilian stereotypes include baiano, nego, the big black guy, mulatto, baiana, nega, and mãe preta. Afro-Brazilian black identity has even been ridiculed in popular songs that convey images of Afro-Brazilians as happy and jovial caretakers, nursemaids, cooks, fishermen, exotic drummers, and dancers.[8] In several Carnival songs, lyrics address Afro-Brazilian women and hair texture. "O teu cabelo não nega" ("Your Hair Can't Deny It") by Lamartine Babo, João Valença, and Raul Valença (1932) and "Nega do cabelo duro" ("Black Woman with the Hard Hair") (1942) by Ruben Soares and David Nasser offer negative descriptions of a black woman who has wavy hair that she is unable to untangle and comb. The woman in the song resorts to straightening her hair with a hot iron. Of course, such stereotypical images of hair texture are not unknown in the United States. The lyrics of "O teu cabelo não nega" and "Nega do cabelo duro" make reference to the outward physical appearance of the black woman without regard to the inner beauty that makes her personal qualities unique.

"Let's Make Some Noise": Young Afro-Brazilians and Their Quest for Racial Equality

Racial identity in Brazil has stimulated many scholars and intellectual thinkers to debate the complexities of racial democracy, skin color, race, class, and identity.[9] In conducting my research, it was important to interact with Afro-Brazilians and learn more about their personal responses to racial identity in Brazil. Many of the Afro-Brazilians that I interacted with were aware of certain stereotypical images of black identity and racial inequality in the Brazilian society and that this was a problem. Furthermore, survival was key to their individuality and identity. "We do the best that we can, but things are so difficult for us here in Salvador," was a response I received from some young Afro-Brazilian males.

Some of the young Afro-Brazilians I met had very little formal education and had a difficult time providing for their families. Some responded with a sense of hopelessness or by engaging in illicit activities. But I also experienced the skill and ingenuity of Afro-Brazilian culture. Many young Afro-Brazilians are skilled merchants and craftsmen who stand for hours on a daily basis in the local squares selling homemade trinkets, food, and garments. Some Afro-Brazilians could take a sturdy tree branch, a rock, a gourd, string, straw, animal skins, metal, and wood and construct well-made musical instruments such as drums, rattles, whistles, bells, and berimbaus.

Afro-Brazilians have contributed to artistic innovation in Brazil. Moreover, in contemporary times many Afro-Brazilian cultural traditions—especially religion, music, and dance—continue to be appropriated as part of the national rhetoric of Brazil. Locals and businesses often commercialize and market these traditions as "Afro-Brazilian products." But in spite of great innovative contributions, Afro-Brazilians continue to be situated at the lowest social and economic strata of Brazilian society, and thus other voices are rarely heard.

While there has been no iconic Martin Luther King–type civil rights activist, many young Afro-Brazilians have attempted to confront racial inequality. There have been historic formations of black protest movements such as the Frente Negra Brasileira, which was organized in the 1930s and led a series of demonstrations. By the 1940s black protest began to be manifested in artistic expression, especially in Rio de Janeiro, which saw, for example, the creation of the Teatro Experimental do Negro (Black Experimental Theater) and Teatro Popular Negro (Black Popular Theater).

In contemporary times many young Afro-Brazilians have a philosophy that I describe as "let's make some noise." They do this by creating vibrant drumming ensembles and participating in different social organizations. Since the 1970s many young Afro-Brazilians have attempted to respond to their social, economic, and political situations in Brazil by participating in black consciousness movements such as the Movimento Negro Unificado (Unified Black Movement, MNU), an organization formed to advocate against racism and brutality and unite the struggles of Afro-Brazilians throughout the country.[10]

Young Afro-Brazilians in the cities of Rio de Janeiro, São Paulo, and Salvador have begun to experience ethnic pride and learn about pan-Africanism, civil rights, and black pride movements in the United States, resulting in a new questioning of racial identity and equality. They have responded with their own struggle for social justice and black identity, an identity dependent not only on ethnic affiliation and attire but also on popular music as tools for validating their African heritage.

In 1988 Brazil commemorated the centenary of the abolition of slavery by holding celebrations throughout the country, but in many areas Afro-Brazilians used the festivities to protest racism in Brazil. In Rio de Janeiro approximately five thousand Afro-Brazilians organized a march called "The Farce Against Abolition" as a way of showing how racial inequality continued to exist in the midst of political agendas touting what was supposed to be "freedom and opportunity for all."[11] In Salvador the negative responses of many young Afro-Brazilians to the centenary resulted in the local government canceling its celebrations.

Although black consciousness movements in Brazil have in a way succeeded in bringing attention to racism and race relations, there continues to be little representation of black leadership on the local, state, and national levels. One positive aspect is that in Salvador, the MNU now annually celebrates a National Day of Black Consciousness in honor of Zumbi, the leader of the Palmares quilombo. While conducting my research in Brazil in November 1998, I had an opportunity to attend this celebration. This particular celebration was a sacred/secular event that involved a special mass, prayers, music, and dancing, bringing together government officials, clergy, the media, political activists, musicians, dancers, and communities. The celebration was held on the steps of the Casa Jorge Armado in the Pelourinho district. Processions began at the Rosário dos Pretos Church and were followed by a Catholic mass, recitations in honor of Zumbi, and musical performances by several local Carnival organizations (e.g., Filhos de Gandhi and Olodum).

For many young Afro-Brazilians, popular music continues to be a main vehicle for expressing local, social, and ethnic identity. Axé music and samba-reggae are among the popular styles that Afro-Brazilians link with a positive black identity. Moreover, since the 1990s the use of rap music as social commentary has also become part of Brazilian popular music, especially among Afro-Brazilian youth groups in large cities—Salvador, Rio de Janeiro, and São Paulo. Brazilian youths often sing rap songs as a way of "doing politics."[12]

In Brazil I interacted with many Afro-Brazilians who believe that if provided with better opportunities they would succeed in achieving their career goals. In some instances this has involved the pursuit of better social and economic opportunities by relocating to the United States and Europe. Many Afro-Brazilians cannot afford to relocate to other areas, but continue to display a great sense of pride in their heritage and black identity as "Afro-Brazilians" and are also proud to be "Brazilian" because they were born into this national identity.

Many Afro-Brazilians I met wanted to acquire more knowledge about their African ancestry as a way of understanding the total intricacies of their racial makeup and identity. This is what I refer to as holistic knowledge—an acute awareness of how African culture has enriched Brazilian society. Although many had not traveled to the African continent and experienced the culture firsthand (as I had done in my own research), their inquiries into African heritage were also multidimensional as they attempted to reinvent and reinterpret African cultural traditions in various expressions—religion, music, and dance within Brazilian society. Moreover, many young Afro-Brazilians become mentors for adolescents in their communities. As mentors they continue to emphasize the importance of axé, its African roots, and Candomblé religion in constructing holistic knowledge of their historical background, racial makeup, and identity within Brazilian society.

The Sacred: Afro-Brazilian Religious Expressions

Religion has made Brazil an even more complex society. The "sacred" is actually something that links people of different sociocultural backgrounds. Here, I am not making an argument that all races in Brazil practice the same or similar religions; what I mean is that even before the dominance of Roman Catholicism, people from European, African, and Native American heritages experienced in their own ways (customs and traditions) certain types of sacred worship that may have influenced their lives in the secular world. In this context I use the word *religion*, but before the experience of colonialism Africans and Native Americans had their own special terminology and ideologies for worshiping the sacred.

When Africans were transported as slaves into Salvador beginning in the mid-sixteenth century, no one could have imagined just how they would impact the sacred/secular landscape of Brazil. With Africans from various regions, the experience of slavery resulted in the creation of a complex, intersecting crossroads that integrated sacred and secular activities. Many of the African slaves were organized into *nações* (nations) based on similarities of ethnicity such as region, language, or culture. As a symbolic reference for the gamut of cultural, social, and religious similarities among African groups, the nações helped many Africans maintain cultural traditions, find spouses, and create long-lasting relationships.[13]

Among the nações in Salvador, the Congo-Angola from the Central African region and West African ethnic groups (Yoruba, Ketu, and Ijexá) over time fused their cultures to become known as Nagô.[14] In addition, the Ewe and Fon people were called Gêge and also fused some of their culture with the Yoruba, which became known as Gêge-Nagô.[15] Each of the various nações was identified by its special ancestral spirits: *orixás* for the Nagô, *voduns* for the Gêge, and *inkisses* for the Congo-Angola. These ancestral spirits have come to influence Candomblé religion.[16]

Candomblé is the result of Africans attempting to make sense of a new environment while celebrating ancestral spirits and reinventing many of their religious and artistic traditions. The term is a product of African and European phonetic linkages; one theory holds that "Candomblé" is derived from a contraction of *candombe* (a dance of African origin performed in Brazil and the Rio de la Plata area) and *ilê* (from the Yoruba word meaning house). Other theories posit that the term stems from phonetic linkages based on the Bantu word *kandombele*, which means to pray. Other variations of this linkage include the terms *kandombile*, which means prayer or veneration, and *kandomide*, a word derived from *kulomba-ku-domba-a* (to pray) and *kò-dómb-éd-à* (to ask the intercession of).[17] All of these theories seem plausible; they illustrate the complexities of the Candomblé religion, which combines European ideas with the varying religious, cultural, linguistic, and ethnic traditions of the Africans imported into Salvador as slaves. In my field research I asked several practitioners of Candomblé about their knowledge of the term. Their responses were similar: most believed that the term stemmed from "mother Africa."[18]

Some practitioners of Candomblé are devout Catholics who at the same time continue to pay homage to their African ancestors. For example, when I arrived in Salvador in 1998 I became acquainted with a local man named Ricardo Oliveria and his wife Maria, who were members of the Rosários dos Pretos Church and also practicing members of Candomblé. Ricardo expressed that he is an elder and devout member of the Catholic Church and also believes that Candomblé is part of his heritage. Both his parents are followers of Candomblé. During the Sunday masses at Rosários dos Pretos, Ricardo continues to wear beads around his neck for health and prosperity that were given to him as a practitioner of Candomblé. I would often see other Candomblé practitioners attending regular Catholic services and on special family occasions such as christenings.

Some Brazilians from outside the city of Salvador continue to be attracted to Candomblé as a religion that offers them emotional and spiritual experiences. Even nonpractitioners often seek guidance concerning finances, family problems, election probabilities, love relationships, and illnesses. Moreover, after they become initiated into the religion, some Brazilians return to cities such as Rio de Janeiro and São Paulo to establish Candomblé houses of worship—another way West African àsé is spread and nurtured in Brazilian culture.

Reinventing Artistic Expression

For many Africans in Brazil, artistic expression served as a tool for the construction of traditional identity, permitting Africans to make alliances, assert themselves, and develop a sense of ethnic consciousness outside of Africa. Artistic expression became a means for adjustment into a new society and an emotional release, and functioned as a cognitive mechanism for revisiting past experiences involving ethics, aesthetics, politics, and culture. One of the most important aspects was the use of African and African-derived musical instruments such as drums, bells, gongs, rattles, and so on. Musicians often played such instruments to evoke spirit possession during divination and healing ceremonies. Along with their native instruments, Africans also brought to Brazil their distinct playing styles and specific attitudes toward music and musicians. They maintained the tradition of virtual male domination in playing the drum and participating in complex religious ceremonies. Women often participated in musical performances as dancers and singers.[19]

Popular music in Brazil is greatly indebted to the African heritage of artistic expression. During colonialism, although the expression of religiosity, music, and dance were most often done in a private and secret setting, on occasions Afro-Brazilians were collectively allowed opportunity to express themselves and maintain certain aspects of their artistic traditions through music and dance. One of the most significant secular forms of music and dance performed by Afro-Brazilians originated in the Central Africa regions of Angola and Congo:[20] *batuque*, in which dancers form a small circle, sing, and clap hands to the sound of large drums. Each participant would enter the circle in turn. When the dancer in the middle was ready to leave, he or she chose the next person to enter the circle with a forward nudge of the pelvis.

The batuque was a manifestation of the communal "African ring" that gave birth to many popular music, dance, and artistic forms in Brazil. The dance's intensity was heightened with hip swings and gyrations, footwork, clapping of hands, and snapping of fingers. One particular feature of the batuque was the *umbigada*, a gesture in which participants touched each other with their navels as an invitation to dance.[21] The stylistic movements of the batuque influenced the lundu, samba, capoeira, carimbó, caxambu, coco, maculelê, maracatu, and samba de roda.

During colonialism Afro-Brazilian artistic creativity was also influenced by European art music. Particularly in Salvador, African musicians were often called upon to provide the entertainment in private homes, and some became proficient in reading music and playing Western instruments such as violins, flutes, bugles, organs, and trombones. These musicians became skilled at performing European repertory such as marches, waltzes, and polkas. Exposure to European styles would prove beneficial to Afro-Brazilians musicians who, after abolition of slavery in the latter part of the nineteenth century, began to migrate to Rio de Janeiro, the city where, over time, the popular music tradition fully developed.

Scholarly Research Focusing on Afro-Brazilian Cultural Traditions

Afro-Brazilian cultural traditions have been continually demystified, dissected, and analyzed in research by social scientists, historians, ethnologists, and ethnomusicologists. Moreover, many Afro-Brazilian cultural traditions of religion, music, and dance were initially embraced and relegated as part of folkloric expression.[22] Raimundo Nina Rodrigues (1990/1896, 1905) was one of the earliest scholars to detail the complexities of Afro-Brazilian religious culture. He was followed by the publication of works by Arthur Ramos (1934), Edison Carneiro (1936), and Manuel Querino (1938).

In the 1940s and 1950s scholars such as Melville J. Herskovits (1944), José Medeiros (1957), Pierre Verger (1957), and Roger Bastide (1958) contributed studies in Candomblé religion.[23] Herskovits included a description of special rituals such as the baptism of musical instruments that even to this day many Candomblé houses continue to observe. What is also significant about Herskovits's research is his album compilation of field recordings of music from actual worship ceremonies.[24] Verger's extensive research on Afro-Brazilian religion provides a comparative analysis of West African religious practices and Candomblé. Bastide's seminal work *O Candomblé da Bahia (Rito Nagô)* (1958) continues to be one of the primary sources for analysis and examination of symbols, rituals, divination processes, and roles of leaders in the religion. In later works Bastide provides sociological analysis of Afro-Brazilian religious traditions.[25]

Alan Merriam (1956, 1963) presented discussions on Candomblé topics that ranged from the significance of musical instruments to rituals to an analysis of song structure. The seminal works by ethnomusicologist Gerard Béhague (1984) placed the study of Candomblé in an ethnomusicological perspective by detailing the functionality of the music within a cultural paradigm. Béhague also compiled an album of music from actual Candomblé ceremonies.[26]

Most of the literature that has focused on Candomblé has provided paradigms that relate to the history, function, and complexity of Candomblé as a religious tradition in Brazil.[27] One of the reasons I undertook my research was to enhance the literature with a conversation and an active engagement with the "voices," feelings, and sentiments of the practitioners as well as the sacred musicians in Candomblé religion as primary agents in spreading and nurturing of West African àsé in Brazilian culture. This conversation was also aimed at connecting Afro-Brazilian religious and artistic expression with other African diasporic areas.

West African Àsé Power/Creative Energy in Religion and Popular Music: African and African Diasporic Connections

As in many African and African diasporic areas, in Brazil religious and artistic expression continues to inform black identity. Thus, the black experience in Brazil, Africa, and other African diasporic areas, and the effects of colonialism, have influenced a growing interest in cultural studies of religious and artistic traditions within paradigms of cultural memory, power, ethnicity, class, identity, gender, and sexuality in local, national, and international settings.[28] Moreover, some scholars have investigated the ways in which people in Brazil and other African diasporic areas reinvent certain types of cultural traditions.[29] Allan Hanson posits that traditional culture is more an invention constructed for contemporary purposes than a stable heritage handed down from the past. Nancy Morris has posited a similar paradigm that music is made in local contexts of mobility and migration, and is the constant writing out and blurring of class and ethnic differences; tradition is always a matter of invention and reinvention.[30]

From colonialism have resulted processes of globalization, musical borrowing and appropriation, fusion, and hybridization.[31] Peterson, Vásquez, and Williams (2001) posit that one of the many side effects of globalization is the production of immigrant diasporas—groups of people who live in host countries but continue to sustain links with their home societies and ancestors. The globalization process happens at the local level; individuals negotiate with these changes by drawing from their cultural and religious resources.[32]

Similar to blacks in other diasporic areas, in Brazil people of African heritage are situated in dual/hyphenated identities (e.g., Afro-Brazilian, African American, Afro-Cuban). In the literature the African diaspora is described as being part of a "Black Atlantic," "circum-Caribbean," a complex African cultural system manifested in diversity and a product of various cultural processes—syncretism, creolization, *creolité*, and culture *metissage*—all of which signify the hybrid, dual/hyphenated identities, and the character of the cultural products of the region.[33] Moreover, Brazil and many Afro-Brazilian cultural traditions are often situated within in the terrains of Latin America.[34] But I believe there is a greater discourse that relates to the African heritage that continues to link Brazil with other African diasporic areas. This linkage is the integration of the sacred and secular influences of black religions and artistic expressions where West African àsé concepts have been spread and nurtured.

Candomblé is part of the African diasporic religious heritage that includes Haitian and New Orleans Vodou, Cuban Santería, and Trinidadian Sàngó. All of these traditions integrate the sacred and secular; all involve worship of a pantheon of ancestral spirits. Such ancestral worship in parts of the African diaspora are manifestations of spiritual and historical memory, which often finds expression via elaborate artistic creative symbols, icons, dances, songs, tales, music, and talismans that channel an imagined source of power and creative energy from West African àsé.[35] Even the language shows evidence of cultural survival: African terminology such as òrìsàs (ancestral spirits), àsé (power, energy), and Sàngó (a warrior deity) have been incorporated and reinvented in the local lexicons as orixá, axé, and Xangô (in Brazil); orisa, àsé, and Sàngó (in Trinidad); orisha, ache, and Chango (in Cuba); and ashé (United States). In these religions, practitioners communicate with ancestral spirits through extensive singing done in call-and-response patterns, polyrhythmic drumming, and ring dancing. These rituals evoke spiritual possession and communication with the spiritual world.

Many Africans who were transported to the African diaspora originated in societies where religious traditions were very much linked with the secular and often were geared to enhance the temporal aspects of life, from adolescence to maturity. People of the African diaspora often defined who they were politically, socially and culturally through various forms of religious beliefs. Moreover, there were various means of cultural and social adjustments, expressions for mediating beliefs and sacred/secular activities.

In examining the social formations of the African diaspora one must consider how commercial interests and different social and cultural situations influenced religious and musical experiences. Religion and music played an important role in European colonialism. Colonists often used religion and music as a way of Christianizing and controlling various groups in the diaspora. One bittersweet aspect is the conglomeration of religious, cultural, and musical ideas that emerged, resulting in the rich artistic expression that today is recognized on both local and global levels.

The practice of importing millions of Africans into Brazil for economic gain and territorial control was similar to slaving practices in other areas such as Haiti, Jamaica, Cuba, Bermuda and many others. For centuries Brazil and other New World colonies participated in the Atlantic slave trade that transported millions of Africans to the New World. A process of globalization began when Africans imported as slaves brought elements from their own cultures with them. In many instances Africans attempted to make sense of their new environment by reinventing the sacred landscapes of their own familiar religious traditions. In the New World, just as in the old, they venerated deities, held festivals, and constructed altars, shrines, and temples.

Reinvention has been a major sociocultural process of artistic innovation and ingenuity in black experience in Brazil and other parts of the African diaspora. Thus, for displaced Africans a primary legacy of reinventing artistic traditions was the use of available resources (bottles, wood, animal skins, animal bones, metal, rocks) to construct traditional musical instruments.

The active engagement of singing, drumming, and dancing is a "musico-aesthetic" that continues to link Brazil with other African and African diasporic areas that share a rich heritage of African artistic tradition. This "musico-aesthetic" of creativity is manifested in constant movement where rhythmic momentum is often energized with hand claps, finger snapping, and foot stomping —all of which may be overlapped with voices and musical instruments engaging in polyrhythmic, syncopated, and melodic innovation of musicians and dancers. The manifestations of this tradition are diverse; various styles of popular music and dance choreography of hand, hip, foot, and pelvic movements have resulted in emergence of rumba and vacunao, salsa, batuque, samba, jitterbug, twist, break dancing, and many others.

For displaced Africans in Brazil (and other African diasporic areas), enslavement did not obliterate many traditional artistic values because these values were sustained in the minds and bodies of the people. In a profound way, music and dance linked the Africans with their home societies and ancestors. Music and dance were important dimensions of reinventing sacred and secular landscapes, crucial for venerating the ancestral spirits. A heritage of African memory remained in musical expression, culture, and religion and was, over time, integrated into the larger society and became part of the Brazil's social and cultural space.

With Carnival organizations such as Olodum, Ilê Aiyê, and Filhos de Gandhi, Brazil is part of a "percussive" community where black artistic expression is often characterized by vibrant drumming. In the colonial experience of the African diaspora, drums and drumming frequently were repressed or banned.

Such repression itself sometimes led to the emergence of popular styles and the creation of alternative rhythmic expressions. For example, the North American style of rhythmic patting juba that involved moving, patting, and slapping parts of the body was created. Drums often were banned in areas such as Trinidad and Tobago, where in the late nineteenth-century British colonial authorities banned percussion performances because the sound produced by the bands was too loud and was believed to provoke immoral behavior. As a result, Africans conjured up other types of performances in tamboo bamboo bands to produce a sound similar to drumming but much quieter. Trinidadians later developed a more African aesthetic percussion through the medium of the steel drum, commonly called the pan.

From processional drumming in funerals to Carnival, I witnessed the richness of the drum in Brazil, Africa, and other African diasporic areas that have greatly impacted black experiences, musical traditions, and music production. In these areas the drum could not have become such a powerful and influential instrument in both sacred/secular settings without dynamic drummers who through their hands and bodies communicate the rhythmic and sonic language of the drum. From Candomblé, Santería, and Vodou to secular popular music, dynamic drummers such as Babatunde Olatunji, Mongo Santamaria, Francisco Aguabella, Max Roach, Carlinhos Brown, and many others enhance the status of the drum and all in some way have contributed to the diversity of musical and stylistic ideas in drum performances.

In Brazil, Africa, and other African diasporic areas, sacred shrines, temples, churches, and houses of worship have often provided aspiring musicians with opportunities to develop and nurture their musical talents as apprentices and master musicians. Furthermore, some black musicians with sacred music backgrounds have also continued to develop their talents and pursued careers in the popular music industry, contributing to the popularity of many secular styles. On occasion the skilled musicianship exhibited by these musicians (e.g., Ray Charles, James Brown, Aretha Franklin, Chano Pozo, Fela Kuti, Carlinhos Brown) has been influential, marketable, and emulated by white musicians (e.g., Elvis Presley, Jerry Lee Lewis, Janis Joplin, the Rolling Stones, the Beatles).

When first innovated, popular styles such as samba, reggae, jazz, blues, funk, soul, and Afro-Beat often received an array of responses and criticisms from artists, local medias, local authorities, and communities. Moreover, many of these styles can be linked with black religious expression. For example, the origins of jazz are linked to African spirituality of Vodou, which was said to evoke secular and sensual passions that conflicted with the sacred foundation of European-American society.[36] In the 1940s Afro-Cuban jazz in the United States developed partly out of the inspiration of jazz trumpeter Dizzy Gillespie (1917–1993), who included in his ensemble the traditional Santería drummer and Afro-Cuban priest Chano Pozo (1915–1948). Gillespie often acknowledged that Pozo's intro-duction of Yoruba, Kongo, and Abakua rhythms into his jazz orchestra trans-formed African American jazz, developing a new genre called Cubop.[37] The in-clusion of the sacred rhythms with the power to call down the divinities infused a heightened sacred element into jazz, enriching and transforming it by linking it with its ancestral heritage. Other Cuban musicians that Santería influenced in-clude Francisco Aguabella, Mongo Santamaria, and Armando Peraza.

In American culture the dividing line between blues and spirituals and the differing roles of blues singers and clergy has never been clearly defined. Some regard the blues as the "devil's music,"[38] but the blues possess the same sacred qualities as spirituals. They are secular in that they affirm earthly passions such as love, sex, and happiness, but spiritual in being impelled by the same search for the truth of the black experience. Like spirituals, the blues affirm and preserve the worth of black humanity through ritual drama. The familiar sexual connota-tions of the blues tend to overshadow the music's equally important role in con-juring up supernatural forces from ancestral Vodou worship—as expressed, for example, in Muddy Waters's "Got My Mojo Working" (1960) or in Jimi Hendrix's blues and funk rendition of "Voodoo Chile" (1968).[39] And, of course, the blues deals with obstacles experienced by African Americans in everyday life.

In the black experience of Brazil, Africa, and other African diasporic areas, some popular musicians appropriate sacred energy to provide a type of "spice," spirituality, and emotionalism to secular popular music performances. But some musicians also appropriate secular energy to provide a type of spice to sacred music (gospel blues, gospel rock, holy hip hop, samba mass). It is interesting to note that African American artists such as Little Richard, Aretha Franklin, James Brown, Ray Charles, Sam Cooke, B. B. King, Tina Turner, Gladys Knight, Patti La Belle, Thelonious Monk, John Coltrane, and others initially performed in the church before pursuing careers in popular music. Many of these musicians incor-porated musical and stylistic features from religious/gospel music in their per-formances of what became known as funk and soul.

Performers such as Ray Charles, James Brown, and Aretha Franklin were powerful symbols of blackness. Ray Charles mixed secular with sacred when, in 1954, he released a recording of "My Jesus is All the World to Me" with the lyrics changed to "I Got a Woman." James Brown was an innovator when he used de-vices characteristic of the emotional preaching style of African American min-isters such as falsettos, screams, shouts, melismatic variations, and parodies of the Pentecostal church and holiness practice of testifying.

Bob Marley calls on the name of Jah (Jehovah) in reggae; Ray Charles, James Brown, and Aretha Franklin have often included references of the Lord, reli-gion, and church within the lyrical content of popular songs as a way of convey-ing a strong sense of emotionalism in performances and recordings. This strong sense of emotionalism is also incorporated in the music of Stevie Wonder, Gladys Knight, Patti La Belle, Al Green (minister and popular musician), and the legendary B. B. King, who often includes in his songs the phrase "let's go to church."[40]

In Afro-Brazilian culture, popular music production often has a sacred/secular connection. Popular musicians such as Gilberto Gil, Maria Bethânia, Carlinhos Brown, and Virginia Rodrigues often begin a performance with special prayers and salutations to the African ancestral spirits petitioning the blessings of axé for a successful performance. In many instances these musicians are highly influenced by the spice, spirituality, and emotionalism of various African and African diasporic popular styles—jazz, blues, funk, soul, reggae, and many others.

There is also what I describe as a sacred/secular "roots" music and a crossroads connection in that many popular musical styles (samba, reggae, axé, jazz, blues, soul, funk, rap, rumba, salsa, soca) partly reflect their African heritage—a continuous transatlantic flow of reinvention and creative energy influenced by religion, music, dance, and social movements. Over time many of these styles were taken back to Africa and fused with the local music, then crossed back over the Atlantic in a continuous cycle of innovation where they may connect the sacred with the secular.

Many types of sacred/secular "Africanisms" continue to connect Brazil with other African diasporic areas. But I must emphasize that each area has its own complexities of racial identity, struggles, sociocultural/sociopolitical experiences, and artistic creativity. Brazil is distinguished by what I describe as the "Afro-Brazilian experience," that is realized in Candomblé religion and artistic expression that are very much part of Afro-Brazilian racial identity. This experience has given way to innovations in popular music and the creation of an assortment of musical instruments. In the popular music Afro-Brazilian musicians have their unique ways of integrating various types of rhythms and musical instruments to create an Afro-Brazilian sound that is culminated in dynamic expressions of music and dance. In the Afro-Brazilian experience another distinction is the manifestation of West African àsé that has been reinvented in Afro-Brazilian culture as axé, a tradition that continues to connect the sacred and secular.

Secularizing "Àsé/Axé"

This book is a culmination of several years of research on the sacred/secular influences of àsé/axé, Candomblé religion, popular music, and Afro-Brazilian culture. It examines how Candomblé emerged from the religious sanctum of Afro-Brazilian culture and has influenced artistic creativity in various styles of Brazilian popular music and dance, from samba to ijexá, samba-reggae, and axé. Brazil's popular music is distinguished by the high energy of the samba music and dance produced there. With the increasing popularity of Candomblé, some young Afro-Brazilians have appropriated and secularized aspects of it in their art as a means of constructing and articulating regional, social, and ethic identity. Practitioners of the religion in cities such as Salvador achieve wide dissemination of their religious practices when they hear popular music that incorporates Candomblé sacred drum rhythms, or when they encounter Candomblé-type rituals such as the observance of special foods and prayers offered to the ancestral spirits to celebrate secular public events such as the annual Bahian Carnival. Through commercial recordings and live performances, Candomblé has come into contact with the open borders of urbanity, politics, globalization, tourism, and consumerism.

Many prominent Brazilian artists such as Dorival Caymmi, Gilberto Gil, Caetano Veloso, Maria Bethânia, Carlinhos Brown, Daniela Mercury, Margareth Menezes, and Virginia Rodrigues have included in their repertoire songs that relate to the sacred themes, imagery, and symbols of Candomblé. This religion has also become an iconic part of the Negritude movement in Brazil. Furthermore, because of the importance of musical expression in Brazil and the global marketability of African-derived music, the musicians and musical styles associated with the religion have in many ways also influenced popular music. And yet, despite the commercialization of their art, many Candomblé musicians—who are initiated, trained, and dedicated to perform music in special ceremonies—maintain their spiritual quality. The musicians play a major role in the experience of worshipping a pantheon of deities that now have widespread iconographic significance in Brazil. Even the musicians themselves have in a sense become iconic figures in their communities and among local musicians, who often attempt to emulate Candomblé musicianship.

In Salvador, local churches such as the Rosário dos Pretos and the Catedral Basílica are sites for many of the city's religious and popular festivals. Many of these festivals pay homage to both Catholic saints and the ancestral spirits of Candomblé. These popular and exciting festivals often attract large crowds who attend prayers and then enjoy popular music performed by many local groups. During these festivals it is not unusual for local churches to be filled with participants dressed in Candomblé's traditional white garments and wearing beads around their arms and necks for protection by ancestral spirits. In many of these festivities axé is popularized and secularized. Furthermore, during these festivities many people (practitioners and nonpractitioners) petition through prayers, music, and dance "the positive blessings of axé" for success in their lives.

In this book, chapter one examines the ancestral origins of the religious context of West African àsé and how it has been reinvented, negotiated, altered, secularized, and accommodated in Brazilian culture as axé. Chapter two examines the importance of music in Candomblé and discusses how some of the sacred rhythms have been appropriated and secularized by Brazilian popular musicians and by Bahian Carnival organizations such as the *afoxés*. Chapter three examines the appropriation of sacred themes, imagery, and symbols from Candomblé religion in Brazilian popular music.

Chapter four discusses Candomblé musical performance, the role of drummers in Candomblé, and the influence of Candomblé musicians as popular music icons in their communities. Chapter five examines how young Afro-Brazilian drummers of the *blocos afro* in Salvador have taken the art of sacred drumming into contemporary popular music production in Brazil and how many of the young musicians are "making noise" as part of the Negritude black-consciousness movement in their communities. Chapter six examines the many facets of Bahian Carnival and how various artists, Carnival organizations, and young Afro-Brazilians celebrate their "re-Africanization" with performances of popular music and appropriation of sacred themes, imagery, symbols, and iconography from Candomblé in public celebration. Chapter seven examines axé as an innovative contemporary style of Brazilian popular music. Combining elements of samba and other styles, axé is one of the contemporary popular music styles innovated within the locality of Salvador.

The sacred designation axé has been appropriated and secularized by the popular music industry and is now associated with many Bahian artists that include Daniela Mercury, Margareth Menezes, and Carlinhos Brown, and Carnival organizations such as Olodum, Timbalada, É o Tchan, and Ara Ketu. Outside of a religious context axé music is a thriving, youth-oriented popular style of electronic instrumentation and dance choreography that has gained mass-audience appeal and continues to influence a new generation of aspiring musicians. The final section of the epilogue concludes with a bestowal of hope, prosperity, and success from spiritual axé on all who read its contents.

1 | Sacred/Secular Influences
The Reinvention of West African Àsé in Brazil

I**T MAY SEEM** perplexing to examine the influences of a religious tradition on popular music. However, I believe that a conversation between the sacred and secular is an appropriate way to begin an exploration of what I refer to as axé and its African roots. I use the terms axé and African roots to examine aspects of Afro-Brazilian religious, cultural, and musical traditions that in many ways have influenced those of Brazilian culture and popular music. To comprehend the gamut of these influences, in this chapter I examine the ancestral origins of the religious concept of West African àsé and how it has been spread, reinvented, negotiated, altered, secularized, and accommodated in Brazilian culture in what is known as axé. With the spread of West African àsé, Brazil shares a legacy of African ancestry with other African diasporic areas.

Religion transforms people's lives by providing social dimensions and behavioral norms. Moreover, it provides sources for repentance, atonement, faith, devotion, reverence, and spirituality. Religious practices are geared to enhance the temporal aspects of life, from adolescence to maturity. Believers define who they are politically, socially and culturally through various forms of religious beliefs. These beliefs are often pervaded with myths: of an "omnipresent spiritual force" and the creation stories that surround it; of sacred forces that function as assistants to a Creator; of natural phenomena and the earthly and spiritual explanations for them.

Much religious talk centers on the dichotomies of good/evil, sacred/secular, and sin/redemption. The major goal of most religions is to redeem people during their earthly lives so they can move, after death, to a higher order that reconnects them with the spiritual world. "Good" actions correspond and are not in conflict with the laws and order of spirituality; certain "good" beliefs and practices that work in concert to ensure the integrity of religions are deemed sacred by religious dogma. The concept of "evil" comes in when people find themselves in a condition of unbalance, conflict, and interests that lie beyond the sacred, usually as a result of becoming more integrated in the activities of the secular, earthly world. The consequences of this integration can be described as sin or a "falling away." In many religions this unbalance can be remedied, as people are forgiven and receive redemption from the spiritual world.

In West African Yoruba religion, àsé is imagined as power and creative energy that mediates between the sacred and secular worlds and that can be channeled through many sources including human beings, plants, animals, blood, and inanimate objects (rocks, buildings, paper, soil). In addition, àsé is a boost of energy that can be charged through various types of rituals that appease a pantheon of ancestral spirits. These rituals include special ceremonies, animal sacrifice, anointing of herbs and special liquids, blood offerings, food offerings, recitation of prayers, musical performance, the sound of musical instruments (especially percussion), dance, and spirit possession.

In the secular world the manifestations, power, and energy of àsé are embedded in spirituality, creative energy of musical talent and artistic innovation, wisdom and knowledge, perseverance and survival, birth, family, lineage, prosperity, good fortune, and good health. Through the power of àsé people prosper and live in harmony with nature; the universe is allowed to exist. Some practitioners also believe that àsé is a powerful link between past, present, and future. They believe the protection of àsé is the force that has sustained Africans in many parts of the world from slavery to independence and into the present day.

Origins of West African Àsé

One of the major reasons I conducted research in West Africa was to trace the origins of àsé back to its cultural roots and to compare similarities and differences in the preservation of àsé in Brazil, West Africa, and in African diasporic areas. I began my inquiry by traveling to the Cape Coast of Ghana to Elmina Castle, built by the Portuguese in the fifteenth century as a trade station and a major point of embarkation for Africans transported to the New World.[1] Because various ethnic groups were housed together, the first attempts at maintaining African cultural traditions may have been made within the confines of Elmina. Experiencing the confines of Elmina was a solemn experience. Gazing out of the tiny barred windows made the voyage of displaced Africans and the "dangerous crossroads" over the Atlantic more vivid. My journey led to the àsé regions of Togo/Nigeria/Benin.

The origins of àsé concepts and philosophy stem from the Yoruba people of West Africa, who reside mostly in parts of southwest Nigeria and in communities scattered throughout Benin toward the Togo border.[2] The major religious center is located at Ile-Ife. In Yoruba tradition, as in other parts of Africa, there is a nebulous distinction between the sacred and secular realms of life and between the material and the spiritual. Acts of religiosity are celebrated and imbedded in all aspects of communal life—education, politics, harvesting, hunting, homemaking, and community welfare.[3] Philosophical principles that surround the foundation of àsé not only enhance religiosity and spirituality but also thrive and function in all aspects of life in the secular world.

In the Yoruba religion, the spiritual power and energy of àsé is bestowed upon devotees by a pantheon of ancestral spirits called *òrìsàs*. The Yoruba conceive àsé as having an important role in the cosmos: it is a single unifying entity that embraces human society, nature, and transcendental powers in a continuous cyclic movement of interaction and regeneration. The earth is connected with the sky and with generative forces such as rains, the sun, and the rivers that nourish humanity.

Nature is comprised of powerful living forces superior to man. They inhabit prominent natural objects such as mountains, rivers, and trees, which are generally regarded as temples or abodes of deities and ancestral spirits. The forces of nature in many instances personify specific human qualities—male, female, husband, wife, son, daughter, hunter, and martyr. These forces are not considered separate from humans; rather, the worlds of deities, ancestors, and human beings form a complete unity.

Àsé is conceptualized as fluid, like a river that never rests, a continual, flexible flow of powerful and energetic charges. The river flows within the framework of two inseparable realms: the visible, secular world of the living (*aiyé*) and the invisible, sacred world (*orun*) of the ancestors and òrìsàs. The ancestors, spiritual beings who dwell in orun, are imagined as having the ability to return to the physical world when family members designated as maskers (*eégun* or *Egúngún*) become the partial reincarnations of their predecessors.[4]

In myth, àsé was created by a Supreme Creator, known as Olódùmarè (or Olorum, Olorun), who presides over the affairs of nature and Mother Earth. Olódùmarè is omnipotent and wise, a father figure who represents a nonphysical and spiritual world. Olódùmarè has a pantheon of òrìsàs who possess àsé and who act as intermediaries between the spiritual realm and Mother Earth. According to myth, in the beginning, all the òrìsàs lived with Olódùmarè in heaven. The earth was covered with water and Olódùmarè commanded the òrìsà named Orishnala to form the earth. However, Orishnala was found intoxicated by his younger brother, Oduduwa, who then assumed the tasks of completing construction of the earth.[5]

Later, Olódùmarè intervened in a quarrel between the two brothers and made peace between them. To Oduduwa, who finished creating the earth, he gave the right to be king and ruler of the earth. This resulted in a royal lineage passed through Oduduwa's sixteen sons. To Orishnala he gave the power to mold bodies; he became the creator of humans. In these stories, Olódùmarè possesses the àsé of authority, power, and resourcefulness. He can be compared to the Christian God and Christian prophets. His great àsé of wisdom makes him a Solomon-like figure with the ability to settle spiritual disputes for the good of mankind.

Olódùmarè is a supreme king (*Obá*) and is often regarded as remote and difficult to approach. Although he is prayed to, no shrines are erected in his honor, no rituals are directed toward him, and no sacrifices are made to placate him. This can be explained by the belief, in Yoruba cosmology, that the remote and powerful creator can be approached only indirectly, through lesser deities.

The creation story of Olódùmarè presents various dichotomies: good/evil, sacred/secular, and sin/redemption. In the beginning, when Olódùmarè was in heaven and the earth was formless and covered with water, there was a sense of goodness and innocence. Evil and sin appeared when Oduduwa was given the responsibility for constructing the earth because of his older brother Orishnala's drunkenness. When chaos and conflict surrounded the completion of the earth, Oduduwa appeared as a savior figure. Olódùmarè models redemption when he intervenes and makes peace between the two brothers by assigning them different tasks for the good of the earth and its inhabitants.

The Òrìsàs: Possessors of Àsé

Despite the separation between heaven and earth, humans are able to petition Olódùmarè through mediation with the òrìsàs, the guardians of àsé. Religious life is based on and externally manifested in ritual through worship of the Supreme Creator, veneration of ancestors, and calls upon divinities to assist humans in making contact. Practitioners make sacrifices and offerings to ensure the òrìsàs' favor for the daily activities of the community, and believe that the òrìsàs are able to manifest themselves and transmit àsé at any geographic location when summoned through rituals of prayer, musical performance, dance, food offerings, spirit possession, and animal sacrifice.

The word *òrì*, root of the term òrìsà, has dual significance: It means "head," as in the physical head, but it also refers to forces responsible for controlling one's being. The physical head is representative of the inner person. The òrì is the personality—the soul that rules, controls, and guides the life and activities of a person. In essence, the òrìsàs represent an individual's own deep nature, as opposed to the roles and styles of behavior the individual has been taught by society. They provide the full spectrum of possibilities within an individual and the potentiality of the true self.[6]

The pantheon of òrìsàs includes Èsù, deity of disorder; Òrúnmìlá, sometimes referred to as Ifá, deity of wisdom; Yemoja, mother goddess of sea; Òsun, river deity; Osóòsi, the hunters' deity; Òsùmàrè, the rainbow serpent of the underworld; Oya, river deity; Sàngó, solar and storm deity; Òsanyìn, deity of herbal medicine; Sòpònnà, deity of smallpox and earth; Ògún, deity of war and iron; and Ibeji, deity of twin births.[7] These òrìsàs are not only a continuation and extension of the continual flow of àsé through life and death but also the ultimate personification of an unending cycle that moves in all directions in a circle of cosmic order. They are the imagined àsé of natural forces—thunder, storm, fire, water, wind, rainbow, and rain. They are also the conceptualization of living beings: husbands, wives, mothers, sea creatures, warriors, hunters, and martyrs.

The cosmology of àsé includes a trickster/guardian known by names such as Èsù, Elegbara, and Legba. This trickster/guardian, who knows the secrets of divination, possesses both positive and negative àsé; he stands at the crossroads of the sacred and secular. Both feared and loved, he is the messenger of ancestral spirits and the guardian of temples, houses, roads, and crossroads. During ceremonies, songs and special offerings are first given to the trickster/guardian to ensure a successful celebration.[8] Despite these special offerings, the trickster/guardian often double-crosses those who put their faith in him. Nevertheless, he is considered the protector of the people; those who abuse their power are at the mercy of the trickster/guardian, who can bestow negative àsé.

Mediating Àsé in the Secular World

Important to appeasing the òrìsàs are spiritual leaders called *babalaô*, who act as mediums between the sacred and secular worlds. In some communities the practitioners often refer to the leaders simply as baba (father) and ìyá (mother) as an enduring indication of a spiritual parent/guardian. Because of their spiritual powers, mature women are often imagined as being equal or superior to the ancestral spirits. In this capacity they serve as mothers, nurturers, and caretakers of the spirits, echoing a human mother's strong relationship and bond with her children. For example, Mama Yemoja is regarded as a great mother in the Nigeria area; practitioners describe her as a leader with "her hands full of àsé" and possessing special powers to summon the òrìsàs from the spiritual realm.[9]

The spiritual leaders also act as diviners and venerate the òrìsàs through the process of divination called Ifá. They preside over special houses and shrines and act as mediators over divination processes and ceremonies that appease the deities. Each of the shrines that I was allowed to visit was distinct and had a special character. Some shrines were adorned inside and out with special colors and decorations associated with a particular òrìsà. Some were constructed with several rooms where ceremonies were held, and with living quarters for the spiritual leader and other officials. The shrines in the communities were often the major centers of communal interaction. Membership in these shrines varied from approximately fifty to one hundred. Members sought the advice of the spiritual leader for various reasons, such as predicting future health or prosperity through special rituals that included the tossing of cowry shells in a number of combinations.

Àsé in the shrine is regenerated by anointed practitioners designated to serving the òrìsàs. These practitioners receive a "calling" or summons to serve the àsé world. There is commonly an initiation where leaders such as Mama Yemoja would preside over training the practitioners to serve the òrìsàs. Depending on the shrine, the length of the initiation may vary; initiated practitioners are often required to learn musical repertoire, drum rhythms, special repertoire, and participate in rituals that may include eating special foods and praying.

The life/death cycle is important for the continuation of àsé in the community, in that the experience of dying is imagined as a transformation into an ancestor deity and thus continues the life/death cycle. In this transformation àsé is nourished and transmitted to the living and the deceased through celebrations with elaborate processions, ceremonies, and festive drinking and dancing. Some communities have artisans trained to construct an array of distinctive coffins lined with the finest fabrics that symbolize the worldly accomplishments of the deceased. For example, if the deceased was successful and employed in an occupation such as a poultry farmer or taxi driver, the coffin may be constructed in the shape of a large fowl or an automobile. This and other rituals ensure that the deceased will be sent to orun with distinction.

West African Àsé and Artistic Expression

Music (singing and drumming) and dance are important for generating àsé power and creative energy in the shrine, the community, and in individuals. Moreover, this expression allows practitioners to communicate with the òrìsàs through spirit possession. Music and dance have mimetic qualities in that, through expression, initiated practitioners mimic the movements and personalities of the òrìsàs being celebrated.

Because of the significance of artistic expression in communicating with the spiritual world, in special ceremonies that celebrate the òrìsàs practitioners place a heavy emphasis on the text of chants, praise acclamations, and songs. Two vocal types, *orin* or song and *oríkì* or praise song, as well as several vocal styles, are available to singers. The oríkì òrìsà are praise hymns for the ancestral spirits in which a singer recites the names and deeds, status and power, characteristics and appearance, and likes and dislikes of a particular òrìsà.[10]

The sound of musical instruments (drums and bells) can evoke the power and energy of àsé. Together with voices, they are a means through which religiosity is expressed. Musical instruments are invigorated by the spiritual world and gain vestiges of power related to the àsé of healing, physical strength, and spirit possession. Constructed to resemble human beings or animals, instruments are in essence deified as the àsé of life. Occasionally they are given male or female names, even birth dates that the community celebrates with food and sacrificial offerings.

Instruments also have power to summon the spiritual realm. In producing àsé, the constant rhythmic pulsations of the drum are imagined as having special powers to provoke the òrìsàs. It is in essence a symbol of the community and symbolically forms a family—father, mother, son and daughter—and often graphically details the history of lineages. Drums are formed in various shapes and sizes. They are categorized as either single-headed, with an animal skin fixed on only one end, or double-headed, with an animal skin fixed on both ends of the drum. Because of their symbolic quality, proper care is given to construction and maintenance. Skilled craftsmen prayerfully construct drums with bells, string, cord, or pegs that may be attached around the instrument.[11]

In West Africa, many practitioners I spoke with regarded music (the sonic) as sacred sound and dance (choreographic movements) as sacred movements that are the culmination of an active engagement with the spiritual world. Many believed that such expressions offered to the spiritual world mediated positive àsé in their experiences of religious and sociocultural identity in the shrine (sacred) and community (secular). Moreover, by actively engaging in music and dance for the òrìsàs in the shrines, many believed that they would continue to be successful in the secular world.

Many practitioners revered drums as having spiritual qualities. In my interpretation, drums often were revered as "holy beings." Performance of the music by skilled musicians was also important for generating positive àsé. The male musicians that I interacted with often assumed roles as special/anointed drummers. Some practitioners believed that these musicians were specially chosen by the òrìsàs to perform the music. In the same way that drums were considered sacred, drummers became empowered by òrìsàs with the power and creative energy of àsé. Even during special rehearsals that practitioners were allowed to observe, performing drummers were highly motivated and seemed to be empowered by the òrìsàs.

Omofolabo Soyinka Ajayi describes three functional stages of dance in West African–influenced religions—invocational, transcendental, and celebratory—that I believe can be applied to some of the ceremonies I observed in my research. According to Ajayi, in many West African–influenced religions invocational dancing is performed to summon the presence of the òrìsàs and prepare practitioners for worship. Transcendental or possessive dance signals that communication with the spiritual world has been reached. This dance is executed in an altered state of consciousness in which an òrìsà assumes control of the body of a practitioner. The change can be subtle, marked only by changes in dance patterns. Elements of the òrìsà's personality, including habits, emotional dispositions, and the social mores he or she symbolizes, appear in the dancing, along with the òrìsà's physical features. Finally, celebrative dance culminates the wor-

ship service. It is a means of giving thanks and praise for a successful completion of the ceremony.[12]

In many of the ceremonies I observed in West Africa, the music and dance
could be described as invocational, transcendental, and celebratory. But in many,
music informed dance expression as a means of appeasing the spiritual world.
During the special ceremonies musical performance often culminated with ring
or circular dances that symbolized community, solidarity, affirmation, and innovation. Some could be described as processional in that, at the beginning of ceremonies, initiated practitioners entered the shrine in a uniform fashion in what
seemed to be a procession (often dressed in white garments), followed by other
dances to summon the òrìsàs. The intensity of the music (singing and drumming) informed dance as spirit possession was evoked; some practitioners experienced a type of personality transformation and took on the spiritual attributes of the òrìsàs they were serving. When possessed, female participants often
dressed as males and mimicked the movements associated with male spirits;
similarly, male participants sometimes dressed in feminine apparel and hair-
styles and mimicked the movements associated with female spirits.

Àsé concepts and philosophical principles continue to guide the lives of
many people in the West African region. These concepts and principles are embedded in everyday life. The religious experiences and belief in àsé expressed
by the practitioners that I observed play a vital role in transforming their lives
by providing social dimensions and behavioral norms. Furthermore, belief in
àsé provides sources for repentance, atonement, faith, devotion, reverence, and
spirituality. This belief also enhances the temporal aspects of life, from adolescence to maturity. In the secular world people often define who they are politically, socially, and culturally through various forms of religious belief. The vitality of these beliefs is pervaded with myths: of Ólodùmarè, the "omnipresent
spiritual force," creation stories, and the òrìsàs, the sacred forces that function as
assistants to the Supreme Creator. For many practitioners, sacred àsé keeps them
connected with the spiritual world and enables them to thrive and survive in the
secular world.

Sacred/Secular Connections: The Internal and
External Spread of West African Àsé

The spread of West African àsé concepts to other areas may have begun to occur
before the arrival of Africans to the New World. Here I am not making an argument that the entire continent of Africa was comprised of West African àsé; but
with constant migration (voluntary and forced) of Africans from the West African region to other areas due to kingdom decline, famine, wars, and enslave-

ment, àsé concepts may have spread to various parts of Africa even before the arrival of Africans to the New World. For example, I interacted with several communities outside of the Yoruba as far as the Cape Coast of Ghana, who were enriched in the àsé tradition and who expressed that, because of the migratory flow of Africans from many parts of the Western region, their ancestors may have been descendants from this tradition. This is what I refer to as an internal spread of West African àsé. Moreover, the establishment of Elmina Castle, built by the Portuguese on the Cape Coast of Ghana (in the fifteenth century) as a trade station and a major point of embarkation for Africans to the New World, also prepared the way for an external spread of West African àsé to the New World.

My major goal in writing this book was to examine the ancestral origins of the religious concept of West African àsé and how it has been spread, reinvented, negotiated, altered, secularized, and accommodated as a concept in Brazilian culture. But in conducting my research I also found what I refer to as a type of "global spreading" of West African àsé concepts and imagery through commercial recordings and performances. In contemporary times West African popular musicians with international status have reinvented, negotiated, altered, secularized, and accommodated àsé expressions—religion, music, dance, imagery, and symbols—in popular music and culture. For example, Babatunde Olatunji (1927–2003), perhaps the most prominent Nigerian drummer, had an extensive career and recorded with jazz musicians that include John Coltrane, Horace Silver, Cannonball Adderley, and Max Roach. Olatunji's album *Drums of Passion: The Invocation* (1989) incorporated elements of the sacred and secular with several songs dedicated to the òrìsàs. This album is part of the *Drums of Passion* series released in 1986 as *Dance to the Beat of My Drum*.[13]

Other West African musicians of jùjú music and Afro-Beat have incorporated sacred/secular imagery and symbolism of àsé in popular music performances.[14] On his album *Live Live JùJú [Live]* (1988), King Sunny Adé combined imagery of the sacred/secular with his inclusion of the popular song "Àsé." Another album, *Get Yer Jùjús Out* (1989) by Chief Commander Ebenezer Obey, included the song "Òsé Olorum Obá," which pays homage to the Supreme Being in Yoruba religion. The legendary Fela Anikulapo-Kuti (1938–1997)—creator of Afro-Beat, a fusion of jazz, soul, highlife, and jùjú—often looked to the power and creative energy of àsé for inspiration as he observed rituals before performances such as pouring a libation to honor the òrìsàs.

The external spread of West African àsé, expressed through religious worship, shrines, music, musical instruments, dance, spirit possession, and devoted practitioners, is part of a legacy manifested in Afro-Brazilian culture that in many ways has influenced popular music in Brazil. In Brazil, sacred energy has often invigorated secular creativity. My case in point is the influence that Candomblé religion has had in the sacred and secular landscapes of Afro-Brazilian culture, racial identity, and popular music production. In the experience of slavery, Africans attempted to make sense of their new environment by reinventing familiar sacred landscapes. For the Yoruba this was a reinvention of àsé nurtured in Brazil's mixed cultural and religious society comprised of Central Africans (from the Congo-Angola region), Native Americans, and Europeans. In the new landscape of Brazil, just as in the old, the Yoruba attempted to venerate òrìsàs by holding special celebrations where àsé could be generated. In these celebrations, recreation of a nebulous distinction between sacred/secular activities resulted in the emergence of Candomblé religion.

The Sacred: Reinventing West African Àsé in Brazil

Candomblé religion is a reinventing in Brazil of the sacred landscape of African religiosity and spiritual guardianship. In Candomblé, Afro-Brazilians have reinvented àsé concepts and philosophy as axé. As in the Yoruba tradition, in Candomblé axé is the imagined spiritual power and energy bestowed upon practitioners by the pantheon of òrìsàs (in Brazil *orixás*, e.g., Exú, Yemanjá, Iansã, Oxóssi). Many Candomblé practitioners believe these ancestral spirits can become manifest and transmit West African àsé to any geographic location when they are summoned by invoking the proper ritual—music, dance, and spirit possession.

Devoted practitioners believe in a strong relationship between human beings and cosmic totality. This and other Candomblé beliefs are informed by African heritage and conceptions of nature, unity, and life. Candomblé forms a collective sense of communal consciousness with the sacred, the origins and foundations of cosmic order exhibited through holy things such as images of the orixás and sounds of sacred musical instruments. Communication with the sacred involves an initiation process in which elders teach younger practitioners the foundations of religious worship and the history of the religion. During the initiation process, the younger practitioners may form an emotional bond with each other, resulting in a common group with unified experience.

Candomblé is a complex religion that has emerged under different sociocultural experiences in Afro-Brazilian culture. The origins of the religion are based on a mixture of historical, social, and cultural experiences—forced importation, colonialism, master/slave relations, cultural memory, ethnic affiliations, religious conversion, Roman Catholicism, Native American religious mythology, and the reinvention of ancestral worship.

Candomblé emerged in the midst of the different Brazilian nações (nations)— Congo-Angola, Nagô (Yoruba, Ketu, and Ijexá), and Gêge (Ewe and Fon)—that contributed to its vibrancy and complexity in Brazil. Even before the spread of West African àsé, in the mid-sixteenth century Africans imported from the Central African (Congo-Angola) region attempted to maintain many of their religious traditions and worship of ancestral spirits. These traditions also were grounded in a belief that secular structures were intimately linked with religious ideas.[15]

Similar to West African mythology of the secular living world (aiyé) and the sacred realm (orun), Central African mythology was centered on a pantheon of ancestral spirits that mediated between the sacred and secular worlds. In Central African mythology, the Supreme Being was Zambi.[16] The universe was divided into two worlds, the world of the living and the world of the dead, which were separated by a large body of water through which the dead had to pass. Although the souls of the departed moved to the other realm to join the souls of deceased ancestors, they never completely abandoned the secular world of the living. The ancestral spirits retained their power and influenced the fortunes and continual growth of their surviving relatives.[17]

Human beings were considered "double beings," with visible outer and invisible inner shells. The soul was an eternal force that acted independently of the outer being. When the outer person slept, the soul flew off to pursue its own labors and adventures. In appeasing the sacred world, initiated spiritual leaders (*xinguila*) served as mediators between humans and the sacred world. Moreover, the spiritual leaders were highly dependent on music because only musicians playing various types of musical instruments (e.g., bells, drums) could provoke spirit possession.[18] Thus, as Candomblé emerged some of these beliefs and practices from Central African mythology were integrated with West African àsé concepts.

There are many plausible explanations for the spread and persistence of West African àsé concepts over other African-influenced religious beliefs in Brazil. Àsé may have persisted in Afro-Brazilian culture because of the late arrival of West Africans who displayed a tightly ingrained "psycho-aesthetic" devotion to àsé in their minds and bodies. By the time a large number of West Africans began to be imported in Brazil in the mid-eighteenth century, some of the spiritual leaders and culture barriers associated with Central African religious traditions were gone, leaving a younger generation of Africans and their offspring who in many ways were "Brazilianized" and could now be identified as "Afro-Brazilians." Thus, cultural memory of this younger generation may have been less vivid than their elders.

West African àsé encompassed an entire body of philosophical principles (religious worship, health, family, talents, and prosperity) that individuals could incorporate in their lives for survival in the secular world of Brazil. With the constant influx of Gêge and Nagô Africans (Gêge-Nagô) in the later centuries of Brazilian slavery, a significant religious mixing began to emerge. Many arrived with a vivid sense of their cultural heritage of àsé and attempted to find common ground in religious worship in a shared core of cultural beliefs while attempting to maintain specific traditions. For many Africans already established in Brazil, perhaps intermingling with practitioners of West African àsé as a life and energy source may have stimulated a deeper reconnection with African religious beliefs.

West African òrìsàs were venerated alongside other deities—voduns for Gêge, and inkisses for Congo-Angola—many of which had similar spiritual attributes linked with natural forces (thunder, storm, fire, water, wind, rainbow, rain). However, with the dominance of slavery and religious conversion, to protect the continuance of African worship in Brazil, many of these ancestral spirits were often concealed and reinvented through the syncretism of combining spiritual qualities from African ancestry with the saints of the Roman Catholic Church.[19] Ancestral spirits such as Yemanjá became linked with the Virgin Mary, Iansã with St. Barbara, and so forth. By conjoining ancestral worship with rites from Roman Catholicism, enslaved Africans reconnected themselves with West African àsé but at the same time extended their African sensibility of worshiping the ancestral spirits through religious and artistic expression of music and dance in Brazil.

Some Candomblé practitioners also venerate Native American spirits such as the Caboclo, which represents the Native American population. Some believe that Native Americans are the true "owners of the land," since they occupied Brazil before the Europeans. Thus, in Candomblé special ceremonies should be given to honor Caboclo spirits and acknowledge this ownership.[20] This type of worship may have resulted from the earlier arrival of the Central Africans, when Native Americans still largely inhabited Brazil. Caboclo spirits may have been adopted in Candomblé as a religious act of the Africans adopting the divinities of other people.[21] During the Caboclo ceremony (Candomblé de Caboclo), several Native American spirits (e.g., Tupinamba) are celebrated with singing, drumming, and dancing in a manner similar to the African orixás.

The Reinvention of West African Artistic Expression in Brazil

In Candomblé religion, music (singing and drumming) and dance are vital sources for generating positive àsé and communicating with the spiritual world. Moreover, for many practitioners music and dance connect the sacred and secular worlds. In Candomblé there is a distinct West African artistic influence in that the Yoruba had a large body of music and dance repertoire to celebrate the ancestral guardians. But because of the sociocultural affiliation with the different nações (nations), there has also been an intermingling and mixture of artistic ideas and stylistic techniques. This may have resulted from the conjoining and celebration of ancestral guardians that are imagined as possessing similar spiritual attributes such as Yemanjá (West African) and Dandalunda (Central Africa). For example, ijexá, a drum rhythm that is highly regarded in the Candomblé repertoire, was performed in many ceremonies that I attended in Salvador to celebrate ancestral guardians—Oxum, Oxalá, Yemanjá (West African), and Dandalunda (Central African).

The designation "Ijexá" (Ijesha) refers to one of the West African nações (nations) where àsé was nurtured. However, in many ceremonies I observed that practitioners referred to Ijexá as a drum rhythm performed in a Congo-Angolan style in moderate tempo using an open-palm drumming technique.[22] Practitioners expressed that the songs that accompany this rhythm are sung in Yoruba to honor the West African guardians, and often in Kimbundu to celebrate Dandalunda. Although there is a distinct West African artistic influence, music and dance in Candomblé is also an example of how Africans from different nações constructed and reinvented artistic expression for their new experience in time and geographic space within Brazilian society and the sanctum of their religion. This type of construction (reinvention) links Brazil with other African diasporic areas where there are different manifestations of West African àsé.

The Sanctum: Reinventing Sacred Spaces

The *terreiro* (Candomblé religious center) is a reinvention and recreation of the Yoruba sanctum, sacred shrine, compound, and space where axé is nurtured through religious ritual, music, dance, and spirit possession. Each terreiro is part of the sacred "holy things" in the Candomblé religion. Each has its own axé that caused it to be established and to continue and flourish. Many practitioners believe that axé is buried in the soil under the terreiro. The terreiros that allowed me into their sacred world were some of the oldest religious centers for Candomblé worship in Salvador. These terreiros accommodate approximately fifteen to three hundred members. The shapes and size of the terreiros vary. For example, Tira Jima is a small, one-room edifice, while Ilê Odô Ogé can hold three hundred or more attendees. Architecturally, Ilê Odô Ogé resembles a temple with statues of the orixás, water fountains, and what seem to be marble floors. The terreiros are located in a variety of socioeconomic neighborhoods.

Some terreiros hang a white flag or scarf from a pole or around a tree to indicate that a terreiro is in the vicinity. At the entrance, special foods such as manioc flour, eggs, and beer may be left for the orixá that is being celebrated on a given day. Dried coconut leaves are hung in the doors and windows to ward off evil forces. The room where Candomblé ceremonies take place is often painted white, with colorful strips of crepe paper hung from the ceiling. When the wind blows

Interior of a Candomblé terreiro in Salvador.

through open windows, the rustling sound of paper gives the room a feeling of awe and mysticism.

Although in most terreiros ceremonies are conducted in private, on a few occasions some do allow media coverage, for example, during the visit of an elected official. In 1998, during my initial study of the terreiros, I visited the Gantois, one of the oldest terreiros in Salvador. The local media were allowed to interview some older practitioners with television cameras present about the grave illness of their leader and the succession process to elect a new leader.[23]

Terreiros are major repositories for history in the community. Members take pride in their chronological wall displays of photos of all past officials, along with items such as animal horns and skins, religious pictures, and crucifixes. Each of the terreiros I visited has special rituals for celebrating the orixás on specific days, including sprinkling liquids and sacred powders in the sanctum and on the musical instruments, feasting on the favorite foods of the orixás (e.g., goat, chicken, okra), and smoking cigars (charutos) as a healing agent. In addition, some terreiros have special altars that hold straw baskets where practitioners deposit money as a symbol of good fortune and prosperity.

The interior of most terreiros is distinct, with a square or star-shaped stone marker (the entoto) in the middle of the floor. Many believe this is a sacred space where axé is nurtured. In this most sacred area of the terreiro, practitioners dance, experience spirit possession, and kneel in reverence to the orixás, lead-

Special altar constructed inside a Candomblé terreiro in Salvador.

ers, and musicians. Vases filled with sacred liquids and bowls of manioc flour are left here as special offerings during Candomblé ceremonies. At various times during the ceremonies, purified water from the vases is sprinkled on the floor in this area.

Similar to West African Yoruba tradition, the success of the religion depends to a large extent on a hierarchy of leaders who nurture axé. With responsibilities ranging from administration to overseeing musical training, leaders also function as diviners in a capacity similar to that of the babalaô, who act as consultants in ailments and future predictions. Although males have played a major role in the organizational leadership and makeup of Candomblé, female leaders continue to offer an image of "mother and nurturer."[24] Female leaders are known by names such as *mãe de santo* (saint mother) or *iyalorixá* (mother of the orixás); males by *pai de santo* or *babalorixá* (father of the orixás).[25] Many terreiros also have what is known as a "little mother" (*mãe pequeno*) or a "little father" (*pai pequeno*), a person who serves in a secondary leadership capacity. The secondary leaders are often expected to assume a primary role after the death of the leader.

Leadership is established in various ways, including proprietary ownership, heredity, seniority, or a combination of all three. Some leaders establish small houses of worship within the confines of their own homes.[26] This gives them primary authority to choose their successors. In many terreiros, leaders are given royal or chiefdom status or both; leadership is often handed down from parent to offspring.

The death of a leader is a solemn experience. The axé must be rechanneled to the future leader by means of the axêaxê ritual. One practitioner I interviewed was able to describe his own experiences with the axêaxê traditions in his terreiro, Ilê Oya Gei, which is located in São Martins in Salvador, and which follows Gêge (Ewe/Fon) traditions.[27] He said when a leader dies in his terreiro the only sounds that are produced during the axêaxê come not from drums but from clay pots that are beaten softly on the side.[28] Other practitioners explained that during an axêaxê, the musical repertoire is somber and geared to sending the person to orun, the spiritual world of the ancestors. During an extensive period of mourning following the axêaxê, most terreiros will not provide ceremonies to the community, usually until a successor has been chosen. Other local terreiros may pay their respects to the deceased by refraining from holding ceremonies and silencing various types of music for a given time.

Sons and daughters of the orixás also regenerate axé in the terreiro. These practitioners symbolically experience two births, one by earthly and one by spiritual parents. In this way they are designated as the spiritual children of their orixás. Honoring the spiritual parents is a great part of devotion in Candomblé. It should be noted that not everyone in the religion is allowed to become a son or daughter of the orixás. As in West African tradition, practitioners receive a "calling" or summons to serve the spiritual world. This summons may be the result of a catastrophic experience deemed as the orixás' way of attracting the attention of a practitioner. The practitioner then consults a spiritual leader who recommends a solution through prayer and meditation and through the *jogo dos búzios* (casting of cowry shells), which determine the initiate's particular orixá.

The initiation process is a long series of events by which the leader transmits the axé to the initiates. This involves learning a body of music repertoire, drum rhythms, dances, and special chants and songs of the orixás; participating daily in several types of ritual bathing with sacred herbs; eating special foods; and praying. In undergoing this extensive process, the initiates form a communal bond and allow themselves to become subservient and submissive so that they may be ridden and tamed as horses of the orixás.

One practitioner described his initiation as a solemn experience. Before he was initiated into the Candomblé religion he was a devout Catholic, even serving as an altar boy in the church. But at twelve years of age he received a calling from the orixás. Although his mother was an initiate in Candomblé, she felt that he was too young to become an initiate. However, in a dream the orixás revealed themselves to her and informed her that her son had a special mission to perform. After this she was more receptive to the initiation of her son, allowing him to begin the process when he was fifteen years old.[29]

Other practitioners say that during the initiation process they became aware of the sacred "holy things" (images, objects) and sacred abilities. Female and male initiates constantly experience spirit possession. They are kept in different areas within the terreiros and are constantly guarded by the orixás. On occasions when the orixás leave the initiation room, Erê, the spirit of innocence, protects the initiates. They continue to experience spirit possession but their movements and emotional behavior are childlike. After an extensive initiation period, each initiate's head is shaved and white dots are painted on their heads, foreheads, and cheeks. The dots symbolize the orixás arriving and placing themselves in the heads of the initiates.[30]

New initiates participate in special ceremonies such as the one I observed at Terreiro Amazi tuá de Unzambe Mãe Lau. The initiates were presented to the community with a procession led by the mãe de santo.[31] Their heads were clean-shaven and painted with white and black spots; they had long beads around their necks. They all moved in circular motions as the leader of the terreiro constantly rang an adjá bell. The initiates then entered a quiet, solemn state with their eyes closed. Following this was a hearty welcome from the community and the spiritual guardians. Then began a ritual cleansing in which the new initiates were sprinkled with sacred powders and rolled on straw mattresses, covered in a white sheet and holding a leaf from a sacred plant as the leader continued to ring the adjá. The second time that the new initiates entered the room, their heads were covered with feathers and they went through the ceremonial process again.

Ogans, men chosen by the leader and a particular orixá to act as protectors and elders of the terreiro, play similar roles as the initiates. Ogans are also required to undergo an initiation that lasts approximately twenty-one days to one month. During the initiation period they become pure vessels of the orixás and are required to abstain from intimate relations and to participate in ritual bathing in sacred herbs. Ogans also learn proper religious etiquette for worshiping the orixás and for offering animal sacrifices to their orixás. Each eventually becomes what is known as an *axogun*, a person responsible for sacrificing animals on the day when the orixás are celebrated. Ogans also play administrative roles: they make sure that the terreiro continues to be provided for financially and spiritually. They also learn musical repertoire of the orixás; the ones who perform music in their respective terreiros and are known as *ogan alabê*.[32] With such responsibility, ogans are given great respect—they serve as role models and act as advisers to younger members in the terreiro.

Over the years I conducted research on Candomblé, I encountered many experiences in attending ceremonies at different terreiros. I have chosen three memorable experiences to discuss some of the ways axé can be generated in a terreiro and how practitioners celebrate the ancestral spirits with an active participation in singing, drumming, and dancing. The first ceremony took place in October 1998 at Ilê Axé Opô Afonjá, one of the oldest Candomblé terreiros in Salvador. Many practitioners and families live on the grounds of this terreiro. The room where the ceremony was held was large enough to hold approximately five hundred people. During the ceremony, the entire floor of the sanctum was covered with sacred leaves. Several chairs were placed in the front of the room. One of them, the mãe de santo's chair, resembled a queen's throne. On opposite sides of the room was special seating for other officials of the terreiro. For ceremonial purposes, men and women in the audience were not allowed to sit in the same areas.

Preparations for the ceremony began long before the start time of 7:00 p.m. Chickens and goats were prepared for sacrifice, special foods were cooked, participants were dressed, and the musicians were rehearsed. When the ceremony began and the musicians began beating the Candomblé rhythms, the terreiro immediately filled with people from the community. The leader purified the room with pemba, a powdery substance that was blown over the room and the musical instruments.[33] The initiates knelt three times at the entrance of the terreiro to ask the orixá Exú (the trickster/guardian) for permission to begin. Once the ceremony began, it lasted until the next day. This was because many practitioners believed that, from midnight to early morning, the orixá Exú is most active at the crossroads of good and evil, with events such as robbery, fights, police brutality, and narcotic trafficking making it dangerous for anyone to leave the protection of the terreiro during these hours.[34] But it is also believed that the orixá Ogum has the power to control Exú's trickery by dispatching two types of spirits who act as policemen: Da Roda and Xorokquê.

The first part of the ceremony began with a procession of initiates that lasted approximately forty minutes. After this, a barrage of fireworks announced the entrance of approximately twenty women led by the mãe de santo, all carrying a large wooden bowl of food. As they entered the room, they placed the bowl in the sacred area and knelt to honor the orixás. Practitioners from the audience were allowed to assemble in this area to eat from the contents of the bowl, which was filled with okra, one of the favorite dishes of Xangô, the orixá that was being celebrated. While all this was going on, the initiates experienced spirit possession and were assisted by the *ekede*. When a female initiate went into possession, the ekede removed her scarf and wrapped it around her head, then placed a special white garment around her waist. When a male initiate went into possession, his shirt was removed and a white scarf was wrapped tightly around his upper torso. While in possession, jewelry and shoes were also removed. This was all done to ensure that the initiates remained neatly dressed and poised throughout the rituals and spirit possession.

The ceremony climaxed when the initiates entered the room a third time carrying a long red cloth called the *ojá abalá*. People in the audience again were allowed to gather in the sacred area of the room, this time to encircle themselves with the cloth. This was an empowerment of axé ritual. After the ritual the initiates, dressed in elaborate clothing, entered the room holding sacred objects such as mirrors, swords, amulets, bows, and arrows. Flowers were given to each initiate as they danced.

In November 1998 I attended another ceremony at Ilê Axé Opô Afonjá. This ceremony was given in honor of orixá Oxóssi, the spiritual guardian of the mãe de santo of this Candomblé. As in other ceremonies, the initiates danced. But what was unusual was that the mãe de santo danced also. In other ceremonies she sat in her special chair and the initiates passed by her, paying homage by kneeling in a prayerlike position. In this ceremony axé was mainly transmitted through spirit possession of the mãe de santo. When the mãe de santo went into possession there was great excitement in the room. The initiates immediately stopped dancing and fell to the floor in a circle, bowing their heads and not moving from this position. The only person in the middle of the ring was the mãe de santo, whose choreographic movements were similar to riding a horse as she imitated the spiritual qualities of her orixá. At this time the initiates did not experience possession but only stood in the ring and clapped their hands while the mãe de santo experienced spirit possession.

In July 2002 I witnessed a ceremony at Tira Jima where both African and Native American (Caboclo) spirits were celebrated. This particular ceremony was special in that it also was given to celebrate the installation of a new mãe de santo, Sonia Santos, who had assumed the position after the demise of her mother Luz. The first part of the ceremony was dedicated to summoning the orixás, but the second part was dedicated to celebrating the Native American spirits (Candomblé de Caboclo), with the initiates dressed in elaborate costumes and headdresses. Special foods such as fruit, vegetables, beer, and nuts were prepared for the Native American spirits and placed in a special area of the terreiro, where it remained for several days and was then deposited in the woods. Another part of the ceremony involved smoking large cigars (charutos) and drinking beer. The axé of health and healing was transmitted to the practitioners, as smoke from the cigars became a healing agent when it was blown in the faces and on the bodies of practitioners who sought cures from illness. Another remedy was rubbing leaves from special trees on the body of the sick. This part of the ceremony was called a Girô.

Heightened spirit possession in the Candomblé de Caboclo celebration involved active participation in singing, drumming, and dancing. The choreographic movements were similar to samba, with fast movements from the feet and hips. One of the most unusual aspects of the celebration was that initiates often encouraged participants seated in the audience to participate in the dancing.

Participants in this terreiro relayed to me fascinating stories about their experiences of possession when celebrating Caboclo spirits. In one, when the initiates experienced possession they were possessed by Marujo, a spirit that manifested himself as a drunken sailor who smoked excessively. Initiates possessed by Marujo stumble in a drunken manner. A mediating spirit named Martin, often depicted as a bird, descends as an agent of Marujo to control the drunken manner exhibited by initiates.[35]

In all three of the ceremonies I have just described, axé empowerment was central to the celebration but was generated in different ways. All of the terreiros, and their Candomblé ceremonies, were unique. Practitioners responded in various ways. For many the active participation of singing, drumming, dancing, and spirit possession were a type of service and devotion and acts of "doing" and "being"—sacramental offerings of one's self. Some practitioners believed they were vessels and sources of encouragement in the community and terreiro. Thus, in these acts of service and devotion they experienced an embodiment of axé that was manifested in a variety of beliefs and practices and that offered them protection from evil forces and rewards of good fortune and prosperity.

In most terreiros the ritual protocol was very specific for all ceremonies. This included public ceremonies that involved animal sacrifices to orixás on designated days of the week. The sacrifices were most often done in private before the ceremony commenced. In ceremonies, participants invoked each orixá in a fixed order (from Exú to Oxalá). Many ceremonies were similar to what I witnessed in West Africa in that there was an active engagement with the spiritual world that culminated with singing, drumming, dancing, and heightened spirit possession. The ceremonies normally ended with a communal meal after the orixás had been sent away through special songs. All of this assured the generation of axé in the terreiros.

In many terreiros, spirit possession was distinctive. Initiated practitioners in possession often shivered, moaned, screamed, and made contorted movements. Although their bodies and arm movements moved rapidly, they never seemed to bump into or touch any other person. On occasion some terreiros celebrated both West African and Congo-Angolan spirits. Practitioners described that the initiated experience spirit possession in different ways. When a West African spirit (orixá) possesses an initiate, the initiate normally places both hands in a cupped position behind the back. But while in possession by a Congo-Angolan spirit, the initiate normally places the hands on the right side of the body as they sway back and forth. The music and dance informs these complex experiences with some songs that may be sung in Yoruba and/or Kimbundu and drum rhythms played by the musicians employing various stylistic techniques (e.g., open palms, drumsticks).

Although leaders, initiates, and musicians played an important role in ritualizing the orixás, I believe that noninitiated practitioners (the audience) served as active participants and contributed to generating axé. The noninitiated were also part of the community that continued to keep Candomblé religion, music, and dance vibrant. They attended the ceremonies for many reasons; they legitimized axé experiences by witnessing the initiates' communication with the spiritual world. In essence, noninitiated participants can be regarded as the "receivers" of the axé blessings of good health and fortune that the orixás bestow on the secular world. This is why in many terreiros noninitiates are encouraged to participate in ceremonies by singing, clapping, and encouraging the initiates. The enthusiasm that they produce is a catalyst for generating axé energy in the terreiro.

Similar to the West African tradition, in Candomblé ceremonies music, dance, and spirit possession make up an important tripartite that work together to call forth the presence of the orixás and produce positive axé. Music is part of the sacred and, along with dance and spirit possession, makes up what I describe as a "holy trinity." Music informs dance and allows practitioners to mimic the movements that they believe represent the orixás incarnate. In essence music (singing and drumming) and dance bridge the sacred and secular worlds. Through music and dance practitioners communicate with the divine, give praise and thanks, petition for general or specific blessings, appease, atone, acknowledge, and celebrate the existence of the axé in their lives.

In Candomblé, music is a "spice" that energizes the expression of dance that follows a pattern of processional/invocational, transcendental, and celebratory. Moreover, Candomblé continues the West African tradition of ring dancing, which symbolizes communal unity. In ring dancing, initiates move in a circle around the center of the room similar to their West African ancestors as àsé energy is produced.

Candomblé distinguishes itself within West African àsé tradition as the product of Africans who were forced to survive in the different and new environment of Brazil. These Africans attempted to make sense of a colonial environment and maintain a sense of their historical consciousness and cultural values by re-creating aspects of their religious and artistic expressions. To do so, the traditional values and customs that served them at the "crossroads" of sacredness and secularism had to be renegotiated within the new environment. Candomblé was the result: an Afro-Brazilian cultural tradition where the sacred space of the terreiro continues to function within the Brazilian society.

Axé and Candomblé Religion in Brazilian Society

Beyond the sacred space of the terreiro, the reception and perception of axé and Candomblé in Brazilian society have been manipulated from the outside—within the secular world and beyond the terreiro. Candomblé initially emerged within the urban context of Salvador, where Africans and mulattos made up a majority of the population. Within this urban context certain powerful elite and social players involved in politics, local authority, religious settings, and social groups became involved in perpetuating ideological perceptions about the religion.

As facets of Afro-Brazilian culture, the presence of axé and Candomblé religion in Brazil have been utilized in political and commercial propaganda linked with the affirmation and valorization of national identity, local and communal identity, and marketing of products that are distinctive with the state of Bahia's cultural praxis (baianidade), and as part of a global outreach and connection with pan-Africanism and black identity (Negritude). All of this has occurred over different periods of time in Brazilian history.

Roberto Motta, a professor at the Federal University in Recife, Brazil, whom I had an opportunity to interview, agrees that Candomblé has functioned within an urban context:

> Candomblé has always been an urban religion and to this day it is the most urban religion in Salvador. This is because in the city blacks interact in such a way as to perpetuate their African legacy. Whereas in the countryside people have been isolated from one another and there is more control from the Church and the "powers that be." The city with its anonymity has always favored Candomblé. Candomblé [axé] is important in Salvador as a whole because it came to be treated as a character of Salvador [Bahia], something that expresses "Brazilianhood." It has become a national religion in Brazil. People use Candomblé [axé] symbols in everyday conversation even though they are not believers.[36]

Motta's responses make references to Candomblé being part of the true fabric of Brazilian culture. Outside the confines of the Candomblé terreiro, nonpractitioners often call upon the power and energy of axé in order to achieve their goals in terms of employment, music, family, health, and prosperity. The empowering rituals that channel the blessings of the axé into prosperity and success used to be observed only within the confines of the Candomblé terreiro. Now these rituals in many instances are performed in secular settings such as by many Carnival organizations in Salvador within the context of public annual festivals. Before many local festivals in Salvador participants often observe Candomblé sacred rituals such as the Padê, which involves special liquids and food offerings given to the orixá Exú to secure a successful festival season. Also, perfumes, garments, and trinkets are commercially marketed as products of axé and in many instances can be purchased at local malls.

In Salvador the iconography of the Candomblé religion is evident: Buildings bear images of symbols from Candomblé such as the mirrors, amulets, bows and arrows of the orixás. Buildings and streets are named after the orixás. One of the most important sites in the city is the Dique de Tororó, a lagoon where statues of the orixás are erected. These images give the city a special kind of ambience;

Dique de Tororó in Salvador.

they act as guardians to attract locals and tourists. They are also displayed in museums and shopping malls, on travel brochures, and on the Internet.

Figa, a good luck charm constructed to resemble a clenched fist with the thumb extended between the index and middle fingers, is a symbol that demonstrates how African religion and culture have influenced Brazil. Although this symbol originated in Afro-Brazilian religion, it has become popular with many Brazilians. Because it is one of the adornments that people wear around their necks, merchants in tourist shops in many areas of Brazil sell woodcarvings of the figa.

To comprehend how Candomblé as a religious institution and its inner workings have been received and perceived in Brazilian society outside of the terreiro, the appropriated festivals, iconography, and cultural symbols must be examined within a historical perspective. Historically, the reception and perception of Candomblé in Brazil has ranged from legal prohibition to tolerance. Thus, when one examines Candomblé as an Afro-Brazilian tradition, this tradition must also be viewed within the constructs and complexity of racial identity in Brazil that for many years has been enshrouded in a myth of racial democracy and governmental denial of inequalities.

Brazil is a country that has celebrated miscegenation and whitening and has often discouraged the establishment of social organizations based on racial identities. With regard to racial identity, Brazilian intellectuals and elites have often attempted to offer explanations about Afro-Brazilians in terms of racial and physical characteristics, and about social and cultural differences through literary, scientific, sociological, anthropological, and theoretical types of approaches. This can be seen especially in the early part of the twentieth century, with the prevalence of Eurocentric paradigms that centered on the "excessive" African population and discriminatory myths surrounding the inferiority of Afro-Brazilians, and the imposition of "whitening" precepts.

Governmental and legal sectors of cities such as Salvador and Rio de Janeiro tended to preserve the conservative structures of the Catholic Church. As an Afro-Brazilian tradition, Candomblé was often regarded in the realm of witchcraft/sorcery, devil worship, animism, syncretism, and survivalism. Local authorities responded to the practice of this religion with harsh and prejudicial treatment. However, under the Vargas regime (1930–45), the ideologies of national identity and the New State (Estado Novo) began to embrace Afro-Brazilians and mulattos as distinctive facets of Brazilian society and culture. In the mid-1930s this distinction led to Presidential Law Decree 1202, which recognized Candomblé as a legitimate and significant religious tradition and practice in Brazil.

The decree resulted in improved public support for Candomblé by proponents that included city officials, journalists, and ethnographers. Furthermore, with proponents such as journalist and ethnographer Edison Carneiro, Candomblé became part of a campaign for the recognition of Afro-Brazilian religious traditions and was envisioned as a unified body that had rights and privileges equal under the Brazilian constitution to other forms of religious expression. Carneiro's efforts resulted in the creation of the União Brasileira de Estudos e Preservação Dos Cultos Africanos da Bahia (Brazilian Union for the Study and Preservation of African Religions of Bahia, or UBEPA). This governing body consisted of representatives from the Candomblé community. The UBEPA began to issue certificates of membership to Candomblé terreiros. Many terreiros I visited displayed their official certificates of membership on the wall along with other important religious memorabilia.

In the 1940s Candomblé received national attention with conferences made up of foreign scholars, prominent Brazilian leaders, and Candomblé officials that envisioned it not simply as a religion but also as a place for community growth for Afro-Brazilians. In a secular setting, cities as far as Rio de Janeiro began to appropriate Candomblé iconography of dress and regalia during the national celebrations of Carnival. Candomblé as an Afro-Brazilian tradition became part of the public domain—indeed, part of Brazil's national community.

In the 1950s Umbanda, a popular syncretic religion that was created in Brazil, attracted some Brazilian whites in Rio de Janeiro and in other parts of Brazil. Umbanda combines Candomblé beliefs, Roman Catholicism, spiritualism, and

Kardecism (a Brazilian spiritualist movement based on the teachings of Allan Kardec). In Umbanda the orixás are invoked through song, though not so much through polyrhythmic drumming. Umbanda music shows stylistic changes that result from the permeation of nationalistic values in regional and urban cultural settings. The music and dance is highly influenced by urban samba.[37] Umbanda places emphasis on communicating with spiritual beings that take the form of old slaves, Indians, gypsies, and Turkish kings. Like Candomblé, Umbanda emphasizes solving the everyday problems of people, providing avenues for them to consult a spiritual advisor (babalaô).[38]

Although Candomblé received national attention during the 1940s and 1950s, in certain urban areas local authorities continued to discourage the practice of this religion. Some of the older practitioners were able to describe to me some of their early experiences as practitioners and expressed that when Candomblé received attention as a national religion, many practitioners were still unable to practice Candomblé religion freely. In some communities of Salvador (during the 1940s and 1950s), Candomblé was seen as a source of racial and social danger, and numerous stereotypes (e.g., witchcraft/sorcery, devil worship) were used to justify actions against practitioners. Many feared attending Candomblé ceremonies because of the threat of incarceration and confiscation of sacred vestments. Candomblé practitioners continued to be restricted from openly celebrating their faith and had to receive permission from local authorities to perform public rituals involving drumming and dancing. This often resulted in some terreiros relocating to the outskirts of the city and holding ceremonies late at night to avoid being confronted by local authorities.

Raymundo Nonato De Souza, seventy-four, a practitioner I interviewed in the summer of 2002, became a member of the Alzidi Juncara Candomblé terreiro when he was twelve years old. De Souza stated that when he began to practice Candomblé only the poorest Afro-Brazilians were interested and involved. De Souza remembers that from the 1940s through part of the 1970s attending Candomblé ceremonies was a difficult experience for the community, because the police would often raid certain neighborhoods, interrupt the ceremonies, and confiscate musical instruments. Most ceremonies were held late at night in the fear that the participants would be arrested and jailed for practicing Candomblé. This discouraged many people and is why De Souza believed that in his local terreiro a vast amount of Candomblé ritual practices continue to be secretive to this day.[39]

As a religious institution Candomblé received a total "liberation" in 1976, when the mayor of the city of Salvador, Jorge Hage, the cardinal of the Roman Catholic Church, Brandão Villela, and two Candomblé officials gathered to witness the governor of the state of Bahia sign a law guaranteeing the rights of Candomblé practitioners to practice their religion freely. The religion was transformed into a valued cultural heritage, supported by the church and state.[40]

While the total liberation of Candomblé can be seen as something positive for the acceptance/legitimation of Afro-religion within Salvador and in the Brazilian society, in spite of this recognition Afro-Brazilians have remained at the lowest sectors of the society. One of the major paradoxes is the national rhetoric and acceptance of certain aspects of Candomblé as part of the national aesthetic of Brazilian culture. For example, the white costume worn by the baianas often associated with the women of Candomblé—laced dresses and elaborate turbans—have been appropriated in popular culture. Many agencies that feature advertisements about Bahian and/or Afro-Brazilian culture often include in travel brochures photos of women dressed as a baiana. The typical baiana dress has become a nationalist and folkloric costume, especially during festivities such as the annual Carnival celebration.

In cities such as Rio de Janeiro and Salvador there are popular celebrations and festivals pervaded with Candomblé iconography and intertwined in a sacred/secular dichotomy—for example, in Rio de Janeiro, where the annual Carnival celebration has become world renowned, with spectacular competitive performances of escolas de samba and parades of thousands of energetic drummers, vocalists, and dancers. There is also a sacred element in this celebration, most often a major parade unit comprised of the *alas das baianas*: mature women dressed in traditional baiana-style costumes with turbans and long, laced dresses. These women represent the Bahian tias (aunts), who practiced Candomblé religion in Rio.

In Salvador nonpractitioners often wear the costume of the baiana. For example, women who may not be practitioners sell merchandise (foods, trinkets) on the streets or work as local tour guides and greeters wearing the costume as a type of work uniform. During many of the local festivals some males may also dress as a baiana: some are practitioners of the religion while others (nonpractitioners) parade in the costume as a type of masquerade or creative play.

The women of Candomblé are honored throughout Salvador in November of each year with a secular public celebration. Most of the women dress in their usual laced white garments and elaborate headdresses. During this celebration, an event that attracts members of the community and tourists, the city comes alive with women dancing to Candomblé music. The syncretism of Catholicism and African religion is evident. The celebration begins with a Catholic mass held at the Rosários dos Pretos Church. As the mass commences the baianas often participate in procession and dance behind a man, also dressed in white, who carries a large crucifix. During the procession, church bells constantly ring and crowds cheer. After the mass, the women assemble at city hall and are greeted by the local mayor and other officials, who all share in a meal of Afro-Brazilian cuisine such as acarajé.

The *Lavagem do Bonfim,* or Washing of the Bonfim, held in January of each year, is a celebration that honors the Catholic saint Senhor do Bonfim, who is syn-

Baianas—women of Candomblé in Salvador.

cretized with the orixá Oxalá. The celebration commences with a procession from the Conceição da Praia Church to the Bonfim Church, approximately six kilometers. What makes this festival spectacular is that the women associated with Candomblé, along with Catholic priests, carry large vases of flowers.

The thousands of people who attend the procession to the Bonfim Church also enjoy secular activities—drinking, eating, dancing, and musical performances by local Carnival organizations. The procession culminates with women affiliated with the Candomblé religion washing the steps of the Bonfim Church. After this, the entire crowd is allowed to approach the steps and tie fita ribbons to the door of the church.[41]

"The baianas are hard workers in their communities," is a response given to me by some of the locals in Salvador about the women that identify themselves baianas in Afro-Brazilian culture. Other responses varied: some practitioners (both men and women) expressed that in Candomblé the baiana, particularly those that become initiated devotees, are important to the religion because they are regarded as the mothers and caretakers of the orixás. Several examples related to how, in many terreiros, women have the responsibility of preparing the special foods that are presented to the orixás during ceremonies. Other interesting responses I received from some young Afro-Brazilian men (nonpractitioners) associated the baiana with the aesthetics of local identity and Afro-Brazilian culture (baianidade) as something of beauty (beleza) and with the typical black woman from the Salvador region.

Although Candomblé continues to influence Brazilian culture and has in a way become an acceptable religion, practitioners still debate many issues, just like in many other religions. The reception and perception of Candomblé outside of the terreiro have caused many practitioners to confront issues of commercialism, tourism, re-Africanization, Afro-Brazilian youth movements, secularization, and global experiences. Some older practitioners expressed to me that even local officials in their communities now accept Candomblé as a traditional religion, a strong popular expression, and a tourist attraction, and that this has influenced the secularization of Candomblé. During certain local festivals in Salvador where the orixás are celebrated there is sponsorship by corporations as well as participation in the festivities by local officials, including the mayor. This has caused more tourists to seek out Candomblé ceremonies, and many terreiros feel that they can make a profit by allowing tourists to visit.

Terreiros are not always blameless in the popularization and secularization of aspects of Candomblé. Some of the larger ones have web pages that describe history, sacred rituals, and symbols to locals and tourists. Moreover, many terreiros profit by allowing tourists and the local media to visit and attend special ceremonies. Even some local government officials attempt to profit from affiliation with Candomblé, especially during election time, when they seek out terreiros to solicit votes from the Afro-Brazilian community. Some tourist agencies in Salvador maintain a list of weekly celebrations that allow tourists to observe ceremonies for a nominal fee. The money received aids in the maintenance of the terreiro.

I asked several practitioners for their opinions about allowing tourists to attend ceremonies, and received a wide range of opinions. Luiz Badaró, a Candomblé practitioner for over thirty years, believes that several changes have taken place in the religion and this is partly due to secular aspects of popular culture. He noted that the religion "has been taken out of the hands of the blacks that created the religion and has become part of the social and cultural constructs of Brazil":

> When my parents were practicing Candomblé forty years ago, for example, it was much more religious and more rigid. It was much more looked at as a religion. Candomblé was first introduced in Salvador because of slavery, by the Africans coming to Brazil. Salvador was a good land for the Africans. It was similar to where the slaves came from. At that time only blacks participated in Candomblé. It was marginalized by the slave owner and the white society. But for the Africans, this was their belief system. Candomblé was created by blacks.
>
> Now presently the African culture has become part of Brazilian culture and the origins of Candomblé have somehow gotten mixed with European culture. European participants, Indian natives, and other religions as well have caused Candomblé to become different and more rigid. Now it is for everyone. This is not a problem for me. In Candomblé there are ways of making money

and I say this with all due respect. In many ways Candomblé has become a cultural organization that can make money for itself. For example, there is a time in Salvador where Candomblé is not played musically. This means there are no public ceremonies going on, but let's say twenty tourists come into town, some terreiro will say, "sure, this is a way to make money." They will have a ceremony. There are other terreiros that will do ceremonies for tourists, but before the ceremony is held they will do some kind of work asking permission from the orixás to be able to perform that ceremony. This is the difference between the commercial Candomblé and the traditional ceremonial ritual of Candomblé.[42]

Luiz Murisoea, a seventy-five-year-old pai de santo who had been a practitioner of Candomblé most of his life, responded by saying: "I am not at all offended when a visitor wants to come to my terreiro to see a ceremony. If they conduct themselves with respect during the ceremony, that makes me feel good. But if they come to make fun of Candomblé, that offends me and the person will never be allowed to return to the terreiro."[43]

Edvaldo Pain, a twenty-six-year-old Candomblé musician and also a practitioner for most of his life, made some interesting comments about Candomblé and the new faces in the religion. He described a growing interest in the religion as "the revolution of the society" and commented:

> Now people feel they must act a certain way to be accepted in Salvador. Oftentimes Candomblé is always accepted especially among the rich. In the past, Candomblés were not accessible to tourists. Now, tourists come into terreiros with ideas of what they think the religion is or should be. I believe that if they come to see a ceremony, they should come in with an open mind.[44]

All of the terreiros I visited did allow tourists to attend Candomblé ceremonies, and thus provided me with greater insight into various aspects of the religion than if I was not allowed to observe. However, I must emphasize that there are numerous terreiros that do not allow tourists and prefer to maintain the privacy of their specific ceremonies.

Axé, Candomblé Religion, and Afro-Brazilian Identity

Candomblé religion has been referred to as a matrix of Afro-Brazilian identity.[45] In essence, it is a signifier of the black experience in Brazil. In recent decades groups of young Afro-Brazilians have been inspired by black activism and the way African Americans, Africans, and other African diasporic areas have assigned symbolic meaning to various African-influenced religions, popular music styles, and social movements. Outside of the terreiro, Candomblé religion has been linked with black identity and new Afrocentric roots as an icon of African heritage.

While Brazil has included some Afro-Brazilian traditions as part of its national heritage and identity, it has often discouraged social groups that encourage various expressions of ethnic nationalism and racial equality. In the 1970s the emergence of the Movimento Negro Unificado (Unified Black Movement, MNU), which advocated against racism and brutality and united the struggles of Afro-Brazilians through the country, played a role in the perception of Candomblé as among the ideologies of new Afrocentric roots and black identity.

In Salvador, since the mid-1970s and with the emergence of the MNU, many local Carnival organizations have been drawn to Candomblé religion as part of a new black identity. Some members of these groups are Candomblé practitioners and, before celebrating special festivities (e.g., Carnival), perform Candomblé sacred rituals such as the Padê offerings to the orixá Exú to secure a successful festival season.

The concepts of power and creative energy inherent in axé have been appropriated by some social organizations that advocate racial equality and better economic opportunities for the Afro-Brazilian community. For example, Projeto Axé, a nonprofit organization located in the Pelourinho district of Salvador, was founded in the 1990s to address and seek solutions to the problems of homeless children. The organization normally serves children and teenagers mostly from low-income Afro-Brazilian families. The major emphasis of this organization is empowering children (the future generation) with the creative energy of axé to make positive things happen in their lives.

Projeto Axé was inspired by the Brazilian thinker Paulo Freire (1921–1997) and the philosophical principles taken from his books, *Pedagogia da oprimido* (*The Pedagogy of the Oppressed*) (1970) and *Pedagogia da esperança* (*The Pedagogy of Hope*) (1994). Artistic creativity is envisioned as a spiritual activity through which individuals can examine the experience, quality, and meaning of life. Projeto Axé has special ties with the Casa de Sons (House of Sounds), which provides musical training to some Projeto Axé members in hopes that they may become members of some of the local Carnival organizations.

I also asked several practitioners about their opinions of the social organizations that are attempting to empower young Afro-Brazilians with educational skills. One prominent leader who shared her sentiments was Edna Portela Oliveira Silva, sixty-three. A practitioner for her entire life whose parents and grandparents were members of Candomblé, she led the Ilê Obirigenan terreiro. Silva felt strongly that her job as a leader was not only to preside over rituals and worship, but also to teach and train young practitioners. Silva noted that some young practitioners are being influenced by their experiences outside of the terreiro, especially through social organizations. Moreover, she felt that younger practitioners had changed everything, and that worship was much different from when she was a girl. Everyone wants in some way to be involved with axé

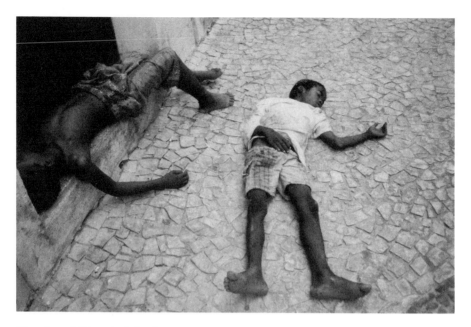

Homeless children in Salvador.

energy as part of his or her identity, she felt, but not truly involved as dedicated practitioners of Candomblé as when she was a girl.

Although many things had changed since Silva was a young girl, she did express that young people in her community needed to be inspired to achieve high goals in life. For years she had constantly observed young people without any types of goals, many from low-income families who could not afford a proper education. Silva stated:

> Our children are affected by what happens in our community. If we cannot provide for our children then they will not have a future. Things have changed since I was a girl. When I was a girl, most young people would accept their situation. But now young people are becoming more aware of their surroundings and want more out of life. This is good. Candomblé and axé are now part of what is good in Brazil. So I think that if young Afro-Brazilians can continue to respect the religion and the ancestors they will have much success in life.[46]

Afro-Brazilians have contributed greatly to Brazilian cultural, social, religious, and artistic landscapes. But it is perhaps the heritage and legacy of West African àsé that has had the greatest impact on Brazilian culture. In a secular sense there is also what I refer as the "axé mystique" in Brazilian culture, where identification with axé has become fashionable as an emblem of black identity and commercially lucrative for local businesses in Salvador, who often market imagery and symbols of Candomblé and Afro-Brazilian cultural identity as something exotic and enticing to appeal to international tourism. In many Brazilian cities, billboards and advertisements (e.g., Axé Chevrolet) announce secular Carnival events and other festivities using greetings and blessings of axé. Furthermore, in daily interaction, people often greet each other with the word "axé," which in this context means hello, good luck, peace, and prosperity.

I believe that axé concepts often mediate racial identities and social classes. In the sanctums of Candomblé religion, many Afro-Brazilians pay homage to a pantheon of African ancestral spirits with prayers and petitions for the blessings of axé. But in popular culture people from different social classes and racial identities who regard themselves as white, pardo, Afro-Brazilian, mestiço, or mulatto often appropriate, reinvent, and reinterpret axé concepts in their everyday lives and participate in popular festivities where they petition axé blessings and engage in secular music and dance activities to celebrate ancestral spirits such as iconic Yemanjá.

Ancestral spirits from Candomblé religion are often imagined as having a type of racial identity influenced not only by religious mythology and syncretism but also by the commercialization of illustrations marketed to popular culture (locals and tourists) via photos, paintings, and postcards. In some illustrations ancestral spirits are depicted as having fair skin textures, straight hair, and blue eyes; in others as having dark skin textures, curly hair, and with more pronounced African features; or as having Native American physical characteristics. Yemanjá is an example of an ancestral spirit often depicted in various ways—fair skin textures, blue eyes, and straight hair that I even observed in many terreiros as part of a sacred display of the ancestral spirits.

Some musicians (individual artists and Carnival organizations) have reinvented and secularized sacred axé—music, drumming, dance, iconography, symbols, imagery—of Candomblé in popular songs that they link with African roots, black identity, and Afro-Brazilian culture. Many of these songs communicate religious and aesthetic expression of a poetics of place (Salvador) and attempt to reconnect Afro-Brazilian culture with West African àsé heritage. Also, similar to several West African popular musicians (e.g., Olatunji, Adé, Obey, and Fela Kuti), in Brazil there is a type of "global spreading" of axé in popular culture through commercial recordings and performances by international artists and Carnival organizations.

2 | From the Sacred to the Secular
Popularizing Candomblé Rhythms

In Candomblé religion, music is an important vehicle by which the orixás are appeased. In special ceremonies axé is generated through a series of sacred drum rhythms, songs, and dances that are offered to the orixás. During the ceremonies practitioners revere the "sonic" as axé embodiment and deem the music as the "voices" of the orixás. When music is performed practitioners often lift their hands to orun, the world of the ancestors, bow in reverence to the sacred musical instruments, or experience spirit possession. For many practitioners music validates their religious experiences and enables them to reconnect, speak, and communicate with ancestral spirits. The importance of music in Candomblé religion in communicating with the ancestral spirits reflects its African heritage and links the religion with similar types of worship in African diasporic areas.

Candomblé music is often intertwined in a sacred/secular dichotomy. Just as practitioners are emotionally moved by the music in the terreiro, nonpractitioners in secular public spaces dance to sounds that are reminiscent of Candomblé music. In this chapter I examine how sacred Candomblé musical expression that is realized in complex drum rhythms, songs, dance choreography, and musical instruments are often appropriated and secularized in popular music and have influenced many performers and artists outside of the confines of the terreiro.

In Salvador the use of Candomblé drum rhythms, songs, dance choreography, and musical instruments by local fraternal groups and Carnival organizations has an extensive history and is embedded in the sociocultural and sociopolitical constructs of religious, racial, and ethnic identity. Moreover, since the emergence of the Negritude movement and influences from pan-Africanism and black pride movements in the 1970s and 1980s, many local performers place aesthetic valorization on the Candomblé musical repertoire to express local, social, and racial/ethnic identity in their communities. Thus, practitioners of Candomblé are faced with the secularization not only of sacred themes, images, and symbols, but also of the "voices" of the orixás.

In the Pelourinho district of Salvador, some practitioners hear the sounds of Candomblé rhythms resonating outside of the terreiro, from the open rehearsals of local drumming groups. Music stores in this district sell recordings of Candomblé music and various types of musical instruments—drums, bells, and rattles marketed as traditional Candomblé musical instruments—to locals and tourists. In spite of this, Candomblé music continues to play a major role in contributing to the vibrancy of the religion.

Creating Musical Axé

The Candomblé musical repertoire is vast and consists of complex drum rhythms and songs that can be categorized according to ceremonial function: music for calling/summoning the orixás, music for sending them away, and so forth.[1] The music involves an intricate activity of auditory symbols—melody, rhythm, tone color, texture, structure, and dynamics—that can be regarded as a vehicle to provoke various types of emotional states and experiences in the practitioners.

Communication with the orixás involves what I refer to as a "musicalization" process, achieved through a variety of textures and timbres, distinct instrumentation, and song and drum repertoire. During the ceremonies the music informs dance, heightens spirit possession, and allows initiated practitioners to mimic the movements that they believe represent the orixás incarnate. Music in Candomblé religion can also be thought of as an active engagement with the dance and spirit possession that bridges the spiritual with the earthly. Through music practitioners communicate with the divine, give praise and thanks, petition for general or specific blessings, appease, atone, acknowledge, and celebrate the existence of the divine in their lives.

The music also enhances the drama of the dance choreography, as the initiated practitioners are being possessed with axé.[2] Rhythm and movement are very much integrated. Depending on a particular orixá, the basic choreographic movements may be simple; the initiated practitioner may simply execute foot and hand motions in circular patterns. The movements may be fast, slow, or contorted; they may include shuffling, twirling, and circular motions; they may represent activities such as shooting a bow and arrow, galloping, sweeping, and holding special sacred objects such as mirrors, amulets, or whips.

The movements executed by an initiated practitioner have a mimetic quality and dramatize a particular orixá's personality, physical, and spiritual characteristics. For example, to represent the physical characteristics of the orixá Ossanha, who is imagined as crippled with one functioning leg, while dancing the initiated practitioner often bends one leg while jumping up and down on the other. For an aggressive orixá such as Iansã, the dance movements are very fast, erratic, and involve constant swaying motions from the hips, twist and turns of the upper body, and hand movements that imitate the orixá swinging her *isan* (switch).

For an orixá such as Oxóssi an initiated practitioner may imitate galloping motions with the body positioned as if one were riding on a horse and with the hands positioned as holding the reins. As the intensity and tempo of the music increases, galloping motions executed by the dancer become accelerated. Other movements may involve simple circular motions. Thus, as the music is performed the initiated practitioners may move in a circle (ring) around the center of the room where axé energy is produced.

For the initiates—those chosen to communicate with the spiritual world—the power of music is emphasized at all intervals of the initiation process. In the same way that the orixá arrives to take up residence in the initiate's body, music is placed in the initiate's head. This begins with a process of ringing various bells near the initiate's head to familiarize them with the sounds and nuances associated with each orixá. In addition, initiates spend many hours learning to sing specific songs and distinguish the various drum rhythms that are used in ritual to appease the orixás. In this way, music becomes part of the mental conditioning required to receive axé energy and communicate with one's orixá.

In the Candomblé ceremonies I observed, practitioners expressed that music is a life-giving source that acts as *magia* (magic), an elixir for communicating with the spiritual world. Moreover, many expressed that the ceremonies would not be complete, and communicating with the spiritual world would not be achieved, without music. Music plays a major part in religious rituals that channel the power and energy of axé to devoted practitioners as they communicate with ancestral spirits.

The practitioners also expressed a variety of reasons for attending Candomblé ceremonies: to celebrate their spiritual guardians, to enjoy the ritual meals, to socialize with friends, and to be inspired by the power of music that induces spiritual axé. Most often, terreiros' doors are open to any practitioners who desire to attend. The music serves as a formal invitation to members of the community, who are welcome if they abide by the integrity of the ceremony.

During the ceremonies I observed, the music seemed to mediate between different social classes so that all practitioners who attended the ceremonies in some way contributed to the sacredness of the ceremony. When people responded to the music, they seemed less concerned with their social status and more geared to receiving the power and energy of axé and becoming part of the Candomblé community. As some terreiros are small in size, occasionally practitioners must stand outside and observe the ceremonies from an open door or window; but this is not usually a deterrent, as the music can be heard for several blocks. On several occasions I observed practitioners standing in the rain. This inconvenience did not seem to matter once the music began. Some practitioners believed that even the sound of the music attracts good fortune and prosperity, and were inspired to donate money to the terreiro as a symbol of their gratitude.

Practitioners expressed varying opinions about the importance of music in

Candomblé. For example, one practitioner who had been a member of the religion for most of his life linked Candomblé music with spirit possession. He said the music "makes people feel good."[3] In a different terreiro a practitioner stated that, although music is a very important aspect of Candomblé ceremonies, it is not indispensable. What is interesting about this comment is that the practitioner who offered it is a musician in his local terreiro. He believed that the words spoken in Yoruba act as an incantation to invigorate the spiritual world, and suggested that, if people continuously spoke lyrical or poetic verses in Yoruba directly to the orixás, they could successfully communicate with spiritual world.[4]

Many practitioners described that the music has the capacity to influence sensations and emotional responses. For example, one practitioner explained that sometimes when she attends ceremonies in the terreiro she may not be in a positive mood because of the problems (e.g., work, family, finances) that she experienced on a particular day. However, often when she hears the music and participates in Candomblé ceremonies, her emotional state changes and she feels more encouraged to deal with her everyday problems in life.[5]

For many practitioners, Candomblé music is powerful and can evoke special powers to heal, soothe, inform, negotiate, inspire, and provide a sense of belonging. In the terreiro it can influence a sense of historical memory of African cultural traditions. Many practitioners that I spoke with expressed that music in Candomblé religion is a link with African societies and ancestors. It is another form of reinventing a sacred landscape that for Africans in Brazil is crucial for venerating the ancestral spirits. For many practitioners music is a sacred space that has allowed them in the terreiro to continue to experience axé embodiment.

Sacred Musical Instruments

The music in Candomblé religion is heightened with musical instruments that many practitioners imagine as life-giving sources. The most important of the instruments are a set of drums known as atabaques and a bell, which may be single or double-headed, called agogô and played with a metal stick. The instruments are symbolic of creation and birth and are mythologized as sacred "living beings." Many practitioners believe that the atabaques are possessed with axé and vested with powers related to healing, physical strength, spirit possession, and dance choreography. Because they are part of the community, these instruments are also endowed with human characteristics such as male or female, happy or sad, hungry or satiated, dressed or undressed. They can also evoke good or bad spirits.

The atabaques vary in size and shape; each size has a symbolic significance. In terreiros with a strong Yoruba influence, the largest instrument is named rum

Agogôs—bells used in Candomblé religious ceremonies.

(also called ìyá lú, the "mother instrument"), the medium one rumpi, and the smallest lê. The sounds of the rum, the mother instrument, enliven the spiritual world. In terreiros with a Congo-Angola influence, some practitioners expressed that the smallest instrument is considered the closest to the "earth." These atabaques are named rumpi (smallest), contra-rum (medium), and rum (largest). Other names given the instruments are ngoma (drums) and gan (bell). When I asked why the drums are named, most practitioners did not know the answer, but indicated that the tradition of naming instruments had existed for many centuries.

Other instruments include various bells, such as the adjá and gan, and the shekere, a large beaded gourd rattle. One of the most interesting musical instruments used to evoke spirit possession and summon the orixás, the adjá is normally played by the spiritual leader in some terreiros and is constructed of two triangular-shaped pieces of very thin metal. During ceremonies, the instrument is played by hitting the two pieces together as if clapping; the sound produced is similar to a very thin brass cymbal.

Because instruments are so significant, special craftsmen construct them. Each terreiro has specific rituals for the construction of musical instruments using materials such as sacrificial animal skins. One practitioner said that in his local terreiro, instruments are constructed by craftsmen known as tanoeiros (atabaque makers). Their task is to construct the frame of an atabaque, which normally takes a day to make. Putting on the drumhead takes more time because the

Atabaques.

skins from the sacrificed animals must be fully dried and in many cases shaved before they can be placed on the drum. This practitioner felt that everything in Candomblé was sacred. Thus, when a terreiro is established, a special offering must be made to the musical instruments.[6]

In many terreiros the power and energy of axé is transmitted to the instruments by means of special ceremonies that may involve pouring blood from a sacrificial animal over the drumheads, since blood is considered a living source. Melville J. Herskovits (1944) and Gerard Béhague (1984) are among scholars of Candomblé research who documented how the power (axé) of musical instruments is conferred through baptismal ceremonies. Herskovits indicated that special power is transmitted through sacred offerings of blood, palm oil, honey, and holy water that are sprinkled on the instruments. In his study of baptismal ceremonies (between 1967 and 1979) of musical instruments, Béhague indicated that musical instruments have a "voice" of their own and their power (axé) needs to be reinforced through nourishment. This involves not only a baptism but also occasionally naming of the instruments (atabaques) and annual feeding to prolong and assure the power received at the baptismal ceremony.[7]

In my own study of the baptismal ceremonies I found a combination of what Herskovits and Béhague had described, but also instruments such as atabaques that are assigned special guardians carefully selected by the leaders and responsible for care and maintenance of the instruments. Similar to practitioners, musical instruments often undergo a type of initiation process before they are

Atabaque constructed with animal skins.

Atabaque encircled with ojá.

deemed worthy to serve the spiritual world. During this initiation process, the instruments often receive an "anointing" from the spiritual world in that a leader may bless the atabaques by sprinkling them with special liquids or with special power known as pemba. Even the skins of animals that are used for drumheads are considered sacred and are also sprinkled with pemba. During the special ceremonies atabaques may or may not be encircled with a cloth called ojá, which is equivalent to the cloths tied around the breasts of possessed initiates.[8]

The atabaques are considered sacred instruments even when they are not in use. After any given ceremony, practitioners cover them to protect them from evil forces within the confines of the terreiro.

Axé power and energy is also transmitted to the agidavis (drumsticks) that

Atabaques covered for protection.

are constructed from special woods and placed symbolically at the feet of the orixás, where they remain until the ceremony commences. When the ceremonies commence, most practitioners believe that, when a musician is performing, the instruments are being fed and are enlivened. As the music resounds, the room is filled with the enticing energy of axé.

Candomblé Sacred Rhythms

Each orixá has its own distinctive ceremonial rhythms. For any given ceremony, the selection of specific repertoire to be performed is chosen by the leader in consultation with the musicians. Like the classification of musical instruments, in many terreiros practitioners classify the rhythms into several categories such as Nagô/Ketu rhythms, influenced by West African Yoruba tradition and played with the agidavis (drumsticks), and Congo-Angola rhythms, influenced by Central African drumming and played with the open palms to get a brisk sound.

Candomblé rhythms are combinations of complex rhythmic parts played on the atabaques and agogô. The rhythms act as a type of "speech surrogacy"—they serve as the imagined "voices" of the orixás. Musicians produce these speech-like qualities with a variety of timbres, techniques, nuances, and dynamics. Like the dance choreography the rhythms have a mimetic quality, dramatizing

Agidavis (drumsticks).

motion and movements in order to portray characteristics of the orixás such as Oxum's graceful movements, Ogum shooting a bow and arrow, Iansã swinging her isan, or Omolú's imagined ailments. Spirit possession also seems to respond to various rhythmic tempi and colorful dynamics.

The rhythms are a symbolic affirmation of the power of the music. In ceremonies, the music constantly speeds up and slows down. These shifts in momentum accentuate and punctuate the rhythmic sensations. Most practitioners associate the speeding-up sensation and faster rhythm tempi with spirit possession while the slower ones are often associated with a sense of calm, beauty, and tranquility. The slow and moderate rhythms of an orixá such as Yemanjá produce a feeling of fluidity and movement, like the waves of an ocean.

One of the most popular calming rhythms is ijexá, a rhythm that is performed for the orixás Oxum, Oxalá, and Yemanjá.[9] Although the ijexá rhythm is complex, there is also simplicity in the flow of the basic timeline played by the agogô, which seems to represent the orixá's graceful and fluid movements. The atabaques are played with open palms in the Congo-Angola drumming style and produce a variety of percussive sounds. Ijexá is one of the Candomblé rhythms that can be played in a steady and moderate tempo. This particular rhythm fits neatly into a 4/4 metric pattern. Music example 1 is a diagram of the ijexá rhythm as the atabaques are played in a steady and moderate tempo against the timeline.

1. The ijexá rhythm of Candomblé.

2. Candomblé rhythm—atabaque parts for the orixá Exú.

3. Candomblé rhythm—atabaque parts for the orixá Nana.

Other rhythms are performed in compound meters, such as those for the orixás Exú and Nana, where the drum rhythms have a more marchlike feel in 6/8 meters.

Propulsive rhythms like those played for Iansã and Xangô convey a feeling of aggressiveness, exemplifying the tempestuous nature of these particular orixás. The complexities of both rhythms are mainly in the rum and rumpi drum parts. The Iansã rhythm fits into a 2/4 duple rhythmic pattern but its complexity is in the syncopation and metric accents of the different atabaques parts. In the execution of this particular rhythm the musicians employ different techniques such as accenting the first beat of the measure followed by a weaker accentuation on the second beat with what sounds similar to a staccato.

4. Candomblé rhythm—rum and rumpi parts for the orixá Iansã.

5. Candomblé rhythm—rum and rumpi parts for the orixá Xangô.

The Xangô rhythm incorporates sound that many practitioners described as grave (deep and serious) that captures the personality of this particular orixá as being of royal lineage, wise in making decisions, and wielding his double axes. The rhythm for this particular orixá fits in a 12/8 rhythmic pattern.

Each of the rhythmic parts serves a particular function to enhance the musicalization of the orixás. For example, the agogô bell is a constant timekeeper. The rum, the largest atabaque, is the lead instrument for improvising and controlling spirit possession and choreographic movements, inviting the orixás to dance. The rumpi, the medium-sized atabaque, plays a basic rhythm called markings and gives distinct accentuations. The lê, the smallest atabaque, adds intricate rhythms that often control the dance steps for the feet.

Candomblé Songs

Many of the songs in the Candomblé religion tell a story and express praises to the orixás. In many of the terreiros I observed practitioners employing several techniques in the performance of the songs. These techniques included call-and-response singing and speechlike chanting of certain Yoruba words. In the ceremonies the rhythms, songs, and stylistic and musical techniques all worked together to produce axé.

In many of the terreiros the ceremonies began with *avaninha* or *bravum*, rhythms that served as a call or summons during which the initiates entered the sanctum in procession. The summons began with the agogô maintaining an ostinato timeline. The atabaques then entered with sounds and nuances integrated with mixtures of call and response, rhythmic dialogues, and the overlapping conversations of voices and dancers.

Although the atabaques have a primary role of "calling/summoning" the orixás, they function as accompanying instruments to the vocal repertoire. In ceremonies several songs were performed for a particular orixá. For example, in many terreiros, in what is known as a xirê, during the first part of the ceremony the musicians performed several songs dedicated to Exú, the trickster, including a despacho, a special offering requesting permission to begin the ceremony.[10] Then the singing and dancing commenced. Once the ceremony began the music was continuous, pausing only to change from one song or drum rhythm to the next. The ceremonial musical repertoire was extensive, and in some terreiros several songs were sung for each orixá.[11] These songs were generally composed of simple phrases and utilized small vocal ranges, and most often were sung in unison.

In many ceremonies each song began with a verse sung by a leader, bell player, or a special soloist. The leader often ornamented the verse with what sounded like semi-spoken dialogue incorporated into the melody. After the verse was sung, the leader sometimes made symbolic hand and arm gestures to the audience and the initiates, placing his hands on or near his heart or on top of his head. The verse was normally answered by a chorus composed of the initiates, who were also dancing, and by practitioners in the audience, who contributed intensity of the music by clapping, singing, and cheering.

In the performance of songs the musicality was not static. Instead, to add drama and contour to the music, a lead singer often used various vocal techniques such as approaching pitches in stepwise motions and or leaps and bending and flattening different pitches. Because of the constant repetition of text, many of the songs seemed longer. However, although there was much repetition many of the songs seemed to follow a format of a phrase and cadencelike structure in binary (AB) form. The first part of the phrase (A section) was the verse sung by the leader and this was followed by the response (B section) sung by the initiates that ended the phrase and cadence. The verse (A section) that was performed by a leader (bell player, special vocalist, etc.) was often short and was basically a summons or call to the orixá. The response by the initiates (B section) often consisted of more textual material that was intended to give thanks, appease, or a prayer petition. When the leader repeated the verse, the singing embellished on certain words and pitches as follows:

Verse (A section) performed by the Leader:
    Ori-o axé!
    [Power of the orixá]

Response (B section) performed by the Initiates:
  Abèté gbeni kòòsà
  [You who give blessings to your devotees more quickly than other gods]

Text is repeated:

Verse (A section) embellished by the Leader:
  Ori-o-o-o-o-axé!
  [Power of the orixá]

Response (B section) repeated by the Initiates:
  Abèté gbeni kòòsà
  [You who give blessings to your devotees more quickly than other gods]

With each repetition, the songs gradually increased in tempo and intensity, and some initiates began to experience axé embodiment through spirit possession. Once they reached possession, the singing often ceased. Only the vibrant sounds of the atabaques and agogô rhythms continued. Instead of singing, noninitiated participants often continued to clap and cheer the possessed initiates. When spirit possession ended, the tempo decreased and the singing recommenced.

In most of the terreiros, Yoruba was incorporated into the ceremonies as the liturgical language.[12] Thus, the songs were made more complex with the use of Yoruba as part of the text. Yoruba is a tonal language with three level tones: High, Low, and Medium. The complexity in this language is that every syllable must have at least one tone. The use of Yoruba in Candomblé ceremonies is also to re-connect practitioners with their African heritage.

In most of the terreiros some of the common liturgical words practitioners were able to describe included òsé, a week that was dedicated to a particular orixá, Olorun/Olorum (supreme deity), olá (honor, dignity), òrí (head), orun (spiritual world), aiyé (living world), àwon (spiritual entities), Obá (King), ìlú (drum), jó (dance), Dará (to be good), emi (breath), àsé (axé). I must empha-size that, although many practitioners are able to sing or speak some phrases in Yoruba, many are not able to give a literal translation of the song lyrics. Instead, many are simply aware of the symbolic and liturgical contexts of the specific texts and phrases as they relate to a particular orixá or musical repertoire.

I believe that noninitiated practitioners (the audience) serve as active partici-pants and contribute to the solemnity of the music. This is why they are encour-aged to participate in ceremonies by singing, clapping, and encouraging the ini-tiates. The axé energy that they produce is a catalyst for communicating with the spiritual world. However, I must emphasize that most terreiros have their special ways of performing music and noninitiated practitioners respond to the music in different ways. In some ceremonies there were practitioners (in the audience) who seemed to be knowledgeable of the musical repertoire, Yoruba phrases, and actively participated by singing and/or clapping, while others chose to participate by listening to the music more quietly and observing the rituals.

In many of the terreiros the older practitioners attempted to pass on the tradition of music to the younger generation. However, the older practitioners expressed concern and have noticed that the younger people are not as enthusiastic about spending time learning to sing songs in Yoruba; they prefer to sing them in Portuguese, which has made the older practitioners unhappy. Because of this some of the older practitioners expressed that young people are becoming "lazy," are being influenced by the secular world and popular culture in Salvador, and are not fully maintaining their African heritage by not learning Yoruba properly.

The younger practitioners responded that they are not lazy and that older practitioners put too many restrictions on the younger generation in Candomblé. They felt that the religion should not control their entire lives. Young people in Brazil when they express their Afro-Brazilian identity, think they should not be criticized for what they think or believe outside of the terreiro. If a young person does not know how to sing a song in Yoruba, this does not mean he or she is less religious or appreciative of the African heritage than the practitioners that are knowledgeable of Yoruba. This type of criticism has discouraged some of the young practitioners.

The younger practitioners were also becoming less enthusiastic about practicing Candomblé because they believed that they would have to dedicate most of their time to the religion and would not have the opportunity just to be young and enjoy their friends and popular music. Moreover, to these young practitioners Candomblé music—especially the sacred rhythms—were symbols of Afro-Brazilian identity, peace and hope, something that should be shared inside and outside of the terreiro.

Ijexá: A Rhythm at the Crossroads of the Sacred and Secular

The ijexá rhythm of Candomblé has become one of the iconic "rhythms of life" outside of the terreiro and in Afro-Brazilian popular culture.[13] This rhythm has been adopted by many community-based secular groups and linked with black pride and struggle. It holds a symbolic power linked to the construction and articulation of local identity and the social and political philosophies of Negritude. Ijexá, as a rhythm of life, epitomizes the importance of musical expression that has come to represent African ancestry, establishment of the nações (nations), and the continuation of many African religious and cultural traditions.

The popularity of ijexá stems from the symbolic significance of the orixás

Oxum, Oxalá, and Yemanjá in Afro-Brazilian culture. The ijexá rhythm is not as jagged-sounding and propulsive as some other Candomblé rhythms. Its moderate tempo is well suited for marchlike processions and conveys a sense of peace, love, tranquility, and stability that many local groups have come to appropriate in popular culture.

The Afoxés and the Ijexá Rhythm

In Salvador the ijexá rhythm has become a signifier of blackness and fraternal spirit for groups such as the afoxés whose members were initially Candomblé practitioners. The term afoxé has several meanings: a carnival-type fraternal organization, a procession, a style of popular music, and a beaded gourd rattle. The first meaning is the one that interests us here.[14] The afoxé percussion groups have a long history of performing Candomblé rhythms such as ijexá in public celebrations. Afoxé groups are manifestations of old and new traditions. In many ways they are the offspring of the irmandades, Catholic lay brotherhoods formed in Salvador in the seventeenth century to help perpetuate African traditions. Voluntary and mainly organized along social, racial, and ethnic lines, many of these groups also functioned as both social clubs and mutual aid societies.

Afoxé groups began to organize themselves in the latter part of the nineteenth century. One of the first afoxé groups was Embaixada Africana (African Embassy), which in pre-Carnival celebrations paraded in Salvador in 1895 to advocate for indemnity for the Islamized West Africans who had participated in the Malê Revolts in 1835.[15] Participants dressed in African-inspired costumes such as African royalty and Zulu warriors armed with shields to symbolically represent their ethnic groups.[16] Afoxé groups that later emerged were Pândegos de Africa (African Merrymakers), Chegada Africana (African Arrival), and Filhos da África (Sons of Africa). These groups dressed in African-style clothes and celebrated African themes. They honored orixás and legendary heroes such as Zumbi, the leader of the Palmares quilombo.

In the early twentieth century the afoxé groups were considered radical. Many members of the upper classes looked upon public Candomblé musical performance and the dressing up in African garb as offensive and distasteful. Local authorities frequently attempted to ban such public performances and often publicly ridiculed the members of afoxé groups and repressed their acts.

In the late 1940s some of the afoxés began to incorporate figures from exotic cultures as iconic symbols of peace. One of the most prominent afoxé groups to emerge in the 1940s was Filhos de Gandhi (Sons of Gandhi), founded in 1949 by Antonio Curuzu and a group of stevedores in homage to Indian nationalist leader Mahatma Gandhi.[17] Members of this group were Candomblé practitioners who normally held ceremonies for the orixás before participating in public festivities. Filhos de Gandhi has been referred to as Candomblé da rua (street Candomblé).

For groups such as these the Candomblé music repertoire may have been appropriated as the music of choice because many of its members were practitioners and had firsthand knowledge and experience in performing the music. Raymundo Nonato De Souza, seventy-four, a musician and devoted Candomblé practitioner of the terreiro Mutuisara in Salvador, was able to detail his experience and membership in the afoxés and Candomblé religion. De Souza became as an active member of the afoxés in the 1950s, but considered himself a very dedicated practitioner of Candomblé religion. His major reason for joining an afoxé was that he was able to perform Candomblé music in a public setting. Several of his friends had become members and this also influenced De Souza to seek membership. Although the religion often experienced repression from the local authorities, at that time Candomblé was a very strong religion and the orixás were powerful in his terreiro. He believed that many of the men that joined the afoxés at the time were truly devoted to the orixás.

De Souza explained that the afoxés were not as involved in commercial activities (such as tourism) as they are today. His membership in the afoxés was also an expression of his pride in being Afro-Brazilian and a member of Candomblé religion. While describing his experience in the afoxés De Souza reemphasized that, similar to Candomblé religion, he learned to express himself freely through music and membership in the afoxés.[18]

By the 1960s, the popularity of afoxés had severely declined locally in Salvador. This decline came in a decade in Brazilian history when both national and local sectors of the society were affected by the 1964 coup that brought a military regime to power and resulted in various types of governmental restrictions. Artists such as Gilberto Gil and Caetano Veloso were active during this time and were proponents against racial inequality and social injustice that resulted in several years of exile from Brazil. These two musicians have played an important role in the revitalization of the afoxés.

In the mid-1970s, Gilberto Gil played an important role in reorganizing the afoxés after his return from exile. He became a member of the afoxé Filhos de Gandhi. Many members of Filhos de Gandhi expressed that Gil was a leader and hero in the community: he had achieved success that many young Afro-Brazilians attempted to emulate. Gil was elevated to one of the highest-ranking officials in the Filhos de Gandhi, and he often participates in the processions.

Part of the Gilberto Gil legacy is his capturing the essence of the Filhos de Gandhi in song on his legendary album *Refavela* (1977), with the song titled "Patuscada de Gandhi" ("Revelry of Filhos de Gandhi"), and another song, "Filhos de Gandhi" (1975), that some members regard as a type of organizational anthem.[19] In the song "Filhos de Gandhi," Gil seems to add a spiritual quality

Member of Filhos de Gan-
dhi dressed in traditional
attire.

by praising and calling out to many of the orixás (Omolú, Ogum, Oxum-maré, Iansã, Yemanjá and Xangô) of Candomblé and all the people to see the Filhos de Gandhi. Similarly, Caetano Veloso has also been very active in the popular music and activities of the afoxés.

In homage to the orixá Oxalá, the members of Filhos de Gandhi normally dress in long white robelike garments with turbans, colorful beads and other ornaments, ribbons, gloves, blue socks, and white sandals. Filhos de Gandhi is an organization of inclusion geared to membership of the old and young and members of different social classes. The organization reveres noted figures that they regard as having made a contribution to world peace such as Mahatma Gandhi, Martin Luther King, John Lennon, Bob Marley, and many others.

Most of their dancing, singing, and drumming are derived from the Candomblé ijexá rhythm and are dedicated to the orixás. Filhos de Gandhi performs the ijexá rhythm as a symbol of its peaceful, fraternal spirit. The instruments that they use during performances include atabaques, agogôs, shekeres (large beaded gourd rattles), trumpets, and whistles.

Before a performance, members of Filhos de Gandhi normally pay tribute to the orixá Exú by observing a special Padê ritual. The observance is normally held in the major square of the Pelourinho district near their headquarters. After several songs are sung and prayers are given, sacred liquids and approximately three bowls of manioc flour are deposited on the square.

Depending on the festivities, Filhos de Gandhi participants can range from approximately a thousand to almost ten thousand members. During public festivals processions often commence at one of the local Catholic churches in the Pelourinho district such as Rosários dos Pretos, and then proceed to one of the major streets in the central part of the city. The musical ensemble often performs on top of trio elétrico vehicles, sometimes with one musician serving as conductor. In processions some members ride upon vehicles designed to resemble elephants or camels, while others carry replicas of goats on their shoulders as they dance and sing. Still others march in the processions carrying live white doves or throw white corn to the crowds. The imagery of the elephant and camel are symbolic and representative of important animals associated with oriental culture. The imagery of the goat, the live white doves, and white corn are intended to represent some of the animals and favorite foods that in Candomblé ceremonies are often sacrificed and offered to appease the orixá Oxalá.

The Filhos de Gandhi musical ensemble has many ways of performing afoxé music. Since the music must be audible enough to be heard above the cheering crowds, members of the ensemble may use microphones and include as many as 150 agogô players who continuously play versions of the basic timeline of ijexá. The atabaque and shekere players, who maintain a constant rhythmic flow and improvise around the vibrant timeline, may also number over one hundred.[20]

The musicians of Filhos de Gandhi often begin performances with the agogô players, who establish and maintain an ostinato timeline. Other musicians in the ensemble then enter playing the various beaded gourd rattles (shekeres), striking the base or the beads attached to the gourds.[21] The execution involves using various parts of the hand with flexibility from the palms, fingers, and wrists. The atabaques of various sizes (rum, rumpi, lê) then enter, played with an open-handed Candomblé technique from the Congo-Angola tradition. The largest atabaque (rum) usually improvises. Most players strap the atabaques around the waist or shoulder while the instrument is being played.

The musical performances of the Filhos de Gandhi are similar to those of Candomblé religion in that most of the songs are sung in Yoruba, some with a mixture of Portuguese, and in a call-and-response style. The singers may use various vocal techniques—approaching pitches in stepwise motions and/or leaps, bending, and flattening different pitches. Similarly, there is a constant repetition of text, and many of the songs follow a format of a phrase and cadencelike structure in binary (AB) form: a verse is sung by the leader (A section), followed by the response by the ensemble that ends the phrase and cadence (B section).

Singers may also embellish and accent certain words and pitches. Similar to Candomblé musical performances, the verses are normally short and may consist of textual material that gives thanks, appeasement, or a prayer petition to the orixás. One of the major differences is that Filhos de Gandhi performances often include fanfares played on valveless trumpets at different intervals in the music. Also, whistle blasts mark the beginnings and endings of musical phrases.

In addition to performing in public festivals, Filhos de Gandhi has become a popular tourist and community attraction. Members of the group perform on Sunday nights at their headquarters in the Pelourinho, which is turned into a

Members of Filhos de Gandhi playing atabaque-type drums, in Salvador.

dance hall. Although admission to this weekly event is free, the organization earns proceeds through the sale of trinkets, recordings, and various types of foods and beverages. On most Sundays the crowds are so massive there is standing room only. Couples, both locals and tourists, dance with swaying hips and arms and shuffling foot movements to ijexá rhythm and dynamic instrumentation. The musical ensemble, comprised of approximately twelve musicians playing the traditional atabaques, bells, rattles, and trumpets, is usually seated on a stage. The songs evoke memories of the orixás and are presented in a mixture of Yoruba and Portuguese in a call-and-response pattern between ensemble and audience.

The Filhos de Gandhi is not the only popular afoxé group in Salvador. In the 1970s and 1980s the surge of interest in the Negritude movement stimulated politically charged afoxé groups such as Badauê, founded in 1978; its members normally wear costumes of golden yellow and white, gold to symbolically represent the orixá Oxum and white for Oxalá. There are also several female afoxé groups that sprang up as a result of the Negritude movement in the 1980s. Like male afoxé groups, the female groups—including the Filhas de Gandhi (Daughters of Gandhi) and Filhas de Oxum (Daughters of Oxum)—glorify African heritage in Brazil. During annual festivities in Salvador such as Carnival, female afoxé groups perform Candomblé-based music and dance in processions along with their male counterparts.

In Afro-Brazilian popular culture the terms *afoxé* and *ijexá* have become synonymous as popular music styles. But even more than this, afoxés groups and rhythms from Candomblé such as ijexá have inspired the emergence of many other types of Afro-Brazilian drumming groups (e.g., blocos afro) and individual artists in Brazilian popular music.

To see the members of Filhos de Gandhi during local festivities is a memorable experience. The pulsation generated from the sound of numerous atabaques and agogôs playing ijexá produces a sense of axé energy and embodiment outside of the terreiro. As the Filhos de Gandhi proceed through the streets of Salvador, for miles all one can see are the white costumes worn by the members as they dance and sing to ijexá. The afoxé groups embody the "crossroads" and the interconnection between the sacred and secular in Afro-Brazilian culture. They connect Brazil to a legacy shared with other African and African diasporic areas where, in different sociocultural and sociopolitical contexts of the black experience, there are also various types of brotherhoods/sisterhoods, secret societies, and fraternities that place emphasis on music and dance.

Secularizing the Sacred: Afro-Brazilian Connections with "Crossroad" Traditions

Blues, jazz, rumba, reggae, soul, funk, rap, soca, and other popular music styles are often imagined as crossroads traditions created within a sacred/secular connection and in some cases linked with ancestral spirits, African and African diasporic religions, the devil, secularization of religious music, and individual performers.

"Rhythm is Gonna Get You" (1992) is a popular song by Gloria Estefan and the Miami Sound Machine that presents a sacred/secular connection. This song invokes an enticing power and energy from bembé, a type of Santería ceremony that incorporates drumming and sacred rhythms. In bembé participants use music to evoke spirit possession and communicate with the orishas.

In Brazil popular musicians—Gilberto Gil, Clara Nunes, Margareth Menezes, Moraes Moreira, Carlinhos Brown, and others—are also intertwined in a sacred/secular connection in that some of these musicians have appropriated sacred rhythms of Candomblé in their popular music. For example, several popular musicians have appropriated the Candomblé rhythmic ijexá ostinato timeline played on agogôs as an idée fixe (fixed musical idea). Some use it as part of a melody that represents an image, mood, or story about the afoxé, African nações, and Afro-Brazilian heritage and ethnic pride. Artists often incorporate the bell and atabaque parts of the ijexá rhythm in samba, samba-reggae, and axé that flows with instrumentation ranging from the sound of low pulsating surdos to keyboard synthesizers.

Gilberto Gil's album *Refavela* (1977) not only is iconic as a type of "re-Africanization" and a musical homage that stemmed from his participation in FESTAC—the Second World Black and African Festival of Arts and Culture in Lagos, Nigeria, in 1977—but was a groundbreaking compilation that incorporated the ijexá rhythm from Candomblé religion. Moraes Moreira, a singer-guitarist whose career in popular music cannot be overstated, was one of the most popular musicians of the *frevo baiano* in the 1980s. Moreira amplified the sound of ijexá. In the late 1960s and 1970s, as Afro-Brazilian popular music emerged, he achieved fame as a member of the group Novo Baianos (New Bahians). In 1979 Moreira and Antonio Risério, the author of *Carnaval Ijexá* (1981), composed "Assim Pintou Moçambique" ("Thus Arrived Mozambique"), a song that fused the ijexá rhythm with the trio elétrico sound using drums and electronic and amplified instruments such as guitars and cavaquinhos.

Clara Nunes incorporated ijexá as a major rhythmic motif in her rendition of a song entitled "Ijexá" (1982), which pays homage to afoxé groups in Salvador. The song also uses Yoruba words (Obá, ilê, aiyé). Margareth Menezes, one of the major innovators in the new trends of axé music, incorporates the ijexá rhythm in some of her recent recordings. For example, in her recording of the song "Ifá, Um Canto Pra Subir" (1990), the ijexá rhythmic timeline played by several agogôs recurs throughout the song. The instrumentation is extensive, with an array of instruments that include congas, timbales, drums, trumpets, trombones, surdos, electronic keyboards, and saxophones. The song also incorporates digitized sounds. Synthesizers highlight the ijexá rhythmic timeline with an echo effect played against the interlocking parts of the percussion instruments and trumpet and saxophone riffs.

Some artists have incorporated the sound of funk and soul with influences from Candomblé music and other local styles. Carlinhos Brown, one of the most prominent musicians in axé music and from a Candomblé background, explained in an interview with *Down Beat* magazine (2000) that African American funk/soul musicians share similar cultural connections and experiences with Afro-Brazilians. Moreover, Brown felt connected with funk/soul music that he changed his name after James Brown. For him, singers such as James Brown, Ray Charles, and Aretha Franklin were particularly inspiring during the military coup and dictatorship in Brazil in the 1960s and 1970s.

Brown believes that Brazilian music was influenced by African American music, and vice versa. In particular, he believes that funk was influenced by Afro-Brazilian music because many of the funk rhythms are similar to Candomblé rhythms. The changes are the result of the musicians' own experimentation:

"What might surprise Americans is that Brazilian [popular music] has always been inside [African] American music and the other way around. I believe that Funk was influenced from Candomblé, because the rhythm is very much like it. I think that all these rhythms—dance, jingle—are very similar to what we have been doing in Brazil."[22]

One of Brown's most recent and innovative albums where he experiments with elements of sacred and popular music is *Presents Candombless* (2005), a compilation of Candomblé music that he incorporates with a contemporary sound of funk, electronic, and techno-mix. The title of this compilation conveys a sense of religiosity with the designation of "Candom[bless]." But the secular feeling pervades in some of the songs as Brown incorporates the ijexá rhythm with funk-style bass played on various types of electronic instruments.[23]

Some of the popular musicians from Salvador explained to me how and why they incorporated Candomblé songs, rhythms, and dance choreography in their popular music repertoire. For example, in addition to his position as a sacred musician at the Ogum Ja Tuluyaê terreiro in Salvador, Antonio Carlos, thirty-nine, taught African music and dance at the Escola de Dança da Fundação, a cultural institution located in the Pelourinho, the historical district in Salvador. He also played various percussion instruments in a popular music group with two other musicians, a German guitarist and a Brazilian vocalist. The group mainly performed blues; asked why they chose this style, Carlos responded that samba, blues, funk, reggae, and rock were all connected and derived from African music. Moreover, to Carlos the rhythmic structures of these styles sounded similar to Candomblé rhythms. For Carlos this made many popular styles easy for him to perform.

Carlos explained that he has many ways of working elements of Candomblé rhythms into the popular music repertoire that his group performs. He attempts to find Candomblé rhythms that fit into a 4/4 metric pattern because many popular black styles fit into the similar rhythmic/metric scheme. He described that he can transform a Candomblé rhythm (ijexá) into something new simply by using the timeline of the agogô part together with a rhythmic motif on a bass guitar to get a funk sound. Carlos also explained that even a complex rhythm such as Xangô that follows a 12/8 rhythmic pattern could be transposed into a 4/4 rhythmic pattern by altering note values to quarter and eighth notes. For Carlos, this is a type of improvisation on the Candomblé rhythms. Depending on the song style (e.g., blues, samba, funk, R&B), another strategy is to manipulate the rhythms with more accentuation and shorter note values, adding syncopation and incorporating a variety of instruments such as drums, trumpets, and rattles.

Lula Almeida, thirty-two, was a popular musician who performed regularly in Salvador and in Los Angeles, California. Performing for audiences in the two cities presented different experiences. In Salvador, Almeida performed on the trio elétrico vehicles that required amplification and larger instrumental ensembles. But in Los Angeles he performed mainly in local clubs with smaller audiences. Almeida considered his renditions of Brazilian music, in which he incorporated elements from Candomblé, "new sounds" in Los Angeles that represented a sense of ethnic pride in his Afro-Brazilian identity. This was culminated in his use of African-derived rhythms, timelines, drumming techniques, traditional musical instruments (rattles, whistles, bells, and tambourines), and songs he sometimes sang in the Yoruba language. But Almeida described that he attempts to keep his music contemporary with modern electronic instruments. Almeida also expressed that, in a sense, when he incorporates elements and fragments from various popular styles with Candomblé rhythms, his music is an illustration of African, African diasporic, and global connections.

Because of his success in the popular music industry, Almeida had a generalized view of appropriating of Candomblé music. He felt strongly that having knowledge of Candomblé music was important to his musical innovation and also in many popular music styles found in Salvador. Almeida stated the following about playing Candomblé music in both sacred and secular settings:

> Both my mother and father practiced Candomblé. That is how I learned the rhythms and songs and how to play the atabaques. I was only eight years old when my father brought me to a musician at the Candomblé terreiro and asked him to teach me how to play Candomblé music. I was really happy about this. I believe that all good musicians in Salvador have some experience in playing the Candomblé rhythms. I believe that if you can't play Candomblé rhythms, you will not be able to play styles like samba-reggae, axé music, afoxé, or ijexá.[24]

Edmilson Lemos, forty-four, had been associated with Candomblé religion as a devoted practitioner, musician, and drummer for over thirty years. When he was thirty years old he became an ogan, an official in his local terreiro. Outside of Candomblé, Lemos had other interests and took contemporary dance lessons with an instructor outside the terreiro because he was interested in learning capoeira and classical ballet. He made his professional debut as a dancer in 1979 with Brazil Tropical. Lemos had also traveled and lived in several countries, including the United States, Korea, France, Germany, Italy, and Angola. He had also performed with such musicians as Paul Simon, Olodum, and Baden Powell. Lemos relocated to Salvador in 1992 because he married a local woman; they had one child.

Lemos was the leader of a female percussion group in Salvador known as Kalundu whose members ranged in age from fourteen to twenty-three. He chose to organize a female group outside of the afoxé tradition because he believed that an all-female group would be commercially appealing in the popular music industry. This particular group was nonpolitical and had no platform regarding ethnic identity in Salvador. Instead they performed various types of love songs as well as samba and reggae. Some of the musical instruments used by the group included electric piano, bass, and various drums.

Kalundu incorporated some Candomblé rhythms in their music. Lemos stated that it was very easy to identify the rhythms used in the group's music. For one of their primary rhythms they chose a rhythm associated with the orixá Iansã as symbolic of ideal womanhood, a female with ambition, success, and talent. Normally the group used this particular rhythm during processions at annual festivals, where they often included a corps of female dancers adorned in special garments and holding isan switches that symbolically represented Iansã. Lemos described that the Iansã rhythm played at a fast tempo is highly appropriate for their processional marches. When the group performs at events such as the weekly *festa da benção* (the blessing party) held in the Pelourinho district on makeshift stages, they may perform love songs and incorporate electronic musical instruments into their performances.

Lemos felt strongly about the appropriation of Candomblé in popular music, particularly the sacred rhythms. Like Almeida he had a generalized view of Candomblé rhythms in popular music and said the following about the importance of Candomblé music and rhythms in popular music:

> In Salvador the Candomblé rhythms are important to popular music styles as afoxé, ijexá, samba-reggae, and axé music. If you want to be a good musician here, then you must know how to play the Candomblé rhythms. With my group [Kalundu] there is a lot of mixing of the Candomblé rhythms with other styles of music. The sound that the group creates is different and people really enjoy the music.[25]

Luiz Badaró, thirty-five, was another devoted Candomblé practitioner and popular musician who was very positive about using Candomblé rhythms, dance, and songs in popular music. Badaró also performed in Salvador and in Los Angeles, California. With rhythms such as ijexá, Badaró combined axé, samba, reggae, afoxé, capoeira, and jazz to create what he described as symbolic movements of orixás in popular dance choreography:

> What I do is stylize the orixás in popular dance. As a popular musician and choreographer, I create movements that are similar to the orixás that I am teaching. This is how I create a positive sense of black identity incorporated with contemporary dance movements. I feel strongly that one can take from the traditional such as Candomblé music and dance and make it even more their own. So I create and put more things [various styles of popular music] on top of what I already know from the Candomblé [music and dance] base. A good example of this is that it is easy to develop more movements and musical improvisation for the orixá Ogum because he is looser and has a variety of movements that allow me to be creative. The movements of the orixá Xangô are also loose. But on the other hand the movements of the orixá Oxalá are more restrained so I create extra movements.[26]

Axé and the African Roots of Candomblé Music

Music is a powerful source that is itself often revered as a religion. In many instances music devotees are as devoted to music as religious followers are to their religion. Within many religions, music informs rituals of worship, prayers, dance, and emotional states. Music in the Candomblé religion is endowed with meaning, significance, ritual, and community. Its ceremonial music has conversational qualities that evoke certain emotional states in practitioners. Music links them with the spiritual axé via communication with the orixás. This tradition of music and spirituality is the long-lasting legacy of the spread of West African àsé.

The sacred can influence secular creativity, activities, individuals, beliefs, symbols, images, national and ethnic identity, iconography, music, performers, trends, aesthetic taste, and stylistic ideas in popular music.[27] Axé and the African roots of Brazilian popular music are also embedded in Candomblé music (the imagined voices of the orixás), which has often been appropriated, reworked, and reinterpreted as one of the ingredients of contemporary Brazilian popular music. Candomblé music greatly informs Afro-Brazilian identity. Furthermore, sacred rhythms such as ijexá can be thought of as a type of simulacrum. In the sacred space of the terreiro it brings forth a sensation of reverence, remembrance, and spirituality of African heritage and celebration of the ancestral spirits. Outside of the terreiro in the public space, ijexá brings forth sensations that are steeped in ethnic pride, the afoxés, the Afro-Brazilian sociocultural and sociopolitical struggle in Brazil, the Negritude movement, and popular music and dance.

Before ending this chapter I must also mention that in Salvador, Candomblé music and dance are also appropriated and secularized in popular folkloric shows. For example, the Teatro Miguel Santana is one of the major venues for performances by the Balé Folclórico da Bahia, a professional dance company founded in 1988. This dance company tours throughout Brazil and internationally. While in Salvador I had several opportunities to experience their dynamic programs, which they performed to sold-out audiences.

Balé Folclórico da Bahia incorporates Candomblé music, dance, and iconography into its repertoire. This group is working to spread Candomblé music and dance throughout the world.[28] Several members of the group expressed to me that they were from a Candomblé religious background, one reason why the music and dance are so authentic. The group attempts to dramatize axé embodiment when they perform artistic renditions of songs, drum rhythms, and dances dedicated to the orixás.

In a religious sense, Candomblé music is an example of how a displaced community uses musical expression to transmit history and reinvent aspects of its home culture in its new environment. Music is vital to the Candomblé religion; most ceremonies would not be complete without musical expression. The sounds of the music and the musical instruments are like heartbeats—living sources that continue to channel the creative power and energy of axé.

Candomblé music links practitioners with the past and demonstrates how traditional aesthetic values were not obliterated by the conditions of enslavement but instead were sustained in the minds and bodies of the people. In a profound way, Candomblé music is comprised of dynamic "rhythms of life" that continue to vibrate in both sacred and secular spaces.

3 | Axé Embodiment in Brazilian Popular Music
Sacred Themes, Imagery, and Symbols

For practitioners in Candomblé religion, the power and creative energy of axé is embodied and manifested through their devotion and reverence for particular themes, imagery, and iconic symbols. This chapter examines the appropriation of sacred themes, imagery, and symbols from Candomblé religion in Brazilian popular music. In Brazilian popular music there is a sacred/secular connection in that many popular musicians have appropriated sacred themes, imagery, and iconic symbols associated with the orixás, axé, Candomblé religion, and African roots as topics of songs marketed in commercial recordings, live performances, and public celebrations. This sacred/secular connection also contributes to the uniqueness of Brazilian popular music and Afro-Brazilian cultural identity.

Brazilian popular music is distinguished by rhythmic structure, instrumentation, vocal quality, and styles of individual performers. Brazilians often respond to the popular music as a friend and loved one. Many popular music styles make people want to dance and sing while at the same time conveying a deep sense of its rich and varied history and traditions—traditions that mix European melodic lyricism and poetic symmetry with African rhythmic vibrancy. The popular music often combines traditional and nontraditional musical instruments such as the drum, electric keyboard, piano, surdo, pandeiro, cavaquinho, atabaque, and cuíca.

The Afro-Brazilian presence in the popular music cannot be overstated. Nationally and internationally, Afro-Brazilian music covers a gamut of musical traditions from religious to various secular songs and dances. Many popular music styles in Brazil can trace their origins back to African and African diasporic influences, which can be detected even in their names: samba, pagode, batuque, lambada, fricote, samba-reggae, carimbó, funk, reggae, rap, and so forth. Within the origins of many popular styles is an ever-present sacred/secular connection that stems from Candomblé religion.

The Axé of the Orixás: Iconic Images, Symbols, and Inspirations for Popular Songs

In many religions faith and confession are highly motivated by images.[1] For many Candomblé practitioners, each day of the week is associated with the images of a specific orixá, whose colors are apparent in the clothes people wear or foods they eat. In many of the terreiros I visited practitioners often described that they have two orixás, one male and one female, that protect them throughout life.[2] These two orixás protect the "front and back" of the practitioner. The orixá that protects the front of the practitioner is regarded as the primary guardian orixá. A practitioner identifies his or her guardian orixá through divination and with successive throws of shells known as the jogo dos búzios (casting of cowry shells).

Practitioners are influenced by the mythology that is associated with particular orixás. For example, one of the most beloved orixás in Candomblé is Yemanjá. In many parts of Brazil, this orixá has become an iconic figure even outside of the religion. Yemanjá is the mother of all orixás. A Marian figure sometimes called the Virgin Mary and Our Lady of Immaculate Conception, Yemanjá is often imagined as a great mother.[3] She is sometimes reinvented as Our Lady of Navigators, the patron saint of fishermen and businessmen. If given a suitable celebration and offerings, she brings good fishing and prosperity. Yemanjá is often portrayed with open hands, tossing pearls of good fortune into the ocean. Because of her association with water, she is often depicted as a mermaid with large breasts, fair skin, blue eyes, and long brown hair. She is also represented as a queen who controls the moon and the stars.

Oxum's spiritual qualities include prosperity, peace, love, and beauty. The protector of maternity (motherhood), she is often pictured wearing golden dresses and jewels, and dancing with grace and elegance. Her characteristics are normally transferred to her spiritual daughters such as Mãe Menininha, the legendary leader of the Gantois terreiro.

One of the most powerful male orixás, Xangô is associated with thunder and lightning and often depicted wielding a double axe. Iansã is a female orixá who is syncretized with Barbara, a saint of the Catholic church. Iansã is often described as having a special type of personality: she refuses to stay out of the enclaves of cults reserved for male authority. She has a sharp tongue, which she occasionally wields like a sword, and often spits fire. Furthermore, though she may from time to time stay in the corner where her altars are always placed, she is known to suddenly storm all over the place in a revolutionary furor. She insists on being part of the picture, incorporated into the establishment. If excluded altogether, she turns unimaginably violent.

Yemanjá depicted as a mermaid.

Tempo is an interesting seasonal deity that is often depicted with male and female characteristics, changing sexual identity and orientation during various times of the year. Tempo is syncretized with Lawrence, a saint of the Catholic church who was burned at the stake. As part of the syncretization with this saint, Tempo is often depicted holding what resembles a grill that is representative of suffering and the brutality of being burned at the stake. Some terreiros erect special altars located outside the sanctum to honor Tempo.

Ewá is a warrior who sacrifices for the good of humanity. Ogum, the iron warrior, and Oxóssi, the hunter, have both conquered fear and are great heroes and outdoorsmen. Because of sickness, scarring, and deformity, Omolú is shy and introverted and is covered with straw to hide his deformed features.[4] Nana is old but very wise.[5] Oxum-maré is symbolic of a rainbow and moves like a snake. Ossanha is crippled but loves life and vegetation. Oxalá is the father of all orixás and is associated with leadership, wisdom, peace and tranquility, resistance, and struggle. Many of the local festivals in Salvador celebrate Oxalá's leadership and peacemaking abilities.[6]

Some of the orixás also symbolically represent youth and innocence. Children are important because they represent the continuation of life and tradition. Some practitioners revere Cosme and Damião, orixás who symbolize twin births and childhood. These two children saints also are known as Ibeji and are often adorned with special leaves of life as their sacred objects.[7]

Communicating with the orixás is an important sacred ritual in Candomblé. Within the terreiro and during many ceremonies, I observed that women were more often possessed by numerous orixás, both male and female. Although many of the men were possessed by the male orixás Xangô, Oxóssi, and Omolú, they also had no problem having a female orixá as the primary guardian. Moreover, as part of their obligation to the orixás, some felt it was their duty to serve a particular orixá regardless of gender.[8] However, in some terreiros leaders expressed that problems can occur when a guardian orixá is selected. One leader explained that, in her terreiro, on a few occasions men who considered themselves macho and were chosen as sons by orixás through the jogo dos búzios had problems adjusting to becoming possessed by female orixás as the primary spiritual guardian.[9] For this leader these men had put their personal (secular) feelings before their (sacred) obligations to the orixás.

Many practitioners revered the orixás as the spiritual forces and possessors of axé empowerment. They often were imagined as both external actors upon and interior dimensions of human beings. Some practitioners believed that the orixás were a component of the human soul as well as an agency within every human being. But outside of the terreiro some people related to the orixás in similar ways. For example, some nonpractitioners were drawn to a particular orixá who they believed had the ability to help them prosper or share similar attributes (e.g., mother, father, peacemaker, freedom fighter). For many young Afro-Brazilians the orixás were appropriated as iconic symbols associated with the affirmation of African heritage, pride, and black identity. Popular musicians also drew inspiration from these ancestral spirits by creating secular songs that conveyed mythology, sacred themes, imagery, and symbols from Candomblé religion. Such performances often glorify the orixás to bestow axé's blessing of prosperity on humanity.

The Sacred/Secular Connection of Brazilian Samba

Candomblé religion and the orixás share a deep connection with the creation of many Brazilian popular music styles. For example, when one examines the samba as an Afro-Brazilian tradition, there is a close sacred/secular connection. Under the Vargas regime (1930–45), the samba also became part of a national rhetoric and aesthetic of Brazilian culture. In a secular sense, this popular style came to be regarded as part of national pride, an emblem of Brasilidade (Brazilianness), an ideal artifact of what is "authentically" Brazilian, and the product of African and European miscegenation. But the origins of samba are complex and intersect at a "crossroads" where devoted practitioners continued to keep Candomblé religion vibrant in Afro-Brazilian culture.

The samba developed out of a tradition of practitioners engaging in sacred and secular settings of active worship and celebration of the orixás. Like the Candomblé religion, samba initially took its shape and meaning from the experiences of African people and their descendants, who were forced to make sense of themselves and their condition within a social domain of Brazil. The samba also served as an important foundation from which Africans were able to negotiate space for artistic expression of their identities, both personal and collective.

Similar to the theoretical debates surrounding the origins of the term Candomblé, which suggest phonetic linkages associated with several Bantu terms, there continues to be speculation about the origins of *samba*.[10] The term has also been linked with dance (the secular) and religiosity (the sacred) that also may stem from Bantu (Central African) words such as *semba* and *san-ba* (to pray).[11] However, the origins and development of samba—music and dance—cannot fully be attributed to one ethnic affiliation; it is linked to several cultural traditions, both African and European, that have contributed to the multidimensionality of Brazilian popular music.

In the creation of traditional samba, the integration of sacred and secular activities among Candomblé practitioners was continued outside of Salvador after abolition in the late nineteenth century, when many freed Afro-Brazilians migrated to Rio de Janeiro. There they experienced challenges including outright repression against public displays of Afro-Brazilian artistic behavior. That repression did not halt artistic innovation; Afro-Brazilian musicians were able to perform in neighborhoods such as Praça Onze (Plaza Eleven), where their families would gather at the private homes of the women called tias (aunts) to participate in Candomblé ceremonies. Near Praça Onze was the home of Tia Ciata Hilária Batista de Almeida (1854–1924), a Candomblé practitioner originally from Salvador.[12] Ciata was the spiritual daughter of the orixá Oxum.

Ciata's home was similar to a terreiro; practitioners were allowed to congregate, celebrate their ancestral guardians, and experience axé empowerment. The secular aspect of this experience was that, in addition to the Candomblé ceremonies at her home, Ciata often hosted parties where gifted musicians would perform and experiment with various popular music styles (e.g., lundus, marchas, maxixes).

Some of the musicians who attended the sacred/secular festivities at Ciata's home included the flautist Pixinguinha (Alfredo da Rocha Vianna Jr.) (1898–1973), Donga (Ernesto Joaquim Maria dos Santos) (1891–1974), and João da Baiana (João Machado Guedes) (1887–1974). As the son of Tia Amelia, Donga was closely affiliated with the Candomblé religion. In 1916 he began playing with Pixinguinha at Ciata's home. He gained renown for co-composing the first samba song, "Pelo Telefone," and the samba song "Macumba de Oxóssi." João da Baiana was the grandson of Tia Priciliana and is credited with introducing the pandeiro as a samba instrument.

There are many ways that one can embellish on the sacred/secular scenario, Candomblé ceremonies, and the secular parties that nurtured the samba at Ciata's home. The Candomblé ceremonies were a type of service and devotion, acts of "doing" and "being"—sacramental offerings of oneself. In this way Ciata was a vessel and source for the preservation of axé in her community. Moreover, Ciata's experience with appeasing the orixás outside of Salvador, within the context of urban Rio, follows the myth imagined by many practitioners that the orixás are able to manifest and transmit axé at any geographic location when they are summoned through special ceremonies.

Outside of Ciata's home there was what I refer to as an external spread of "axé samba" to Estácio, a neighborhood in close proximity to Praça Onze and Ciata's home. In Estácio much power and creativity was generated by Afro-Brazilian musicians such as Ismael Silva (1905–1978) and Nilton Bastos (1899–1931), who helped develop samba into a distinct and important genre of Brazil's popular music lexicon. From the Estácio musicians came the first escola de samba (samba school), Deixa Falar. With the artistic creativity of the Estácio musicians, spreading of axé with the innovation of the samba became a major vehicle for the self-affirmation of Afro-Brazilians who were at the lowest socioeconomic status in Brazilian culture. The success and spread of samba in the Estácio neighborhood also corresponds with a myth in Candomblé about the blessings of axé to make positive things happen in the secular world. In Brazilian culture, samba continues to be a positive and energetic style that is expressed in popular songs and dances. Moreover, the style has become an international phenomenon.

There was also a West African reconnection and an internal spread of secular axé energy back to its African roots. After abolition, as samba was developing in Rio de Janeiro, some Afro-Brazilians returned to West Africa and attempted to maintain a sense of their Brazilian identity while living within traditional Yoruba culture. Some Brazilian repatriates held onto their Christian beliefs, constructing one of the first Catholic churches in Nigeria, known by the Portuguese name Igrega do Bonfim (also known as the Holy Cross Church).[13]

Repatriated Afro-Brazilians also influenced popular music styles in West Africa. For example, the samba, brought to Lagos, Nigeria, by descendants of freed Afro-Brazilian slaves, influenced the development of jùjú music, a style that emerged in the 1930s. Jùjú was ensemble music performed by a trio made up of a leader who sang and played banjo, a sekere, and a jùjú (a tambourine).[14] The rhythms of early jùjú were strongly based on the asíkò, a dance drumming style performed mainly by Christian boys' clubs. Some of these rhythms came from Brazilian samba; the associated style of dancing was influenced by the caretta or "fancy dance," a Brazilian version of the contredanse. The square sámbà drum that is often used in jùjú was most likely introduced by Afro-Brazilians.[15]

Axé and the African roots of Brazilian popular music are embedded in the creative energy of samba, the popular style that has come to mediate between African and European heritage in Brazil. Often with the sounds of a barrage of vibrant drumming, a mixture of other percussion instruments, and the fast choreography of hip and foot movements, the energy of samba has distinguished Brazil in the international market for popular music. Samba has continually been reinvented in dance, songs, and festive celebrations. Moreover, samba is the Brazilian popular music style that has continued to mediate racial and cultural identity of people that regard themselves racially in various ways—white, pardo, Afro-Brazilian, mestiço, and mulatto. Without the creative energy of axé, the African roots, Candomblé religion, and the popular music generated at Ciata's home in Praça Onze and in the Estácio neighborhood, perhaps samba would not have been created to influence Brazilian culture and so many other popular styles.

Samba and Beyond: A Historical Perspective of Sacred Themes, Imagery, and Religious Symbols in Brazilian Popular Music

What do musicians like Dorival Caymmi, Ary Barroso, Noel Rosa, Clara Nunes, Gilberto Gil, Caetano Veloso, Maria Bethânia, Sérgio Mendes, Clementina de Jesus, Martinho da Vila, Beth Carvalho, Elis Regina, Gal Costa, Margareth Menezes, Daniela Mercury, Carlinhos Brown, and many others have in common? The answer is that many of these musicians have composed, recorded, or performed popular songs with sacred themes from Candomblé religion. This field of popular musicians is vast; these musicians are not all from the same social or racial classes, religions, cities, regions, or popular music styles.

There are many reasons why popular musicians include sacred themes in their music that may relate to their own personal experiences with the Candomblé religion. Some include sacred themes to capture or convey imagery about the beauty of Afro-Brazilian cultural traditions, to pay homage to a spiritual leader, or to express local, social, and ethnic identity. Topics about Candomblé have ranged from ritual sacrifice, appeasement of the spiritual world, divination processes, admiration for a particular orixá or a spiritual leader, and the power and energy of axé.[16] Songs that focus on Candomblé often situate the orixás within the complexities of the secular world, where they constantly have the task of channeling axé to assist people in accomplishing goals, dealing with each other in relationships (love, family, work, death) and responding to nature (sea, forest, rain). Some of the popular musicians have tended to focus on certain popular orixás—Yemanjá, Iansã, Oxum, Xangô, Oxalá, Ogum, Exú—who in their songs are characterized as archetype deities possessing some kind of authority (mother, father, queen, king, freedom fighter).

Some popular songs convey imagery of the female orixás as being mature, wise women, and symbolic life sources. For example, in the song "Iansã" Gilberto Gil describes this orixá as "Senhora do mundo" (Lady of the World) and "Rainha dos raios" (Queen of the rays). In another song Gil describes Yemanjá as a Marian figure, Nossa Senhora (Our Lady).[17]

Appropriating sacred themes, imagery, and symbols from Candomblé religion has an extensive history in Brazilian popular music. Beginning in the 1930s, a few samba composers attempted to capture imagery of the richness of Afro-Brazilian religion and culture through popular song. Ary Barroso (1903–1964), the legendary composer of Carnival marches and the most famous samba "Aquarela do Brasil" ("Watercolor of Brazil"), was inspired to write several *samba canção* after visiting Salvador in 1934 and experiencing its beauty and the richness of its Afro-Brazilian culture. His Bahian sambas include the music and lyrics of "No Tabuleiro da Baiana" ("On the Baiana's Tray") (1936):

No tabuleiro da baiana tem
[In the baiana's tray there is]
Vatapá, ôi, caruru . . .
No coração da baiana tem . . .
[Inside the baiana's tray there is . . .]
Illusão, ôi, Candomblé
[Illusion, oh Candomblé]

During the 1930s and 1940s one of the popular musicians who wrote songs centered on Candomblé and the orixás was Dorival Caymmi (1914–). A native of Salvador and a practitioner of the religion, his is one of the earliest culminations of cultural expression centered on Afro-Brazilian religion and culture. Often regarded as a father of Bahian popular music, through fisherman songs and sambas Caymmi captured images of the baiano (male) and baiana (female), the history of Candomblé, the mythology surrounding the orixás, festivals and celebrations, dance, and the environmental landscape of the Salvadorian region.

Caymmi's collaboration with Carmen Miranda (1909–1955) on the Brazilian film *Banana da terra* (1938) popularized and secularized imagery of the baiana, women of Candomblé with the inclusion of his samba "O que é que a Baiana tem?" ("What Is It That the Bahian Woman Has?"). Caymmi's lyrics describe a baiana as wearing a turban, earrings, skirt, sandals, bracelets, and other types of jewelry. In the film Miranda appropriated this image of a sensual young baiana, wearing a similar costume that includes a *balanganda* (a silver charm with amulets and trinkets), a long skirt, a short blouse, and a turban adorned with fruit (her famous Tutti Frutti hat).

Many of Caymmi's songs of the 1940s are compiled in *Cancioneiro da Bahia* (1947). Caymmi's songs are examples of works that situate the orixás in the secular world as they assist humans in dealing with each other, nature, and life experiences. There is poetic symmetry in the lyrical content of the songs as he links orixás such as Yemanjá with spirituality and nature—"Senhora que é das águas" ("Lady who is of the waters") or "Rainha do mar" ("Queen of the sea"). Some of the songs are as short as six measures; stylistically, they are melodic and set in a variety of keys and meters. The song "Acontece Que Sou Baiano" ("It Happens That I'm Baiano") contains imagery of a man who attempts to deal with temptation and seduction, seeks to do good by performing a ritual sacrifice of a fowl at the entrance of his home, and petitions a Candomblé priest (pai de santo) to bless a woman with enticing and sensuous hip movements.

Cancioneiro da Bahia also contains songs that relate to consolation, hope, good fortune, and prosperity from the orixás. For example, "É Doce Morrer no Mar" ("It's Sweet to Die in the Sea") is about the loss of a husband who drowned; "Promessa de Pescador" ("Promise of the Fisherman") reflects on the mythology surrounding Yemanjá and the beauty, love, consolation, hope, good fortune, prosperity, and protection she bestows.[18]

Caymmi was a master at capturing many of the sacred/secular public celebrations in Salvador. In this song Caymmi describes imagery of the annual February celebration where many people in Salvador deposit gifts in the sea to appease Yemanjá.

Dia 2 de Fevereiro
[February 2]
Dia de festa no mar
[Festive day in the sea]
Eu quero ser o primeiro
[I want to be the first]
Pra salvar Yemanjá
[To rescue Yemanjá]

In the 1950s other popular musicians wrote samba songs about Candomblé religion. For example, Herivelto Martins and Chianca de Garcia composed the song "A Bahia te Espera" ("Bahia Waits for You") (1950), which exalts Bahia as magical place of Candomblé religion and celebrations for Yemanjá.

Although bossa nova, the popular style that emerged in the late 1950s as an altered form of samba, was mostly associated the white upper and middle classes and with poetic imagery of idyllic Brazil—beaches, love, and beautiful women—some artists produced songs in this style with references to the orixás and Afro-Brazilian religion. Vinícius de Moraes (1913–1980), a white Brazilian and one of the most gifted bossa nova lyricists, identified himself as the spiritual son of the orixá Xangô. In 1966 Moraes and the Afro-Brazilian guitarist Baden Powell (1937–2000) captured the imagery and symbolism of the orixás with their seminal suite of songs titled *Os Afro Sambas* (*The Afro Sambas*). This compilation is what can be described as a poetics of place where song texts and tonality are equally integrated to depict the richness of Afro-Brazilian religion, music, and beliefs.

The Afro Sambas combine the refinement of bossa nova lyricism with rhythmic motifs drawn from Candomblé and Umbanda religions. The compilation includes invocations and devotions to orixás such as Xangô ("Canto de Xangô"), Yemanjá ("Canto de Iemanjá"), Ossanha ("Canto de Ossanha"), and Exú ("Lamento de Exú"). For example, the song "Tristeza e Solidão" ("Sadness and Solitude") tells the somber story of a man from the lineage of the Umbanda religion. In fervent prayer he seeks consultation from an Umbanda babalaô (priest) to rekindle his relationship with a woman and to avoid dying from a broken heart. The encounter depicted in "Tristeza e Solidão" is reminiscent of how some practitioners of Afro-Brazilian religions do seek consultation from a spiritual leader in resolving such matters. The spiritual leader would usually recommend some kind of solution through prayer, meditation, and through the divination process of the jogo dos búzios (casting of cowry shells):

> Ela não sabe
> [She does not know]
> Quanta tristeza cabe numa solidão
> [How sadness fills my solitude]
> Eu sei que ela não pensa . . .
> [I know that she does not give a thought]
> Mas ela me condena
> [But she's condemned me]
> Ela não tem pena
> [She has no sorrow]
> Não tem dó de mim
> [No pity on me]
> Sou da Linha de Umbanda
> [I am of the lineage of Umbanda]
> Vou no Babalaô
> [I am going to see the Babalaô]
> Para pedir para ela voltar pra mim
> [To pray that she comes back to me]
> Porque assim que eu sei que vou morrer de dor
> [If I stay like this I will die of sorrow]

In *The Afro Sambas* some male orixás are warned against while others are often given appellations, such as those for Xangô: Senhor (Lord), Aganju (ancestral spirit of the earth), and Saravá (hail). Some of these appellations about Xangô are expressed in the song "Canto de Ossanha" ("Song of Ossanha") (1966), by Vinícius de Moraes and Baden Powell:

O homem que diz dou, não dá
[The man who says I give, does not give]
Porque quem dá mesmo não diz
[Because he who really gives does not say a word]
O homem que diz vou, não vai
[The man who says I go does not go]
Porque quando foi já não quis . . .
[Because when he went, he did not want to go . . .]
Na manhã de um novo amor
[In the dawn of a new love]
Amigo Senhor, Savará
[My friend, Savará (hail)]
Xangô me mandou lhe dizer
[Xangô sent me to tell you]
Se é canto de Ossanha, não vá
[If it is a song by Ossanha, do not go]
Que muito vai se arrepender
[There is much you will regret]
Pergunte pro seu orixá
[Just ask your orixá]
Amor só é bom se doer . . .
[Love is only good when it hurts . . .]

In the 1960s many more Brazilians had access to popular music via the radio, television, and public festivals in urban areas of Rio de Janeiro and São Paulo, where there was a secular spreading of axé—sacred themes, imagery, and symbols of Candomblé and the orixás to different audiences and popular music consumers. A singer such as Elis Regina was able to perform songs such as "Arrastão" ("The Taking In of the Fishing Net") (1965) to large audiences. Composed by Vinícius de Moraes and Edu Lobo, this song makes reference to imagery of Yemanjá (as "Queen of the Sea"), Senhor do Bonfim, and Saint Barbara:

Ê tem jangada no mar
[Hey there is sailing raft on the sea]
Ê meu irmão me traz Yemanjá pra mim
[Hey brother bring me Yemanjá]
Nha Santa Barbara me abençoai
[St. Barbara bless me]
E é Rainha do mar . . .
[Hey hey it's the Queen of the Sea . . .]
Valha meu Nosso Senhor do Bonfim
[Help me our Lord of Bonfim]

Nunca jamais se viu tanto peixe assim
[We never saw such an amount of fish]

Other musicians during the 1960s incorporated Candomblé themes in performances and commercial recordings for different audiences and popular music consumers. For example, on Sérgio Mendes's jazz–bossa nova album *Mendes & Brasil 66*, there is an arrangement of Dorival Caymmi's "Promessa de Pescador" ("Promise of the Fisherman"), which is about the orixá Yemanjá.

Even in the short-lived Tropicália movement, which lasted from 1967 to 1969 and opened the way for musical and poetic experimentation and diversification in Brazilian popular music, there are examples of songs that incorporate Yoruba phrases and references to Afro-Brazilian religion's sacred symbols and imagery. "Batmacumba," a composition on the 1968 album *Tropicália*, fits this trend. At the center of the text is *ba*, a word that means priest in the Afro-Brazilian religious traditions of Macumba and Candomblé. The Yoruba word *obá* at the end of the first and last lines of text designates a king or a minister of the orixá Xangô. Obá is also a common greeting or exclamation in Brazilian Portuguese. The word *bat*, homophone for the Portuguese word for "hits," is seconded on the musical level by the pounding of conga drums that evoke Macumba rituals.[19]

In the 1970s, Brazilian popular music was more focused on the African roots and Candomblé religion as integral parts of Afro-Brazilian identity. Some popular musicians presented songs about the orixás not as timid spirits confined to the sacred realms but as iconic symbols and as powerful beings (e.g., sword of Ogum, lightning bolts of Xangô) that protect people in the secular world. During this time, Gilberto Gil, Caetano Veloso, Maria Bethânia, and Gal Costa recorded an innovative jazz-funk fusion album *Os Doces Barbaros* (*The Sweet Barbarians*) (1976) that publicly glorified power and spirituality and made symbolic references to Candomblé orixás. Also, in the album *Primal Roots*, Sérgio Mendes and Brasil 77 included invocations to the great mother, Yemanjá.

In the 1970s, Clara Nunes (1943–1983), one of the first prominent female singers in Brazil to achieve international fame, composed and recorded "A Deusa dos Orixás," a samba that delves into Candomblé by recounting the mythology of the orixás Iansã and Ogum. It begins with a recitative, prayerlike call to the orixás ("Iansã, where is Ogum? Iansã, where is Ogum? He went to the sea"). This is followed by an increase in tempo as the verse begins with a traditional duple samba rhythmic pattern. The instrumentation includes the cavaquinho, pandeiro, and the agogô, which plays a timeline similar to a Candomblé rhythm.[20]

Iansã, cadê Ogum?
[Iansã, where is Ogum?]
Foi pro mar
[He went to the sea]

Mas, Iansã, cadê Ogum?
[But, Iansã, where is Ogum?]
Foi pro mar
[He went to the sea]
Iansã penteia
[Iansã combs]
Os seus cabelos macios
[Her soft hair]
Quando da luz da lua cheia
[When the light of the full moon]
Clareia as águas do rio . . .
[Shines on the waters of the river . . .]
Na terra dos Orixás
[In the land of the Orixás]
O amor se dividia
[The love was divided]
Entre um deus que era de paz
[Between a peaceful god]
Entre um deus que combatia
[Between a god who fought]
Como a luto só termina
[A fight only ends]
Quando existe um vencedor
[When there is a victor]
Iansã virou rainha
[Iansã became queen]
Da coroa de Xangô
[Of the crown of Xangô]
Mas, Iansã, cadê Ogum?
[But, Iansã, where is Ogum?]
Foi pro mar
[He went to the sea]
Iansã, cadê Ogum?
[Iansã, where is Ogum?]
Foi pro mar
[He went to the sea]

Other popular songs in the 1970s appropriated the imagery and symbols of orixás. The Caetano Veloso album *Bicho* (1977) featured songs based on Nigerian jùjú music. The album also included several upbeat disco-type songs such as "Odara," a Yoruba term commonly used by Candomblé practitioners to signify "good" and "positive." Gilberto Gil's *Refavela* (1977) exhibited elements of the African aesthetic, especially in the use of Yoruba words and expressions, as well as showing influences from West African musical styles such as highlife and jùjú. *Refavela* included the song "Babá Alapalá," which praises Xangô. This album also supported black social movements that glorified African heritage.

In the popular song "Axé Babá" Gil describes the orixá Oxalá as "Pai," the great father of mankind, and as "O pão da vitalidade do teu axé" (The bread of vitality of your axé). There are many ways to interpret the symbolism of pão (bread), vitalidade (vitality), and axé (power/energy) that Gil uses in this song. For example, the song seems to equate Oxalá as a God/Christlike figure and being a spiritual bread of life that nourishes mankind, similar to verses found in the Christian Bible.[21]

Between the late 1970s and 1980s the appropriation of sacred themes, imagery, and symbols from Candomblé religion was also fueled by the popularity and spiritual leadership of Maria Escolastica de Conceição Nazaré, better known as Mãe Menininha (1894–1986), one the most revered leaders in Salvador's Candomblé history. As the leader of the Gantois terreiro, Menininha became an icon of spiritual axé as the spiritual daughter of the orixá Oxum. In the Afro-Brazilian community she was a symbol of motherhood and spiritual guardianship. Political and military leaders became Menininha's supporters. She channeled her spiritual axé to nurture the creative powers of many artists, writers, and scholars. Even after her death, she is memorialized and praised for her contribution to the preservation of African culture in Brazil. Her ritual chair, which resembles a throne, was placed at the entrance of the Museu da Cidade, the city museum in Salvador.

In popular songs Menininha is petitioned with prayers to mediate blessings of axé from the spiritual world. For example, Clementina de Jesus (1902–1987) and Clara Nunes provided music, lyrics, and recorded "Embala Eu" ("Surround Me"), a song that offers prayer petitions to Mãe Menininha to mediate for blessings and spiritual guidance. De Jesus and Nunes sing prayerlike lyrics to Menininha such as "give me your blessings [of axé], liberate me from my enemies, give me your calling, and guide my footsteps wherever I go."[22]

Beth Carvalho, one of the leading singers who helped launch the pagode movement in the 1980s, recorded "O Encanto do Gantois" (1985), a tribute to Mãe Menininha that links her to the axé of the afoxés whose rhythms come from aiyé (the Yoruba cosmos). Highly influenced by rock music of the 1980s, the instrumentation on this song includes not only the traditional cavaquinho and pandeiro, but also electronic keyboards and guitars.[23] Dorival Caymmi, Gilberto Gil, Caetano Veloso, Maria Bethânia, and Gal Costa are among other popular musicians who have recorded secular songs and ballads praising Mãe Menininha and the Gantois terreiro.

Two prominent female leaders that I interviewed, Alícia dos Prazes Luz and Edna Portela Oliveira Silva, commented on the significance of Menininha in Candomblé religion and why she would inspire musicians to compose secular popular music. At ninety-one years old, Luz recalled many of the female leaders of Candomblé as well as much of its history. Luz started her own terreiro at the age of twenty-two near the city of Cachoeira. Luz was the mãe de santo of Tira Jima, a small terreiro in Salvador. Although Luz was not a fan of secular music, she believed that Menininha may have influenced popular music in Brazil because she believed that females such as Menininha are without a doubt one of the most important aspects of Candomblé religion in that they possess innate skills to train and lead people. Furthermore, Luz believed that female leaders had more insight into their ancestry and the history of Candomblé than male practitioners.

Interestingly, Luz felt that most female leaders in Candomblé were important because they were more "obedient than males." Luz explained that when females are given a task, they do not ask why the task is given to them, they just accomplish the job. Luz stated the following about Menininha: "Mãe Menininha was my spiritual mother and I adored her. She was a saint because through her I learned to be a good leader in my Candomblé terreiro. As a baiana through Mãe Menininha I learned to appreciate my heritage. What made her so special was that she knew and could name all of her ancestors from slavery to the present."[24]

When I met with Edna Portela Oliveira Silva, aged sixty-three, she expressed that Menininha dedicated her life to the betterment of Candomblé and the Afro-Brazilian people and she had a special anointing from the orixás. Silva felt that there were both positive and negative aspects about commercial recordings about Menininha and Candomblé religion. Although she did not listen to popular music, Silva expressed that such recordings are examples of how Candomblé religion is part of the cultural fabric of Salvador.[25]

Some of the male leaders in Candomblé also offered comments about the role of Menininha and sacred themes, imagery, and symbols in secular popular music. Ludinho Ramos, a sixty-six year-old musician at the Gantois terreiro, had much respect for Menininha as his spiritual leader and daughter of the orixá Oxum. The popular/secular songs that were written about Menininha and the orixás did not offend Ramos; however, he preferred that any songs about Menininha should be sacred and should originate from the Gantois terreiro.[26]

Luiz Murisoea, a seventy-five year old pai de santo at the Ilê Oxum terreiro, expressed that it is no surprise that there are popular songs dedicated to a spiritual leader such as Menininha and the orixás. Moreover, he believed that sacred themes, imagery, and symbols in Brazilian popular music stem from the fact that Candomblé has become an acceptable religion in Salvador:

In Candomblé there are some powerful leaders of axé. Menininha was one of those leaders. This is why there are popular (secular) songs about Menininha and the orixás. When I came into Candomblé religion over sixty years ago, I do not believe there were many musicians that would even think about writing a popular song about sacred themes, imagery, and symbols in Candomblé because the religion was looked down upon by the rich. The orixás are powerful and axé is something that is magical.[27]

In addition to songs dedicated to Mãe Menininha, in the early 1980s other songs made reference to Candomblé religion, the orixás, and African roots. For example, the song "Nação" (1982), by João Bosco, Aldir Blanc, and Paulo Emilio, integrates spirituality and ethnic identity with popular music. The lyrics, which refer to the ethnic nation of the Gêge, name Dorival Caymmi as the father of modern Bahian music and describe him communicating with the orixá Oxum. Another orixá, Oxum-maré, is imagined as a god of the rainbow, and a symbol of hope. There are many ways to interpret the meaning of this song. I believe it is an expression of ethnic pride and homage to Caymmi and the orixás.[28]

In the late 1980s there were songs that made reference to Candomblé, the ancestral spirits, and a universalism of axé. For example, Neguinho, a member of the Beija Flor escola de samba, recorded "Aldeia de Okarimbé" (1986), which makes reference to Olorun (Olódùmarè), the supreme deity in Candomblé.[29] The song also refers to Afro-Brazilian drumming, dance, and ritual offerings. Also, in the song "Axé Pra Tudo Mundo" ("Axé for the World") (1988), singer-songwriter Martinho da Vila, a native of Rio de Janeiro, attempts to share the blessings of the power and creative energy of axé with the world through his music.

One of the most popular songs in Brazil in the 1990s was "Nesta Cidade Todo Mundo é d' Oxum" ("In This City Everyone is of Oxum") by Gerônimo and Zezé Calazans. It has been recorded by Gal Costa, Caetano Veloso, and many others. This song makes reference to everyone in Salvador having a close relationship and being part of the orixá Oxum, a water deity who many associate with qualities of peace and motherhood. The song also refers to a universalism in Candomblé and the power of living waters that does not distinguish between (racial) colors.

Nesta cidade todo mundo é d' Oxum
[In this city everyone belongs to Oxum]
Homem, menino, menina, e mulher
[Man, boy, girl, and woman]
Toda a cidade irradia magia . . .
[The whole city irradiates magic . . .]
A força que mora n' água
[The power that lives in the water]
Não faz distinção de cor

[Makes no racial distinction]
E toda a cidade é d' Oxum
[And the whole city belongs to Oxum]

In the 1990s Caetano Veloso's "Milagres do Povo" ("Miracles of the People"), which makes reference to African survival, life, sex, freedom, and the orixás of Candomblé, was used on the soundtrack of *Tenda dos Milagres* (*Tent of Miracles*), one of Brazil's most popular television series.[30] Symbolism and imagery of Candomblé can also be found in songs by the legendary Milton Nascimento, such as "Santos Catolicos e Candomblé," a song that infers a syncretism between Catholicism and African religion.[31] Brazilian saxophonist Ivo Perelman presented symbolism and imagery of Candomblé in *The Children of Ibeji* (1992), an avant-garde free jazz compilation. The selections in this compilation are energetic, improvisational, and free in chord progressions and form. Several of the selections are invocations to orixás. Perelman also includes what he titles a chant for Ibeji. Interestingly, Perelman uses the symbolic terms of "children and Ibeji" in this collection of free jazz.

Sacred themes from Candomblé religion can be found in some of the more contemporary styles such as in axé music. For example, in the album *Elegibô* (1990), pop singer Margareth Menezes conjures up African religion and divination in "Elegibô," a song composed by the bloco afro Ara Ketu that symbolically traces the roots of Candomblé and Afro-Brazilian heritage.[32] Menezes sings of the legend of the mythical cities of Elegibô and Ifá, which flourished in West Africa, overcoming hardships and engaging in battles of good against evil. The song makes several references to the Ketu nation and its years of drought and famine. After overcoming these hardships, the people of Elegibô recovered and celebrated with a special offering to the ancestral spirits.

An initiated practitioner of Candomblé, Virginia Rodrigues is one of the most prominent contemporary popular musicians in Brazil. Her talents have been described as different and passionate, a mixture of African American soul and gospel, combining expressions of the Carnival spirit with spiritual appeals to the Candomblé orixás.[33] Rodrigues recorded *Sol Negro* (*Black Sun*) (1998), her first album to pay homage to her African heritage. Many songs on that album offer praises to the orixás. In an echo of the traditional ritual that opens Candomblé ceremonies, Rodrigues begins her performance with offerings and praises to Exú, the trickster/guardian.

In the new millennium Daniela Mercury composed and recorded a song titled "Dara" (2000), in which she seems to compare women to special qualities of the orixás:

Eu vi mulheres comuns
[I saw common women]

Virando rainhas
[Becoming queens]
Perseguindo a poesia
[Pursuing the poetry]
Eu vi rua bela
[I saw the beautiful street]
Bela como elas
[Beauty as they]
Enfeitadas de Nanas, Iansãs
[Decorated as Nanas, Iansãs]
E Oxums e Yemanjás
[And Oxums and Yemanjás][34]

In the album *Mares Profundos* (2004), Virginia Rodrigues offers a modernized and eclectic version of Powell and Moraes's *The Afro Sambas*. One of the most interesting songs is Rodrigues's version of "Lamento de Exú," which she performs as an extended vocalization on the word "ah." She musically personifies this orixá with a deep sentiment in Wagnerian melodic motif and harmonic progression, first played by the strings and then echoed by Rodrigues. The entire composition is written in a minor mode that seems to convey a sense of awe and mysticism.

Trio Mocotó, a group based in São Paulo, secularized the orixás in a fusion of samba, soul music, and rock that they referred to as SambaRock. In this style of popular music they often include arrangements featuring horns, electric keyboards, drums, and an assortment of percussion instruments. One of the songs on their album *SambaRock* (2001) is "Os Orixás," which delves into the mythology of Candomblé spirituality. In their most recent album, *Beleza! Beleza! Beleza!* (2005), they include the song "Lírio Para Xangô."

Not all musicians in Brazilian popular music have been inspired to appropriate sacred themes, imagery, and symbols from Candomblé religion in their music; such usage seems to be mainly from musicians who have experienced Candomblé religious culture in some way. These musicians may have been drawn to certain songs with sacred themes out of admiration for a composer such as Dorival Caymmi, who is often regarded as the "spiritual" father of Bahian music.

Some popular musicians have used sacred themes, images, and religious symbols from Candomblé religion for other reasons such as to praise, describe, reflect, and glorify the orixás as spiritual guardians and problems solvers, and in some cases to link them with ethnic identity and politicize the history of Afro-Brazilian religion and culture. From samba to the most contemporary style of axé music, in some popular songs a sense of "axé embodiment" and spiritual feeling becomes realized in recordings and performances and when the musicians express prayers and incantations and use lyrical description of sacred imagery and symbols of the orixás.

Although there is a sense of reverence in popular songs where an orixá is regarded as a great father or mother and that refer to the sacred confines of a terreiro, most are created within the secular contexts of the popular music industry, in recording studios and live performances. Moreover, popular songs that appropriate sacred themes, imagery, and symbols from Candomblé are more secularized in that, depending on the particular style and artist, they incorporate Afro-Brazilian rhythms and traditional and nontraditional instruments that are mainly intended to appeal to the aesthetic taste of a secular consuming public.

Local Perspectives: Axé Embodiment in Live Performances of Public Celebrations

In addition to commercial recordings, in cities like Rio de Janeiro and Salvador public celebrations often serve as inspirations for popular musicians to appropriate sacred themes, imagery, and symbols from Candomblé religion in their music. These celebrations are mainly where the axé of the orixás are publicly honored. In these celebrations the sacred and secular often complement each other. For example, outside of the Candomblé sanctum many Brazilians pay an annual tribute of flowers, perfume, gifts, and cosmetics to Yemanjá in order to ensure good fishing and prosperity. It is believed that when the gifts are deposited into the ocean and sink, Yemanjá accepts them and this ensures a prosperous year. This custom plays out in Rio de Janeiro on New Year's Eve at Copacabana beach and in February in Salvador at the Rio Vermelho, local beach where people of different social classes are welcomed to participate with their solemn prayers and gift offerings. In the midst of the prayers and special offerings, stages are set up on the beach where popular bands perform for people engaging in secular dancing to celebrate the orixás. Recordings of popular songs are often played over loudspeakers and boom boxes. There are often innovative exchanges between the performers, dancers, and local participants.

In Salvador I experienced how popular musicians were able to integrate their popular songs about the orixás in public celebrations. Many of these celebrations began with a mass given at the Rosário dos Pretos Church or at another Catholic congregation, such as Our Lady of the Immaculate Conception of the Beach (also known as Conceição da Praia). For example, in early December of each year in Salvador, an annual day of festivities and a special mass is given in honor of Iansã and her Christian counterpart, Saint Barbara. Crowds of people pay homage to Iansã and Saint Barbara by dressing in red and white. The mass ends with a procession of devout Catholics and practitioners of Candomblé carrying large banners, flowers, and statutes of saints, followed by the insignias of many orixás.

Participants sing sacred songs in the background, overlaid by a barrage of local drumming groups performing popular music such as rap, reggae, rock, jazz, soca, and Afro-Beat. Some people engage in samba dancing.

Of all the public celebrations that I observed, I most enjoyed the annual February celebration for Yemanjá where the sacred and secular seemed to compliment each other. In this particular celebration the iconic image of Yemanjá was depicted as a mermaid wearing a crown and surrounded by flowers. Thousands congregated at the local beach, Rio Vermelho, to celebrate, experience spirit possession, and stand in line for hours to lay flowers at special altars made for Yemanjá. People also waited to enter a small shrine, Casa de Yemanjá, to anoint themselves with water from the ocean. At the end of the day, boats took hundreds of straw baskets filled with flowers and gifts and deposited them in the ocean.

During this celebration, Candomblé ceremonies were held in a makeshift terreiro where Candomblé musicians played and people experienced spirit possession to communicate with their guardian orixás. Despite the makeshift setting, the rituals, music, and performances were filled with axé and blessings, bringing the Candomblé religion and music into the secular public space. In this way the public became part of the sacred, and experienced the re-creation of the mythology associated with African ancestral spirituality.

Some used the celebration as a type of reconnection with their guardian orixás, while others participated in the festivities as a type of creative play. Many local bands and Carnival organizations used the occasion to perform new musical repertoire in preparation for the annual Carnival season.

During the celebration I was fortunate to meet and speak with Caetano Veloso, who listened intently to several of the live performances. Although the crowds were massive, Veloso was very cordial and attentive to the performers. For me this experience with the popular music and the celebration was culminated when Veloso remarked "Alegria (Happiness)!" With the excitement of the participants in the background I soon realized what he meant by this remark. This celebration was a type of secular axé embodiment of the people in Salvador, and an expression of baianidade (local/ethnic identity) as some communicated with their guardian orixás in the makeshift terreiro and while others were uplifted by the sounds of commercial recordings and live popular music performances.

Although many people responded to the popular music and festivals in positive ways, the popularity of sacred themes, imagery, and symbols in popular culture has stimulated debates that center on Candomblé religion. For example, some practitioners that I spoke with suggested that Candomblé religion has opened the doors of opportunity for many people and that this can be seen in the different ways that nonpractitioners appropriate sacred themes, imagery, and symbols of the orixás. This includes any local businesses and musicians who regard

The author with Caetano Veloso during the annual celebration for Yemanjá, in Salvador.

the orixás as money makers where they can present an image of a sacred spirit in a song, or on T-shirts and buildings and make some kind of profit. Some practitioners did feel positive about the fact that many people are attracted to the power of axé. A concern is that some nonpractitioners tend to humanize/personalize the orixás in a way that appeals to them in the secular world without regard to the sacred mythology that is associated with each orixá. Furthermore, some practitioners would prefer that nonpractitioners keep in mind the sacredness of the orixás and how significant they are in Candomblé religion, and for African survival in Brazil and in many parts of the African diaspora where there are similar guardian spirits.

Black Religion and Popular Music:
Sacred Themes, Imagery, and Symbols

In many ways the appropriations of axé, African roots, sacred themes, imagery, and symbols from Candomblé religion in Brazilian popular music correspond to black expressions of religiosity embedded in popular styles such as soul, reggae, jazz, Afro-Beat, and many others. Brazil is part of an African diasporic community where black expression, religion/spirituality, and popular music often stimulate many emotions and experiences in popular musicians and consumers. Some consumers often respond to black popular music and musicians as being symbolic of a type of worship, devotion, and commitment. For example, in the African American community, black power was first viewed as secular ideology. However, in the mid-1960s, religious sectors of the community began to give it theological meaning. "Blackness" became an archetypal symbol of righteousness and represented all that is pure and sacred.[35] In popular music, the Godfather of Soul is James Brown and the High Priestess of Soul is Aretha Franklin.

Some popular musicians have been imagined as being sacredly thematic and having "spiritual" qualities that are emotionally similar to a religious experience. Thus, when listened to, these musicians may inspire a type of uplifting, aesthetic transformation, and questioning. When the musicians perform, they break down the barriers between secular enjoyment and spiritual feeling. An extreme example is the Church of Saint John Coltrane, established in the 1970s in San Francisco. In this congregation legendary jazz saxophonist John Coltrane (1926–1967) was revered as the image of a saint-figure whose music and ideas symbolically conveyed the word of God.

Perhaps the best example is the sacred/secular connection associated with the popularity of reggae, the Rastafarian movement, and the iconic status of Bob Marley (1945–1981). Many of Marley's songs incorporate a sense of religiosity through his imagery and symbolism of God, Jah (Jehovah), and the promised land. For example, in the album *Exodus* (1977), Marley presents several songs with prayerlike lyrics that petition Jah to send another Moses from across the Red Sea. In other songs he include symbolism and imagery of Holy Mount Zion ("Jammin'"), mystic blowing of the first trumpet ("Natural Mystic"), giving thanks and praises to Jah, and the crucifixion of Jesus Christ ("So Much Things To Say").

There are other examples of the appropriation of sacred themes, imagery, and symbolism from African-influenced religions such as Santería in popular music where the ancestral spirits are given praises. The legendary Celia Cruz (1925–2003), in her album *Homenaje a Los Santos* (*Tribute to the Saints*) (1994), presented songs based on the orishas of Cuban Santeriá.

In Brazil and other parts of the African diaspora, some popular musicians appropriate sacred themes, imagery, and symbols in popular music to convey a sense of spirituality, question religious dogma, or criticize social problems in the world. In the free-jazz compilation titled *Meditations* (1965), John Coltrane incorporated imagery and symbolism of the Holy Trinity in one of the compositions, "The Father And the Son And the Holy Ghost," that is intended to evoke a mood of spirituality. Another example is "Procissão" ("Procession") (1967) by Gilberto Gil, a song that uses sacred themes, imagery, and symbolism of the

Catholic church and Jesus to question the role of religion, the Church, and the social problems (e.g., poverty, racial discrimination) that people in northeastern Brazil often experience in the secular world.

Musicians in Brazil have drawn on a sacred/secular connection in popular music to capture the beauty, significance, and intricacies of Afro-Brazilian identity and religion. I believe that these musicians have also attempted, through popular music, to link the Afro-Brazilian culture with other black experiences and religions. A example of this is Gil's *Refavela*. Many popular songs have called on the names of the orixás to petition prayers for peace, love, and prosperity. In this way the ancestral spirits are often revered as the guardians of the secular world. With such songs the ancestral spirits often become icons of "blackness" in Afro-Brazilian culture, symbols of righteousness, and represent all that is pure and sacred in the manifestation of àsé/axé and African roots in Brazil.

In many ways the performers, composers, and lyricists who appropriate from sacred Candomblé religion are what I describe as "writers and interpreters" of Afro-Brazilian culture. In popular music, these musicians create a sonic and poetic "musico-aesthetics" of place (e.g., Salvador, the terreiro), religion, worship, and Afro-Brazilian cultural identity. The songs they compose, record, and/or perform that have a sacred/secular connection enrich a holistic knowledge in understanding the intricacies of Afro-Brazilian cultural identity.

In many secular public celebrations and live performances honoring the orixás I observed in Salvador, the popular music stimulated emotions and experiences similar to what I had experienced in West Africa and other parts of the African diaspora where sacred themes, imagery, and symbols from African-influenced religions were secularized in different types of public celebrations (e.g., ancestral spirits and harvest festivals, weddings, funerals). In Brazil during the public celebrations participants regarded popular music—samba, samba-reggae, funk, soul, jazz, and axé music—as symbolic of a type of special offering, worship, devotion, and commitment for celebrating the orixás of Candomblé. In these celebrations the sacred became enlivened with secular commercial recordings, live performances, and the active participation of singing, drumming, and dancing.

Axé Embodiment in Brazilian Popular Music

Many songs in Brazilian popular music convey a sense of Candomblé religiosity. These songs, recordings, and performances keep vibrant the Afro-Brazilian presence in popular music and the mythology of the orixás, axé, and the African roots of Brazilian popular music. From samba to the most contemporary styles, a sacred/secular connection stems from Candomblé religion. Many popular musicians are "musical priests and icons of devotion" whose social, cultural, and musical experiences bring a special type of emotion, spiritual quality, energy, and creativity to Brazilian popular music. Through the commercial recordings and live performances of individual artists such as Dorival Caymmi, Caetano Veloso, Gilberto Gil, and others, there continues to be what can be described as a spread of axé power and creative energy to a consuming public (the audience). In many ways, the consumers are active agents, participants, and also intertwined in a sacred/secular connection. Thus, with the popularity of samba and many other styles, there continues to be axé embodiment in Brazilian popular music.

4 | The Sacred/Secular Popularity of Drums and Drummers

Vibrant drumming is a musical tradition that connects Afro-Brazilians with the black experiences of African and African diasporic areas. Observing dynamic drummers was an experience that enhanced this research. Similar to Candomblé, in religions such as Haitian Vodou, Cuban Santería, and Trinidadian Sàngó there is strong influence from West African drumming where a male-dominated corps of musicians summons the ancestral spirits and evokes spirit possession.[1] In many African and African diasporic religions drumming mediates the tripartite of music, dance, and spirit possession. But, drumming also mediates the sacred/secular experiences of many devoted practitioners. Without drumming, practitioners in the secular world would be unable to petition the ancestral spirits for the blessings of àsé/axé power and creative energy.

The experience of slavery did not obliterate the legacy and significance of the drum. For many people of African descent this legacy was firmly grounded in their minds, hearts, and souls. The drum reflects a type of cultural survival manifested in diversity; this has resulted in construction of the instrument in different shapes, sizes, materials, and stylistic qualities. Even their names—atabaque, bàtá, ngoma, conga, djembe, timbale—reflect different experiences, mythology, environments, and aesthetic tastes. This experience also reflects the diversity of playing techniques—drums may be held, caressed, squeezed, beaten, slapped, and struck with the hands, sticks, and/or open palms.

In the African and African diasporic experience, the role and significance assigned to the drum also reflects various types of beliefs, social and cultural practices, and religions within diverse historical contexts. Drums have often been imagined as powerful sources that stimulate an atmosphere of worship and a sense of popularity in both the sacred and secular worlds. Within the framework of both, communities have often vested the drum with power, symbolism, and imagery as a special instrument that can be prayed and danced to in both sacred and secular settings, worshiped, praised, revered, feared, humanized, and regarded as being part of a spiritual family. But, like the experience of many displaced Africans, the drum has also been a victim of prejudice and inequality; in some areas even the sound of the instrument as a speech surrogate was banned in public spaces.

In the African and African diasporic experience there continues to be a sacred/secular popularity of the drum and drummers that culminates in a distinct black aesthetic and cultural identity. The drum and drummers continue to be iconic symbols of black identity and the essence of struggle and longevity of a cultural tradition passed down from one generation to the next, manifestations of the power and creative energy of West African àsé that survived the Middle Passage and the long voyage of enslaved Africans to the New World, where black identity has often been realized through religious and artistic expressions embedded in sacred/secular connections.

In Afro-Brazilian culture the sacred/secular popularity of the drum and drummers reflects a distinct black identity and an extensive history of struggle and survival with a strong connection to Candomblé religion. In this chapter I examine Candomblé musicians and the artistry of their drumming that has influenced many artists and styles of Brazilian popular music. Candomblé musicians do not simply drum: their performances involve high levels of professionalism, discipline, musicality, and artistic ability that continue to influence the level of technical facility demonstrated by local Afro-Brazilian drummers. Musical performance in Candomblé is an art form in and of itself. The musicians use music to express emotion and to construct local and social affiliation, preserving memory of the African nações (nations). The performers' array of aesthetic and interpretative expression satisfies practitioners, the "receivers" in Candomblé ceremonies.

Candomblé musicians have "performative power" and are a catalyst for axé, transmitting blessings from the spiritual world. One can think of the musicians as major players in a dramatization of the spiritual world.[2] In performance they become unified with the orixás, giving them life and movement and recreating revered ancestral mythology. Performances are constant dialogues, musical moments that allow practitioners to experience these stories and receive axé in the same time and space. The hands and bodies of the musicians possess "cooling fire and white heat" as they become empowered with the creative energy of axé.

Candomblé Musicians

Over the years I have had many opportunities to interact with musicians associated with the Candomblé religion and observe their craft and musicianship. Most terreiros have a corps of trained, initiated musicians who guard the integrity of the music and musical instruments. This corps is similar to a professional guild and functions as a brotherhood, social club, and mutual aid society in its community. In many ways these corps groups are the offspring of the irmandades, Catholic lay brotherhoods formed beginning in the seventeenth century,

Candomblé musicians in Salvador.

whose members (usually from similar ethnic backgrounds) sought to maintain African traditions in Brazil. Musical performance, festivals, and special ceremonies were important events for these brotherhoods.

No centralized authority trains Candomblé musicians; they are all trained within their own terreiros. Each terreiro is independent; each has musicians who bring into the religion their own secular experience and knowledge. The musicians' performance ability is evident; they work as a cohesive group at advanced levels.

Candomblé musicians are artists who prayerfully dedicate many years to perfecting their craft. They serve an extensive amount of time as apprentices and disciples. Their artistry is evident in the technical skill that makes the performances vibrant and energetic. They acquire the ability to make critical and aesthetic judgments about textures, dynamics, and phrasing nuances, and also learn the theories and values of performance etiquette.

These musicians consider ceremonies to be joyous occasions in which they can share music with the community. In most terreiros the musicians have a special seating area that sometimes resembles an elevated bandstand close to the center of the room. During ceremonies practitioners gravitate toward the musicians. Most musicians respond to this with sincerity, excitement, and pride as they observe practitioners experiencing axé embodiment in spirit possession. Some

Candomblé musicians' seating area in a local terreiro in Salvador.

are even moved to tears when the orixás descend and communicate with those that become vested with axé energy. Although in ceremonies there is sincerity among the musicians, in some instances there is also a sense of creative play.

The ceremonies provide opportunities for the musicians to socialize, critique their music and talents, and discuss their training, performance practices, and backgrounds. During ceremonies the musicians follow ritual protocol and choose the appropriate music. Their choices depend on their expertise and knowledge of the function and appropriateness of particular repertoire. For example, musicians are very much aware when celebratory music should and should not be offered, or what types of music should be performed to begin a ceremony. Devoted practitioners in the community are equally aware of appropriate musical repertoire, but depend on the musicians' expertise.

When asked about the gender of drummers in Candomblé, both men and women in terreiros had similar responses: men had a special "anointing" in being chosen by the orixás to play the music, and for this reason women were not permitted to become drummers. Some believed that, if women were drummers, while performing they might easily experience spirit possession, and this would be disruptive since the rhythms performed by drummers summon the orixás and produce axé energy. For most of the practitioners, drumming in Candomblé is a form of masculine empowerment. As the drummers, men control every aspect of Candomblé rituals. They become the dominant partners in the experience, leaving those in possession submissive to vibrant drum rhythms. Drummers also have special power in channeling axé of the orixás because it is through music that they first evoke the orixás' presence and later send them away by ending spirit possession. Moreover, drummers are held in great esteem throughout the community. In essence, musicians are role models for maleness.

Sacred Sounds: Drumming and the "Musical Language" of Axé

The musicians regard themselves as "divine drummers," believing that their bodies (both physical and spiritual) are vehicles for producing musical axé. Many practitioners believe that when the musicians perform they are speaking in a discernable language directly to the orixás. Moreover, when the music is performed the musicians are empowered with energy that enables them to translate the messages sent by the orixás to the practitioners. Vibrant drumming is part of an extensive lexicon owned by spiritual world.[3] In this way, the musicians act as intermediaries between the sacred spiritual and secular human worlds, channeling the power of axé through music to evoke the orixás' presence and to later send them away. Candomblé practitioners believe that certain orixás, while in physical form, created musical instruments for their own enjoyment, and also that the orixás have discretion over who should or should not become musicians.

In many cases, becoming a Candomblé musician is a "calling" or revelation from the spiritual world—both a lifelong commitment and the musician's sole means of employment and support. For example, although Antonio Carlos, a thirty-nine-year-old practitioner, was a performer of popular music he was also a devoted musician in Candomblé religion. Carlos described how he received his calling during a ceremony involving intense spirit possession. Carlos was seated in the middle of the floor when four initiates lifted his chair and suspended it in the air by command of the orixá Ogum. Because of this, Carlos was chosen to be a musician at his local terreiro, a position he has held for approximately twenty years.[4]

Arisvaldo Marques, a thirty-six-year-old practitioner, had been a Candomblé musician for ten years.[5] Although he was from a family of practitioners, in his early years he had no interest in becoming a member. However, one day the spiritual leader in the terreiro performed the jogo dos búzios (casting of cowry shells) and stated that Marques had a special calling as a musician and as an ogan (elder) or axogun, the person who oversees the animal sacrifices. Marques then decided to become a musician and active practitioner.[6]

In most terreiros the master drummer or "divine drummer," known as *alabê*, has the highest social status. With his status comes the responsibility to play the rum, the largest atabaque and mother instrument (ìyá lú) of the ensemble.[7] The alabê is responsible for determining musicians' preparedness for performance during the ceremonies. He acts as father, historian, gatekeeper, and custodian of musical authenticity and integrity. In most instances he is a mature individual, an elder drummer with more experience than the other musicians.

"Elder drummer" is an appropriate description of the role of the alabê. Some practitioners believe that, without the watchful eye of the alabês, other musicians would play inappropriate repertoire—for example, music for the wrong orixá— that would result in practitioners not being able to dance or experience spirit possession. Some practitioners also believe that, when the alabê walks by a person and says a word in Yoruba, that person is more likely to become possessed by an orixá. Respect for an alabê's wisdom often extends into the secular Afro-Brazilian community. Many elder drummers see Candomblé as a way to mediate social levels in Salvador.

In the terreiro, musicians such as the alabê emphasize traditional ways of playing music. As "spiritual father," the alabê is given the task of working with younger musicians. For example, Raymundo Nonato De Souza, seventy-four, was the alabê of Mutuisara terreiro in Salvador. When I met De Souza in July 2002, he had been a musician for over sixty years, and his experience was immediately clear: his age, physical appearance, and demeanor all indicated his status. On the night of the ceremony I observed, De Souza made sure that everything was in order before the ceremony began. As he made his way to the performance area, the musicians stood and greeted him with respect.

During the ceremony De Souza invited me to sit in the special area with the musicians. Since I was not an initiated musician in Candomblé religion, I was not allowed to perform with the ensemble, but sitting in this area gave me firsthand experience of a musical performance at the Mutuisara terreiro. De Souza assumed the role as the conductor of the ensemble; made the decision which instruments the musicians would play during the ceremony; discussed repertoires that would be performed; and made sure that the musical instruments were functioning and in working order. Before the ceremony some of the musicians asked De Souza questions regarding the musical repertoire and playing techniques.

During the performances the musicians often focused their attention on De Souza, making sure that they were incorporating appropriate nuances and tempi. He also led most of the vocal repertoire in Yoruba. As he played the rum at different intervals in the music, he began to improvise on complex patterns that produced a type of call-and-response dialogue between the other members of the ensemble. De Souza also incorporated a variety of playing techniques, such as playing the rum, the largest atabaque, with one bare hand and a stick (agidavi) held in the other. Striking the drumhead with the stick produced a deep vibrating sound, while striking the sides of the instrument with the open palm of his other hand produced a brisk staccato sound. Other techniques included using sticks or open palms in both hands to strike the drumheads.

Musical Training and Apprenticeships

Complementing the leadership role of the alabê, in many terreiros the spiritual leaders also assume a responsibility in the training of musicians. In many terreiros the leader sang devotional songs as well as selecting the repertoire to be performed at the ceremonies. The significance of the Candomblé leader's role in musical performance was evident when I interviewed a group of musicians at the Ilê Obirigenan and Ilê Oxum. Since the leader, Edna Portela Oliveira Silva, had significant authority, the musicians felt that it would be appropriate to have her attend the interview to provide additional information on the importance of music in Candomblé. Silva felt strongly that one of her major responsibilities was to work with the alabê to oversee the musical instruction in her terreiro.

Most terreiros have a corps of musicians ranging in age from approximately fifteen to seventy-five and coming from various backgrounds. For example, Ricardo José, twenty-four, was an experienced Candomblé musician at Ilê Oxummare as well as a virtuoso classical flute and piccolo player who performed with the local military concert band in Salvador. José credited his talents as a classical musician to the blessings of axé and the orixás. Lazaro Roberto, who had been performing at Ilê Axé Opô Afonjá for over twenty-three years, also worked as a professional photographer. His photographs of Afro-Brazilian culture appeared in several local museums in Brazil.

The Candomblé musicians I spoke with had varying musical backgrounds, training, and experience. Some had been practitioners of Candomblé most of their lives; others were recruited first as apprentices and later became members of the religion. Some had families that encouraged them to become musicians at a young age, while others were discouraged from doing so.

All the musicians emphasized that during apprenticeship, musicians must demonstrate the technical ability to perform the rhythms with great precision; for them, this is a rite of passage. This is why they give special care to early training to help young musicians develop proper technical skills. For example, during one ceremony a musician performed with his three-year-old son. He placed the child's hands above his on the atabaques so that the child could feel the rhythmic sensations and drumming patterns. He did this over and over as a way of internalizing the rhythmic patterns in the child at an early age. An experience such as this may seem mundane, but it is part of passing on the musical traditions associated with Candomblé.

The musicians also explained that intensive training is important because they perform continuously for many hours while the orixás are being evoked. To generate axé, musicians are required to play continually and with great force until spirit possession has been successfully reached and ended. During performances musicians exert a great deal of energy, using various muscles in their upper and lower bodies, all of which requires physical stamina. Furthermore, musicians must be mentally alert and sensitive to nuances of the music. They must master the technical skills of playing reiterations of notes, creating sounds similar to drum rolls or trills while the hands remain supple and the arms relaxed. They not only play the rhythms but also feel them throughout the body. Each musician has to demonstrate proficiency in these skills by tapping out or beating basic rhythms as well as performing within the ensemble format and following the rhythms of the other players. The goal of this training is to ensure rhythmic accuracy. If rhythms are not performed accurately, the entire ensemble's performance is affected.

Another technical skill that the musicians judge carefully is the ability to sing proficiently the vocal repertoire that celebrates the spiritual world. Even though a number of musicians have an ability to sing in Yoruba and in other African languages, some are not able to provide literal translations of the text. Instead, they rely on their knowledge of the liturgical context and function of each song offering. The musicians believe that the music is an incantation to invite the orixás to partake in the ceremonies. As one musician stated, "Although I am not able to provide textual translations, it does not matter because the orixás understand what is being presented."[8]

Musicians often extend musical training outside of their respective terreiros by recruiting boys from the surrounding neighborhoods as trainees. Because the training takes so many years, the musicians look for boys ranging in age from eleven to thirteen. The musicians observe the boys who perform in local youth music groups, and also recruit young boys who observe the musicians' performances at Candomblé ceremonies. During ceremonies boys often mimic the performers using sticks and items such as the cardboard cores of paper towel rolls. This is how Nivaldo Dario Nascimento, thirty-five, became interested in performing Candomblé music. His mother would take him to ceremonies where he would observe the musicians performing on the atabaques.

Nascimento began his training by teaching himself to play the rhythms. At home he would take two sticks and beat out the rhythms on small cans until he could play them perfectly. He did this for several years until he was recruited by a musician at Ilê Axé Omisi who, eager to teach him the necessary musical skills of Candomblé musicianship, gave him access to atabaques. Nascimento felt that the music was his friend, and that without it he would be an empty human being. He commented about his experience playing the drums in Candomblé:

Young drummers in a neighborhood of Salvador.

> I feel good when I play for the orixás. Being an initiated musician in Candomblé is so important to me. From playing music in the terreiro I believe that I have become a better person and a man in my community. Playing music in Candomblé has taught me the discipline of hard work and not to give up on my talent of drumming. I believe that there are many drummers that have a special calling [summons] in Candomblé and that is to serve the orixás. Many musicians in Candomblé do not have a choice because they were chosen by the orixás to play the music and they should be the best possible musicians. This is what happened to me. When I was young I felt compelled to play Candomblé music. The orixás kept working on me, influencing me to play the atabaques for them. The orixás and axé are strong and even as a young boy I could not refuse to serve the spiritual world as a musician.[9]

Some terreiros allow apprentice musicians to perform in an ensemble format before actual ceremonies commence so that the more mature musicians may observe their performance techniques for later commentary. Edvaldo Pain, twenty-six, said this type of commentary was beneficial to his musical training. His mother, a spiritual advisor, and his father, a musician at Ilê Axé Omolo Oya Se, encouraged him to begin the training. While serving as his father's apprentice, he mastered the basic rhythms and songs of the Candomblé repertoire, but learned other rhythms from some of his younger peers in the terreiro. In the ceremonies, Pain led many of the songs and often danced with the initiates. He commented the following about becoming a musician in Candomblé religion:

My experience in Candomblé is different than some other musicians because I was born into the religion. Even before I was born my parents prayed to the orixás that I would become something like a musician or axogun in the religion. It turned out that I was chosen to become a musician. As a musician in Candomblé I am very comfortable. I know what my responsibilities are to do the work of the orixás and play the best music possible. As a lead drummer, when I play in the ceremonies I expect the other musicians to be as dedicated as I am and play with precision and skill. In ceremonies if I play without any type of emotion, the practitioners would know it and I would be disappointing the orixás and axé. All I can say is that the prayers of my parents to the orixás many years ago were answered because I consider myself to be a dedicated musician in Candomblé.[10]

Speaking the Language of Drums: Studying Drumming with a Candomblé Musician

In order to better understand the craft of the musicians, performance etiquette, practitioner involvement, and the importance of the musical repertoire, I studied drumming with a Candomblé musician. By actually experiencing a musician's daily routine, I gained a better understanding of the intricacies of musicianship. It also gave me many opportunities to observe how the musicians responded to performances by local Carnival organizations such as Filhos de Gandhi, Olodum, Ilê Aiyê, and Timbalada.

Studying Candomblé drumming was like learning a language spoken through the hands. Since I was not initiated in the religion, I was not allowed to perform music during ceremonies. However, as part of my orientation and training, in addition to my experience at Mutuisara (where I observed the performance of the alabê De Souza and his musical ensemble), in other terreiros I also was invited to sit with the musicians in special designated areas and observe musical performances.

Arisvaldo "Ary" Marques, a musician at Ilê Oya Geí terreiro, was my drumming instructor at weekly three-hour instructions with Marques from early October 1998 until July 1999. The lessons were at Marques' studio, located at Ladeira da Praça near the Pelourinho district of Salvador. Although not a sanctum, Marques's studio was a shrine to the orixás, with their images posted on the walls and incense and candles burnt in their honor. During lessons Marques often shared many of the myths associated with the orixás and how these myths related to the musical performances.[11]

I received both individual and group instruction. These lessons were beneficial not only in developing technical prowess in playing the atabaques, but also in observing Marques's group teaching techniques. Marques emphasized that, although the musicians play recurring rhythmic patterns, there are moments in the music when they improvise on their parts. This was a difficult task to master while performing with the other experienced musicians, who could feel the rhythmic sensations throughout their entire bodies. Marques employed methods such as visual and aural exercises for developing rhythmic techniques. One exercise involved observing the techniques of each rhythm by paying attention to hand positions before attempting to execute a rhythm. In another exercise, the students developed auditory perception of the different rhythmic sounds by identifying each instrumental part with eyes closed.

During the lessons, Marques constantly tightened the drumheads on the instrument so that every finger could potentially produce an array of sounds—thumping, slides, and pops. The most difficult sounds to produce on the atabaque were the open and slap sounds employed in the popular ijexá, the rhythm that is used to summon orixás. The open technique is executed by holding the fingers of both hands tightly together and striking the atabaques in the lower portion to produce a vibrant, sustaining sound. After striking the atabaques, the hands are held in the same position until the next sound is produced. The slap technique produces a brisk sound, similar to a staccato and loud as gunfire. This technique is executed by striking atabaques in the middle area. What makes the technique difficult is that intricate sounds are also produced with certain touches of the fingers.

Rhythms that are used to summon the orixás such as Exú, Nana, Iansã, and Xangô are normally played with agidavis (drumsticks); again the musicians produce a gamut of sounds and textures. The rhythms incorporate techniques of playing reiterations of notes and creating sounds similar to drum rolls or trills while the hands remain supple and the arms relaxed.

I experienced how difficult it is to be a Candomblé musician. The musicians are important because, through their devotion, they keep Candomblé worship vibrant. They transmit stories of the orixás through their music, displaying not only devotion but also the discipline required to learn the appropriate techniques for becoming proficient performers. Marques, my drumming instructor, said the consistency of the drumming in Candomblé was the legacy of its African heritage. From my study with Marques (and interaction with African and African diasporic drummers) I came to realize more vividly how, though situated in different geographic spaces, Candomblé musicians, drummers in West Africa, and drummers in many African diasporic areas shared rich traditions of musicianship that they all desired to pass on to the younger generation.

The Social Spaces of Musical Performance in Candomblé Religion

Musical performances often create spaces for social relationships on many levels between musicians who share similar sets of experiences. These experiences may relate to training, performance practices and etiquette, backgrounds, politics, and critiques of another's music and talents.[12] For most of the Candomblé mu-

Musical performance incorporating the open and slap techniques.

sicians that I interacted with, performances provided opportunities for inter-action, dialogue, and critique, creating social relationships and bonds with their peers. Some younger musicians used performances as opportunities to interact with the opposite sex during rest periods, congregating outside the sanctum sur-rounded by young girls from the community.

Criticisms were also relayed to me about seniority status and dedication to Candomblé drumming. Although the experiences of most musicians are posi-tive, some of the older musicians expressed concern about the dedication of younger musicians. In the past, musicians secluded themselves for years, dedi-cating themselves entirely to serving the spiritual world. More recently, younger musicians have assumed leadership responsibilities earlier and earlier, some be-coming alabês as young as twenty-one. For some older musicians this is prob-lematic; some younger musicians were described as taking liberties in musical performances, "playing too fast and improvising excessively."[13]

Some of the younger musicians who had assumed high status in their ter-reiros at an early age responded that the eagerness of younger musicians to play music was a positive way to continue Candomblé traditions. They pointed out that many younger musicians had been practitioners for most of their lives, and therefore were not as inexperienced as their elders implied. For example, Edvaldo Pain believed he had the right to sit in special designated areas with the older musicians, and that age should not be a crucial factor in being chosen as an alabê. Rather, the major qualifications should be a musician's talent, artistry, and dedication. They were confident that their terreiros' leaders had the ability to make crucial decisions of whether a younger musician should or should not be promoted to a senior-level position in Candomblé. If a younger musician is selected to assume such a position at an earlier age than in the past, he is still obligated to be dedicated to his craft. Age should not necessarily be the primary criteria in becoming an alabê in Candomblé. If he has the talent and skills, and is able to function responsibly in such a capacity, this musician should be allowed to have the distinction of being regarded as an experienced alabê.

Critiques and Criticisms: The Secularization of Candomblé Drumming

In many local terreiros in Salvador, older musicians were concerned that younger musicians were showing a lack of regard for the sanctity of Candomblé drumming. Luiz Murisoea, seventy-five, a pai de santo who had been associated with the Ilê Oxum terreiro for more than sixty years, indicated that his role as a spiritual leader was specific: he taught and explained the songs and rhythms to musicians and members of his terreiro. Murisoea was concerned that younger musicians had begun to combine rhythms in nontraditional ways. For him, there were only twenty-one different rhythms and no others should be added in a ceremony. He also believed that only the Yoruba language should be used in Candomblé and that music was the most important aspect of ritual worship. He also believed that music in Candomblé was a type of "popular music" that should be performed in the confines of the terreiro.[14]

The older musicians were also concerned that the younger musicians were showing a lack of regard for the sanctity of Candomblé drumming—especially when they to play the sacred rhythms outside of the sanctum and give private instruction in Candomblé rhythms to nonpractitioners. Not only have these outside musicians quickly learned how to play the music, many have developed systematic methods for teaching the rhythms. Thus, a major concern was the secularization and popularity of rhythms such as ijexá that in many ways are becoming "sonic" symbols of Afro-Brazilian racial identity. The older musicians pointed out that many Candomblé rhythms continue to be appropriated and reinvented for popular music consumption.

The older musicians believed that some popular musicians who appropriate ijexá may have been initially trained in local terreiros; this possibly explains why these musicians are able to perform the rhythm with such accuracy. There is further secularization when these musicians (originally from Candomblé) teach the rhythms to nonpractitioners who reinvent, interpret, and embellish the rhythms for popular music consumption. This consumption often results in financial gain (money) and the abuse of sacred musical axé. In this way the orixás may not be pleased. Thus, the older musicians emphasized that the appropriation and re-invention of Candomblé rhythms often threaten the integrity of axé, the power-ful energy source that is very much dependent on drumming within a sacred context.

Some spiritual leaders also believed that younger practitioners were being influenced by the popular music industry. For example, Edna Portela Oliveria Silva, sixty-three, a mãe de santo at Ilê Obirigenan, believed that some of the younger musicians and practitioners were being influenced by their interest in popular music outside the terreiros, especially through commercial recordings. This has caused the younger generation to pursue careers in the popular music industry in hopes of financial gain.

Some of the younger Candomblé musicians described rhythms such as ijexá and sacred drumming as a "marketable commodity." One explanation given by the younger musicians for this trend is that Salvador's rapid urban growth, as in other cities, has created more social and economic demands, forcing musicians to explore their financial alternatives. Young musicians want to prosper and be pro-fessionally competitive, and many have family responsibilities that require addi-tional income. Those who are inspired by the commercial success of axé music and samba-reggae turn to popular music; others choose classical music. Some even seek employment outside of the music world, as teachers, policemen, cab drivers, barbers, physical trainers, and dancers.

Antonio Carlos, Arisvaldo Marques, and Edmilson Lemos were among the initiated Candomblé musicians who were also popular music performers in Sal-vador. Antonio Carlos, an alabê, defended the teaching of Candomblé rhythms outside the terreiro as a way to demonstrate to young people the importance of African heritage in Brazil. As an instructor of African music and dance at the Es-cola de Dança da Fundação, the cultural institution in Salvador, Carlos believed that it was his duty to instruct his students about Candomblé religion and music. He further expressed that if his students—many of whom are nonpractitioners—have no knowledge of the inner workings of Candomblé, how can they develop a sense of appreciation for Afro-Brazilian culture?

Carlos's group, which included a German guitarist and a Brazilian vocal-ist, incorporated many styles of music—samba, blues, funk, reggae, and rock—to create his own individual style. Carlos stated the following about playing popular music:

> Just like Candomblé music, playing popular music takes a lot of time to per-fect. A musician must be dedicated to playing popular music, develop skills, interact with audiences, and know the appropriate musical repertoire. In Can-domblé and in popular music, people dance to my music. The difference is that in Candomblé the orixás are present. In popular music, when I play I expect to

Antonio Carlos in his music studio in Salvador.

receive payment for my performances. In Candomblé on some occasions I may receive a small gift or some practitioners may give money because they feel led by the orixás. As an alabê in Candomblé I believe that my role is to assist in the training of the younger musicians, and this is similar to my job at the Escola de Dança. I believe that playing popular music with my group in a secular setting has also aided me in being a better sacred Candomblé musician. I am more attentive to the nuances of rhythms and melodies and how people in different settings are affected and relate to my music.[15]

Although Arisvaldo "Ary" Marques was a dedicated practitioner and musician in Candomblé, he also performed popular music outside the religion proper as an opportunity to earn additional income. Marques was a member of a local music band named Bahia com H, which performed in clubs and concerts throughout Salvador and had recently recorded an album of their music. Although Marques had received criticism from some of the older musicians in his terreiro, he emphasized that his training in Candomblé music was crucial to his ability to play styles of Brazilian popular music. He believed his forays into popular music did not overshadow his dedication to the orixás because they were the ones who had bestowed on him the talent to play, sing, and dance. Marques enjoyed all styles of music and believed that Candomblé music was part of his Brazilian heritage, as well as the African legacy in Brazil.

Although Marques planned to continue playing atabaques for his local ter-

Arisvaldo "Ary" Marques in his music studio in Salvador.

reiro, he also wanted to continue performing popular music with his band. Ary stated the following about his performance of popular music with Bahia com H:

> I believe that I can be a dedicated musician in Candomblé and also a popular musician. I consider popular music to be a form of providing entertainment to people who enjoy the music. But in Candomblé this is different. The surroundings are different and also the mood of the people. It is a sacred type of performance. Bahia com H is a group that I dreamed about organizing for several years and we are trying to make it into popular music. We enjoy performing such styles as axé music and samba-reggae. When I am performing popular music at that moment I do not think about Candomblé but only about the popular music and this is no disrespect to the religion. But as a group we really want to be successful in the popular music industry with the recording of our music.[16]

Some younger musicians follow the trends of popular culture on both local and global levels, adorning themselves with dreadlocks, pierced ears and noses, tattoos, and boots and seeking musical engagements outside of Brazil. For example, Edmilson Lemos, fourty-four, the leader of the Kalundu, the female popular music group in Salvador, had been associated with Candomblé as a musician for over thirty years. However, his experience as a popular musician afforded him the opportunity to contract professional engagements in many countries (the United States, Korea, France, Germany, Italy, and Angola) and with musicians as Paul Simon, Olodum, and Baden Powell. Lemos expressed that, in order to compete in the popular music industry, he felt it necessary to adopt what he described as "the new look" by adorning himself with dreadlocks, boots, and tattoos.

For Lemos, this new look was not only keeping up with the trends of popular culture but also a type of costume that he believed would attract fans in the popular music scene of Salvador.

> When I performed popular music outside of Brazil I made a lot of money. But when I returned, married, and had a child, my outlook of solely being a Candomblé musician changed. I really enjoyed performing for different audiences. This was an emotional experience for me, often seeing people dancing or even sometime singing with the music. Now in Salvador I have a family that I must support. The money that is given to me in the terreiro is not enough to live on. I have the talents to play popular music and this is something that is marketable in popular culture. Most of the clubs where I perform know my background as a Candomblé musician and some pay me more money because they know that I can really play the drums well. When I wear deadlocks, boots, and modern types of clothing people in the clubs seem to relate to my music more as a musician who is current with the styles and trends in popular music and youth culture.[17]

I met Arnoldo Junior and Marcelo Rios as teenagers, after they had been performing and serving as apprentices in their local terreiros for several years.[18] Junior and Rios had many performing obligations and were recruited as drummers into Candomblé because of the potential they had demonstrated while performing in local venues. Junior, eighteen, was a drummer for a local capoeira group when, at thirteen, he was recruited by a musician from a terreiro located in Fazenda Grande and introduced to the atabaques.

Junior felt that his experience with a local popular music group gave him a good foundation for playing atabaques. While he had great respect for the orixás, he believed that performing popular music did not affect his religious commitments. He said: "I am young and I enjoy playing popular music. People my age like axé music, samba-reggae, and rap. Playing in secular groups is my way of sharing spiritual axé with the community."[19]

Marcelo Rios, seventeen, was a Candomblé musician who worked at a tourist shop in the Pelourinho district, selling musical instruments and souvenirs. Rios had been a drummer at the Orixás' terreiro in Liberdade for five years. He was also a member of a local band called Dynamite, consisting of three female singers and several male instrumentalists playing instruments such as timbales, repiques, electric guitar, electronic keyboards, and tambourine. Like Junior, Rios expressed his devotion to Candomblé, but at the same time he wanted to continue performing with his band. He also believed that, with his ability to perform

Arnoldo Junior performing with a capoeira group in Salvador.

popular music such as samba-reggae, he would have more opportunities for employment in Brazil and in other areas.

In addition to the influence of popular music on younger drummers, another challenge in the terreiro in recent years has been females becoming interested in serving as Candomblé musicians. Some of this interest stems from the recent popularity of the all-female drumming ensembles in Salvador such as Didá. In most terreiros females are not allowed to play music in Candomblé ceremonies. One example is Virgínia Lúcia, twenty-five, who was from a family of Candomblé practitioners. Her father, a Candomblé musician, taught her to play the atabaques. In her local terreiro the leader encouraged the females to become initiates and begin their training early, so she began dancing in Candomblé at the age of seven, even though her real interest was to play the music. Despite her skill with the atabaques and the agogô, she was never allowed to perform in public or to reveal to anyone that she could play the sacred instruments. However, she believed that, in the future, female musicians would be allowed to perform in actual ceremonies.[20]

In November 1998 I attended a ceremony at the Ogum Deí Candomblé terreiro where a girl of about twelve was allowed to play the lê, the smallest atabaque. She was the daughter of the musician who played the rumpi; he coached her throughout the performance, demonstrating hand positions. A woman standing next to the musicians also coached the young girl, indicating increases or decreases in tempo and encouraging her to focus more on the dancers and the songs. The young girl played the instrument very well; by her performance one could tell that this was not her first time performing in a ceremony.

The responses I received from older practitioners about the secularization of Candomblé rhythms and sacred drumming in Afro-Brazilian culture are similar in many ways to sentiments that have been expressed in the past about the sacred/secular influences of black popular music in other African and African diasporic areas. Such sentiments have been conveyed from "inside" of religious sanctums (shrines, temples, churches, houses of worship) and "outside" by popular/ mainstream culture. *Devil's music, worldly music,* and *backsliding* are only a few labels that individuals and communities have expressed to criticize popular styles and (black) musicians they believe to be in conflict with religious beliefs and practices.

The debates about the secularization of Candomblé rhythms and sacred drumming will continue. But such debates often stimulate musical innovation, commercial interests, and a mass following/audience. Although many of the older musicians have concerns about the popular interests of the younger musicians in their terreiros, the religion continues to respond to creative energy. Besides, popular interests were not completely foreign to some older Candomblé musicians. Alabê Raymundo Nonato De Souza as a young man was himself an early member of the afoxés that were themselves trendsetters when they organized some of the first fraternal organizations in Salvador, performing sacred rituals and Candomblé rhythms and drumming in secular public celebrations. In return, public performances of Candomblé music and musicianship have continued to inspire a corps of aspiring drummers.

Secular Influences: Candomblé Musicians as Pop Music Icons

In his theoretical notions of theomusicology Jon Michael Spencer asserts that, in religious settings, musicians can provide pure and meaningful experiences, but that secularized versions of these experiences are more typical.[21] Complicating the matter, consumers of popular music often treat their experience of the music as a religious experience itself. Thus, some musicians can be considered "musical priests," purveyors of popular music who, when they perform, break down the barriers between secular enjoyment and spiritual feeling. They make themselves into icons of devotion.[22]

Many Salvador locals (mainly older practitioners) with whom I spoke regarded the Candomblé musicians in their communities as popular icons of pure musicianship. But this was a sacred type of iconicity, assigned to Candomblé musicians by devoted practitioners who regarded the musicians as having special powers to communicate with the spiritual world. This special power was regarded as providing meaningful experience for the devoted practitioners.

Other locals, a combination of young practitioners and nonpractitioners, also regarded Candomblé musicians as having a type of iconic status, but that the musicians' artistry extended outside of the sanctum. Moreover, they also believed that the musicians selected to perform in Candomblé ceremonies have demonstrated (in both community and sanctum) the ability to succeed as professional musicians. This professionalism is extremely evident when the musicians visit the communities and succeed in recruiting young musicians for apprenticeships in Candomblé religion.

Some locals also expressed that because of the talent and professionalism constantly exhibited in their communities, these musicians' charisma was able to attract an audience of devotees. They are also sources of income for terreiros; both locals and tourists often pay a fee or donate funds to the terreiro and attend ceremonies not solely to celebrate the orixás but also to enjoy and partake in musical axé. Thus, if the music is performed inadequately it may discourage locals (and possibly tourists) from attending the ceremonies. Adequate musical performances in many instances assure prosperity for the terreiros.

Some locals believe that many styles and trends associated with Brazilian popular music have their foundations in Candomblé sacred drumming and musicianship. Furthermore, popular music consumers often hear rhythms, timbres, textures, and nuances that they believe are reminiscent of Candomblé sacred drumming and musicianship. Some of the locals I spoke with appropriated, reinvented, and secularized the term *Candomblé* as a type of metaphor to describe secular popular music and musicians influenced by Candomblé drumming and musicianship.

Other reasons were given why Candomblé musicians should be considered icons of popular music in their communities. In popular styles such as afoxé, ijexá, samba, samba-reggae, and axé music, the pulsations of drums provide a constant momentum that enhances dancing. Furthermore, popular music figures such as Gilberto Gil, Caetano Veloso, Maria Bethânia, Carlinhos Brown, Moraes Moreira, Antonio Risério, Antonio Carlos Vovô, and Neguinho do Samba have in many ways have been inspired by Candomblé sacred drumming and musicianship. Many of these musicians have an extensive background as practitioners in Candomblé religion.

Most of the older Candomblé musicians that I spoke with in the sanctum did not desire to become iconic figures in secular popular music. Such sentiment they believed stemmed from outside of the sanctum, mainly from popular culture. Instead they regarded themselves as icons of devotion to the spiritual world. In performances it is the musicians' spiritual responsibility to appease the orixás. When the musicians perform adequately, the orixás become their greatest fans;

in return, the music connects the sacred/secular worlds and axé blessings are continually bestowed on the practitioners. Many older musicians expressed that if locals in their communities consider Candomblé musicians as iconic figures, then such status should be applied to the musicians serving as mentors to an aspiring generation of younger musicians in Candomblé religion, who hopefully will continue the important axé tradition of sacred drumming.

5 | Secular Impulses
Dancing to the Beats of
Different Drummers

In Afro-Brazilian culture axé, Candomblé religion, sacred drumming, and African roots have very much influenced the creative energy of secular community-based drummers. Since the mid-1970s, these young drummers have attempted to link Afro-Brazilian identity with other African and African diasporic areas through popular music and the valorization of Candomblé religion as part of the African heritage. Many young drummers actively engage in dynamic musical performances in association with social movements—Negritude, pan-Africanism, and black pride—in a struggle for racial equality in their communities. With active participation in the social movements, these drummers also stand at a crossroads of the sacred and secular.

This chapter examines how young Afro-Brazilian drummers of blocos afro organizations in Salvador are an important aspect of popular music production in Brazil and part of a black conscious Negritude movement. Many blocos afro are Carnival organizations that contribute greatly to the experimentation of new percussive and innovative sounds in Brazilian popular music. They appropriate, reinvent, and secularize axé, sacred themes, imagery, and symbols from Candomblé religion—and Candomblé sacred drumming and musicianship influences many of these drummers. Many blocos afro have mixed and secularized Candomblé sacred drum rhythms with secular popular styles to create innovative hybrid styles (e.g., samba-funk, samba-reggae, axé music) that are marketed to a consuming public.

The Sacred/Secular Connections of Social Movements

Negritude, pan-Africanism, black pride, and civil rights social movements are all crossroad traditions intertwined within a sacred/secular dichotomy. Many of these social movements are informed by religious ideologies and symbols of hope, faith, love, peace, unity, worship, and tolerance that are integrated into sociopolitical platforms for racial equality. Advocates of these social movements often associate religion as a source of guidance and engage local churches and clergy as proponents and spokespersons for racial equality in black communities. Within these social movements some charismatic leaders (e.g., Marcus Garvey,

Martin Luther King, Patrice Lumumba, Zumbi, Mahatma Gandhi, Bob Marley, Louis Farrakhan) have been revered as prophets and spiritual icons—"Moses" prototypes leading people to a promised land of racial equality and success.

On the other hand, some social movements become more visible, accessible, and readily accepted in black communities through association with secular activities (protests, dances, concerts, popular music) and affiliation with popular musicians—Harry Belafonte, Bob Marley, Fela Kuti, James Brown—who in their own ways support sociopolitical platforms of racial equality for people of African descent.

In some instances drummers have taken on the role of activists inspired to incorporate the rhythmic pulsations of their instruments in protesting against racial discrimination. For example, during the early years of the civil rights movement in the United States, Max Roach's composition *We Insist! Freedom Now Suite* (1960) was a highly politicized jazz, drum, and vocal improvisation in support of sit-in demonstrations by African American students in the South and an outcry for social change. Because the composition was controversial and included a song about the African experience of apartheid, in 1962 South African government officials banned a live performance by Roach.[1]

Many blocos afro organizations are in themselves social movements that use religious ideologies and symbols, song, dance, and drum repertoire to advocate for civil rights, urban renewal, educational opportunity, and racial equality.[2] For these organizations, the drum is deemed an iconic symbol of musical innovation and a "sonic" mechanism for expressing black identity and connecting with the experience of other African and African diasporic areas.[3]

In Salvador during the mid-1970s there was a rapid growth of blocos afro comprised of young lower-and working-class Afro-Brazilians. These organizations became proponents of more Afrocentric types of musical performances, especially during public festivities such as Carnival. What resulted was the formation of new Carnival organizations, such as Ilê Aiyê and Olodum. Many of these organizations developed sociopolitical platforms regarding race, equality, and economic progress that they continue to energize in the public space through musical performances.

Young Afro-Brazilians in the blocos afro were very much inspired by the activism of the Movimento Negro Unificado (Unified Black Movement, MNU) in Rio de Janeiro and São Paulo. As Brazil commemorated the centenary of abolition in 1988 by holding public celebrations in many areas throughout the country, young Afro-Brazilians used the festivities as a forum to protest against racism in Brazil. In Rio de Janeiro groups of young Afro-Brazilians organized marches to protest racial inequality's continued existence and the irony of political agendas with platforms advocating freedom and opportunity for all. In Salvador many blocos afro became active proponents in questioning and confronting the "system" with concerns about the progress and opportunity for young Afro-

Brazilians on the economic ladder. This resulted in the local government canceling its centenary celebrations.

Since the centenary, has there been any progress toward racial equality in
Brazil? There was a variety of responses to this question from the young Afro-
Brazilians I spoke with. Some suggested that what minimal progress there was
was due to the emergence of blocos afro organizations that offered opportunities for young people to develop musical skills as educational tools to succeed in
the community.

"Let's Make Some Noise": The Blocos Afro

In 1998, ten years after the centenary celebration, I arrived in Salvador and experienced the dynamic drumming of the blocos afro. I resided in Praça da Sé,
a neighborhood near the Pelourinho district. This was a prime area for tour
agencies, local clubs, and businesses located in the vicinity. I actually heard the
secular sounds of blocos afro drumming before I experienced sacred drumming
in the terreiros. Many local drummers congregated in Praça da Sé area for rehearsals, performances, and to observe other young drummers. I was amazed to
hear the sound of a barrage of drums during many hours of the day, seven days a
week, and see the enthusiasm of young drummers. There were also social spaces
in the musical performances in that drummers often used these experiences to
learn and dialogue with their peers. Many drummers allowed me to observe the
intricacies of their performances and shared their career goals in music and their
experiences working in their perspective blocos afro organizations.

Blocos afro organizations range in membership and are located in different
neighborhoods. Although these organizations are numerous there is a sense of
hierarchy; many drummers consider the older organizations to be more prestigious. For example, many drummers considered Ilê Aiyê (the first major blocos
afro organization, founded in 1974 by Antonio Carlos Vovô in the neighborhood
of Liberdade) the most prestigious organization.[4] Ilê Aiyê emerged not from Candomblé religion but from the secular atmosphere of the Negritude movement in
Afro-Brazilian culture. Membership in this organization was open only to dark-
skinned Afro-Brazilians. Ilê Aiyê quickly became an important vehicle for expressing black pride in an open forum, especially during Bahian Carnival. Public
displays of black pride and the black-only membership policy by Ilê Aiyê were
attacked in the media as racist. Each year Ilê Aiyê chooses to pay homage to a
single African country or ethnic group in its Carnival presentations of dance,
music, poetry, visual designs, and costuming.[5]

Many drummers believed that Ilê Aiyê had succeeded in helping young Afro-
Brazilians to feel positive about their physical features and dark-skinned color.
When Ilê Aiyê made its debut in 1975 with the popular song "Que Bloco É Esse"
("What Group is That"), written by Paulinho Camafeu, the younger drummers I

spoke with were only toddlers or had not even been born. This song negated and critiqued racial constructs and the ideology of "whitening" (*branqueamento*) in Brazil.

> Que bloco é esse? . . .
> [What carnival group is that? . . .]
> Somos crioulos doidos
> [We are crazy blacks]
> Somos bem legal
> [We are really all right]
> Temos cabelo duro
> [We have hard (kinky) hair]
> Somos black pau . . .
> [We are black power . . .]
> Branco se você soubesse
> [White man if you only knew]
> O valor que preto tem
> [The value that the black man has]
> Tu tomava banho de piche
> [You would take a bath in tar]
> Ficava preto também . . .
> [So black you would be too . . .]

Ilê Aiyê had used popular music as a powerful tool not only to critique racial constructs and equality in Brazil but also as a way of presenting a positive image of blackness. Within the public space of Bahian Carnival, Ilê Aiyê presented a positive image of the black Afro-Brazilian. When "Que Bloco É Esse" made reference to "black power," it was a symbolic identification and connection with outside of Brazil blacks (and especially in the United States). The bathing in tar by whites is a symbolic expression that offers a "black is beautiful" inference while criticizing the idea of Brazil becoming a nation of "whites" through racial mixing and processes of miscegenation.

Most drummers I spoke with in the late 1990s had some knowledge of the song "Que Bloco É Esse" as a signifier of blackness in Afro-Brazilian culture. However, many were not black in skin color but were of different hues and skin textures, mirroring the mixed racial identification and heritage in contemporary Brazil. They were from a new generation who grew up during the blocos afro era that was influenced by the MNU and sociopolitical platforms centered on racial inclusion. Thus, what I refer to as "let's make some noise" is not only a sonic proclamation of vibrant drumming to express black identity but also an ideology shared among many blocos afro who attempted to include drummers of mixed racial heritage into politically effective organizations to combat racial inequality. In this way, many drummers in the blocos afro were provided more opportunities to become vocal about issues of race and inequality than their parents had been.

The members of Ilê Aiyê described the group as trendsetting in its ability to inspire something new in drumming, popular music, group solidarity, youth culture, and black identity, and in influencing young Afro-Brazilians in a positive way. Many young Afro-Brazilians also expressed that when members of Ilê Aiyê participated in local festivities the organization was regarded as royalty and costumes that are traditionally worn by the members are in essence symbolic badges of honor. This is why young Afro-Brazilians very much desired to participate in the Ilê Aiyê organization.

Because of the regular performances and lucrative success by other organizations such as Olodum and Timbalada, many drummers were also aware of their contributions. Because of their weekly performances in the Pelourinho district, I had access to Olodum, the prominent Carnival organization founded in 1979 by former members of Ilê Aiyê.[6] In addition to providing opportunities for drummers, Olodum is an organization where drummers were encouraged to be proud of the African heritage through expertise in drumming, samba, and Candomblé religion.

The contemporary bloco afro Timbalada was founded in the early 1990s by Carlinhos Brown in the Candeal Pequeno neighborhood of Salvador and continues to attract massive crowds.[7] During my research most of Timbalada's performances were held outside of Pelourinho in venues near Campo Grande, a cosmopolitan area of Salvador where parks, businesses, hotels, and outdoor performance arenas are located. Unlike many other blocos afros Timbalada did not present songs and lyrics that made reference to the black struggle in Brazil. During public performances group members dressed in an assortment of costumes, with colorful makeup on their faces and bare chests. They often used extensive instrumentation comprised of trumpets, electronic keyboards and synthesizers, and the timbal drum. Performances feature polyrhythmic layering of vocal parts, timbals, surdos, and other percussion instruments, lyric improvisation by the performers as they dialogued with the audience, instrumental vamps, transitional bridges between sections, and rifflike trumpet melodies.

Blocos Afro and Candomblé Musicians

Many members of the blocos afro organizations are not practitioners of the Candomblé religion per se, but some have experienced Candomblé musicianship, discipline, and performance. Similar to Candomblé musicians, most blocos afro organizations are professional guilds that function like the irmandades—as brotherhoods, social clubs, and mutual aid societies in their communities. Many

Members of Olodum performing in the Pelourinho district in Salvador.

blocos afro envision themselves as more than "music organizations" and function as educational resources for young people in their communities. For example, some promote urban revitalization and remedies for homelessness.

Similar to Candomblé ceremonies, some blocos afro performances provide opportunities for young musicians to interact, dialogue, and critique each other and to create social relationships and bonds among peers. And as in Candomblé, some young blocos afro musicians use performance opportunities as a way of interacting with the opposite sex during rest periods; in organizations like Olodum, young girls from the community and tourists often surrounded them during their weekly Sunday performances. However, unlike what I had experienced with Candomblé drummers, older members of the blocos afro did not express concerns about the dedication of the younger musicians or whether they were influenced by popular culture or their peers.

Ilê Aiyê, Olodum, and Timbalada were among the more established blocos afro organizations I observed during my initial year in Salvador. Other organizations were more visible during several local festivals that commenced the Bahian Carnival season. When speaking to members of Ilê Aiyê, Olodum, and Timbalada regarding the appropriation/secularization of Candomblé themes, imagery, symbols, and music, some described Candomblé religion as a *ponto de referência* (point of reference), an integral part of Afro-Brazilian cultural history. Thus, although some young Afro-Brazilians may choose other religions (Protestantism, Catholicism) as a primary religious preference, Candomblé and axé are part of their heritage. Other musicians expressed that, although they were not active practitioners of Candomblé per se, they often refer to the religion as a resource for *pesquisa e observação educacionais* (educational research and observation) and many attended ceremonies at the terreiros to observe drummers (friends or family members) perform the sacred Candomblé rhythms. Several members of the blocos afro regarded their observations of sacred drumming performances as "mutual exchanges" and pointed out how Candomblé musicians often visited their neighborhoods to observe and recruit talented young drummers as potential musicians for the terreiro.

What I saw in blocos afro organizations was vitality— drumming where the hands and bodies of the musicians were also like Candomblé drummers that possessed a type of "cooling fire and white heat" as they became empowered with artistic energy to perform various popular music styles. Also like Candomblé, for many blocos afro organizations music-making is a form of masculine empowerment and socialization, in that many of the members often serve as role models for young boys in their communities. Also, many blocos afro organizations culminate the black experiences of the drum that has survived as a powerful instrument in Afro-Brazilian culture.

Unlike in Candomblé, there are some opportunities for female drummers, and a few female drumming organizations have emerged in Salvador. The organization Escola Didá was founded in the early 1990s by Neguinho do Samba to empower young people through musical performance. *Didá* is a Yoruba word that means "the power of creation." In this organization there are approximately thirty female drummers that wear uniforms of a woven hemplike garment with their logo embossed on a red background. But Didá is more than a drum corps; it is a community project dedicated to social reform for women and children. The organization has two separate musical ensembles—voice and drum—and an instrumental corps. Approximately two thousand women and children who are members of Didá perform during Bahian Carnival on their own amplified trio elétrico truck.[8]

The female drummers of Didá participated in many of the local festivals in performances along with the male blocos afro. The community encouraged their performances by cheering and dancing to their music, just as they did for their male counterparts. Many of these young girls exhibited strength and endurance, carrying large drums strapped around their shoulders. Their sound and playing technique were as deep and vibrant as those of the male drummers.

Samba-Reggae

In Salvador I constantly heard the performances of songs and drum rhythms of samba-reggae that had become an iconic style for many blocos afro organizations. For many of the drummers that I spoke with, Bob Marley was constantly mentioned as a musical inspiration. With the popularity of Bob Marley, reggae attracted a large audience among young Afro-Brazilians.[9] The popularity of reggae music in Salvador also stems from the Bar do Reggae, a local club founded in 1978 by Albino Apolinário after he purchased Bob Marley's album *Kaya* (1978).[10]

The Bar do Reggae is located in a prime area of the Pelourinho district that attracts locals and tourists who may attend Filhos de Gandhi events. With crowds every day of the week, it was difficult to gain entrance into the bar. Patrons often stood outside and simply listened to the music and dance. Reggae performances were also held as weekly attractions on Tuesday nights during the *festa da benção* (blessing party), when bandstands were set up in the local squares of the Pelourinho. The popularity of reggae and other styles (funk, salsa, soca, meringue) influenced a "sonic appetite" among young/local consumers and musicians hungry to experiment with popular music, and this included the innovative drummers of the blocos afro.

Even in the name *samba-reggae* there is a sense of double/mixed identity and connection that links Salvador with another African diasporic area. As a new and innovative style, samba-reggae came to embody the cultural politics of Afro-Brazilian popular culture.[11] One can think of samba-reggae as a fusion of two vibrant popular music styles both of which stand at the crossroads of the sacred and secular. Both styles draw on the experience of people with extensive African legacies of aesthetic, musical, and rhythmic sensibility. Drummers in the blocos afro contextualized the reggae style in a way that complimented their aesthetic taste in Afro-Brazilian culture. This involved experimentation by adjusting various rhythms, timbres, textures, techniques, and drum instrumentation.

Most musicians revered Neguinho do Samba as the innovator of samba-reggae who innovated new ways of incorporating samba, salsa, merengue, reggae, and Candomblé rhythms into a dynamic voice/drum format. The experimental merging of drumming patterns from samba and reggae music eventually came to be called samba-reggae. Both patterns involved the heavy pulsation of low surdo drums playing four separate but interlocking parts. Other percussion instruments, including high-pitched repiques and snare drums, play additional rhythms.

When many blocos afro performed samba-reggae, the drummers often exhibited high levels of musicality. They were not simply performing popular music that enticed dancing; for many drummers samba-reggae performances provided opportunities to incorporate different nuances and textures. In performances this involved paying close attention to different drum strokes and rhythms of the various drums.

One of the underlying rhythms, patterned after a reggae beat, was performed primarily in a slow tempo. Layered over was an additive rhythm based on triple and quadruple patterns similar to those found in salsa and merengue. Although these were the standard rhythms in samba-reggae, some blocos afro included rhythmic improvisation dependent on their musical and stylistic techniques. For example, Olodum played on high-pitched repiques with thin flexible switches, giving the drums a sharper attack.[12] Other percussion instruments used by this group included a set of three timbales (drawn from salsa) that was added to elaborate the basic pattern and to give cues to the other drummers. These innovations distinguished Olodum's sound from other blocos afro organizations.

Some blocos afro explained that they often incorporated fragments from Candomblé sacred rhythms in performing samba-reggae. This might involve appropriating an agogô part or even a rhythmic line from an atabaque part of their favorite orixá. However, for a novice, distinguishing the Candomblé rhythms was difficult because they were reinvented as something new. Other innovative blocos afro rhythmic patterns included experimentation with Caribbean accentuation of a 2/3 and 3/2 clave feel based on a four-beat rhythmic pattern played on repiques and low surdos.

When Olodum premiered the new samba-reggae rhythm in the popular song "Faraó Divinidade do Egito" ("Pharaoh Divinity of Egypt") (1987), written by Luciano Gomes dos Santos, many of the drummers in this organization that I spoke with were very young and impressionable in the sociopolitical workings of the Negritude movement in Brazil. Because this particular song was a hit most of them were familiar with the lyrics:

Pelourinho uma pequena comunidade
[Pelourinho, a small community]
Despertai-vos para a cultura eqípcia no Brasil
[Awaken us to Egyptian culture in Brazil]
Em vez de cabelos trançados
[Instead of braided hair]
Veremos turbantes de Tutancâmon
[We'll see the turbans of Tutankhamen]
E nas cabeças enchem-se de liberdade
[And our heads will be filled with freedom]
O povo negro pede igualdade
[The black people ask for equality]
Deixando de lado as separações
[Leaving behind the separations]

Although some older drummers expressed the significance of Egypt, Pharaoh, and the black community as important aspects of imagery and symbolism of black identity and the African heritage, younger drummers also associated the song with "the material," Olodum's commercial and recording success that had inspired them to learn drumming so that they too could one day join an organization such as Olodum and become successful. This is indeed not a criticism.

For drummers in general, samba-reggae also provided international exposure. For example, in the early 1990s Olodum collaborated with Paul Simon on *Rhythm of the Saints* (1990), which is similar to his previous album *Graceland*. Other collaborations include Michael Jackson and Bill Laswell. *Bahia Black: Ritual Beating System* is another collaborative project and album compilation that features Olodum's samba-reggae with improvisation from several jazz musicians. One of the selections from this collaboration is an example of how samba-reggae was used as a palette for improvisation with jazz: "The Seven Powers" pairs up Olodum with jazz musicians Herbie Hancock and Wayne Shorter. The samba-reggae rhythms provide an ostinato rhythmic pattern throughout the composition. The piece begins with several measures of samba-reggae rhythms. Herbie Hancock enters on the piano with an opening statement of altered chords played in the middle ranges of the keyboard in a call-and-response with the Olodum musicians. Wayne Shorter on soprano saxophone provides an emotional melody and improvisation that weaves in and out on high notes against the constant drumming of samba-reggae rhythms and increased intensity of the piano chord progressions.

For the young drummers, samba-reggae, songs such as "Faraó," and collaborations with international artists have provided opportunity to develop talent and musicianship. Many were from low-income families and samba-reggae was a symbol of hope. The ability to perform samba-reggae offered young drummers a future. For many of the drummers that I spoke with, samba-reggae was a form of education. Moreover, I believe that by interacting with more mature musicians, many young drummers became aware of significance of "Faraó," the Negritude movement, and the significance of black identity in Afro-Brazilian culture that went beyond monetary value.

The blocos afros continue to be an important aspect of Salvador's black consciousness movement. It should be noted that, while blocos afros offer an educational alternative in many low-income neighborhoods in Salvador, they are not exclusive to Salvador. For example, in the 1980s in Recife, Afoxé Povo was formed as a community-based group that embraced the new trends in samba-reggae as part of local identity. Rio de Janeiro has several prominent blocos, including Agbara Dudu, Dudu Èwe, Òrúnmìlá, and Lemi Ayò. In the early 1990s these groups recorded an album together entitled *Terreiros e Quilombos*. In addition, the Negro Power Gang is one of the largest singing and dancing rap groups in São Paulo. Also, in the 1990s, the city of Olinda saw the birth of a similar group, Lamento Negro (Black Lament).[13]

The Blocos Afro and the Pedagogy of Drumming

Most blocos afro organizations do not simply "drum"; similar to Candomblé musicians, there is a great sense of decorum, and they take systematic approaches in preparing for musical performances. In addition to the drumming, some performances often involve special attire (shirts/or bare chests), elaborate haircuts, and choreography. Adequate preparation is a criterion for successful performances. Most blocos afro spend a great deal of time preparing for musical performances, especially during the annual Carnival season.

Some blocos afro organizations participate in local performances, where they try out new material and choreography and observe the responses of the audiences before Carnival commences. During these rehearsal-type performances special officials (e.g., group leaders, managers) in the organizations may offer critiques and suggestions for improving the musical repertoire.

Many of the blocos afro use the Tuesday night weekly festa da benção (blessing party) as a type of rehearsal, because the event normally attracts large crowds of popular music consumers (both locals and tourists). This event is similar to a mini-Carnival celebration with food, drinks, and music, where people enthusiastically dance to the rhythms of the different drummers. During such an event the musicians are able to judge how the audience responds to their music. The musicians may perform on makeshift stages or engage in processional marches on the narrow streets of the Pelourinho (often drawing attention away from the staged performances).

Some blocos afro organizations have hours of intensive formal rehearsals on a weekly basis. Attendance and active participation in these rehearsals help members develop technical skills that must be mastered. One drummer expressed that, if a musician is not responsible enough to attend scheduled rehearsals, this may result in his becoming lackadaisical in attending actual performances, which may affect the performance of the entire ensemble. Thus, preparation for a performance may involve developing technical proficiency, flexibility, body movement, concentration, rhythmic sensibility, and pitch nuances. A drummer must have the ability to work successfully in an ensemble format, making sure that his rhythms are performed correctly and in sync with the other members of the ensemble. This involves complex skills where the drummer must develop an ability to appropriately integrate the rhythms played by his section with the other drummers/bell players in the ensemble.

In performance a drummer uses his entire body. Technical facility of the upper body not only requires developing flexibility and agility in the arms, head, and chest areas in positioning the instrument and using drumsticks, switches, or mallets; the drummer must develop the stamina to perform on various sizes of drums for many hours—often while participating in processional marches or concerts. Some of the instruments are large and require that the drummers be in physically fit condition. Drummers must be able to follow and balance the pulsations of rhythms with the singing by special vocalists, which must be audible over the sounds of a barrage of drums. Furthermore, because many blocos afro organizations incorporate a lead musician who acts as a drum major and/or conductor—signaling pauses and movements by blowing a whistle or making specific hand signals and gestures—drummers must also be attentive and alert to following specific cues.

Many young drummers/new members often undergo a trial period that may last for a few months or as long as a year. This is the time when the more experienced members may work closely with the neophytes to ensure that they are progressing adequately in their musical training. In some organizations new members may be assessed in various ways that include individually performing their drum parts for critique or performing with other members of the ensemble to be sure that the rhythms are played properly. Assessment by the more experienced players may involve evaluating the artistic development of younger drummers in terms of craftsmanship, understanding the cultural background/history of the blocos afro organization, inventiveness, commitment, expression, and ability to work with others members in the musical ensemble.

I was able to attend several of Olodum's performances and rehearsals. Members of Olodum regarded their weekly performances as open rehearsals that provided opportunities for the younger drummers to perfect their technical skills and learn the musical repertoire before professional engagements and annual festivals. Some of the more experienced drummers in the organization were designated as session leaders and had the responsibility for making sure that the players in their particular sections (e.g., surdo, repique, timbale) were performing the music accurately.

Like rehearsals of Candomblé musicians, Olodum's rehearsals were intensive because drummers had to acquire the ability to perform continuously for many hours in local performances and in professional engagements. Furthermore, the drummers were required to develop a mental alertness to the nuances of the musical instruments and vocal textures, and proficiency in executing a variety of technical drumming skills. The younger drummers were often asked to demonstrate proficiency in rhythmic accuracy, both individually and with other members of the ensemble. In many of the rehearsals it was easy to identify some newer members, because they would look over their shoulders to observe the more accurate performances by the more experienced members.

At Olodum's rehearsals the drummers were encouraged to experiment with various rhythms. This often included the drummers playing complex rhythmic patterns against each other based on duple and compound meters. This type of

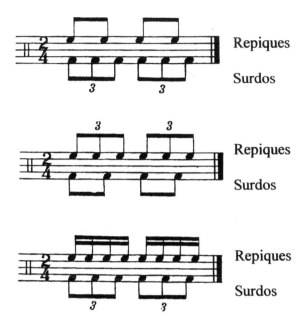

6. Examples of some rhythmic exercises practiced by
Olodum.

exercise was intended to sharpen the rhythmic skills of the drummers, as they
were often required to play interlocking parts with each other during actual performances. Music example 6 illustrates some of the rhythmic patterns played
by drummers in the surdo and repique sections at Olodum rehearsals that I observed. Because of the large number of drummers, the stylistic and technical aspects of particular songs and arrangements may require drummers in a section
to play different parts. For example, in the samba-reggae format the rhythms for
the surdo players may be divided into four different parts. In music example 6,
the upper notations are some of the rhythms that were practiced by the drummers playing the high-pitched repique instruments. For this particular instrument the section leader often encouraged the drummers to execute a light stroke
on the drumheads while the arms were relaxed with supple wrists while striking the instruments with very thin switches. The low sounding surdos that I have
indicated as the bottom lines of each notation represent the high and low pitches
often played by drummers with sounds that are executed with tight forearms,
shoulders, and chests.

During performances, Olodum members often engaged in uniform choreographic movements such as swaying, bending the upper body, waving arms and
shoulders, and leg movements as they played their instruments. All of this required a great deal of energy, precision, and physical stamina. The drummers

who engaged in dancing were required to listen carefully to the rhythmic flow of the vocal parts that were often presented in a call-and-response style while engrossed in the vibrant drumming of samba-reggae.

The Drum as Community

For many blocos afro organizations, the drum is symbolic of community and unity. Blocos afro play an assortment of drums, percussion, and wind instruments. Some of the drums are constructed like the atabaques used by Candomblé musicians and afoxé groups. For example, the timbal, a drum that has become popular with blocos afro, is a single-headed drum similar to the largest atabaque (rum) used in Candomblé religious ceremonies. However, instead of wood for the drum frame and animal skin for the head, this instrument is normally constructed with light metal with plastic drumheads and pegs angled on the sides of the drum that can be tightened for tension. The drum is normally strapped around the musician's upper torso and played with various parts of the hand and fingers. Like the rum, the timbal is constructed so that every finger can produce an array of sounds—thumping, slides, and pops. Like Candomblé and afoxé drummers, timbal drummers use both the open technique, achieved by holding the fingers of both hands tightly together, and the slap technique, achieved by using the open hand to producing brisk sounds. Other blocos afro drums include surdos, repiques, timbales, and djembes.

One of the most unusual drums I observed in a blocos afro ensemble was a single-headed, semicircular instrument constructed of light metal with a plastic drumhead and tension pegs. During processions, drummers normally strap these instruments around their upper torsos. Because of the size of this particular instrument, the sound produced is not as vibrant as an atabaque or timbal. But the playing techniques are similar, employing various nuances and hand and finger motions. In addition to the drums and other percussion instruments, some groups also incorporate trumpets or bugles in the ensembles and special dancers.

Sacred Themes, Imagery, and Symbols of the Orixás

Since the emergence of the blocos afro scholars have presented theoretical notions about the influence of Candomblé religion on Afro-Brazilian cultural identity and music production. For example, Larry Crook (2005) takes an ethnomusicological approach and links the influence of Candomblé and black identity to a stimulus for creating an "Afro" sound. For Crook, Candomblé religion served as an important unifying element among members of the blocos afro. Organizations such as Ilê Aiyê incorporated certain rhythmic and thematic elements from Candomblé religious repertoire to create what became, for them, an "Afro" sound. This involved slowing down the fast samba tempo patterns to a tempo that was more relaxed and syncopated, more African sounding. The groups also maintained an acoustic texture of drumming, percussion, and vocals without adding string and wind instruments. This texture was acoustically consistent with the basic performance ensembles of many African-influenced traditions that had been maintained within Brazil's black communities since colonial times.[14]

Livio Sansone (2001) takes a sociocultural approach in his theoretical analysis of the blocos afro and black identity. He suggests that, since the emergence of black identity and black pride movements and the blocos afro, young Afro-Brazilians tend to evaluate presentations of "blackness" as trends rather than identifying with and participating wholeheartedly in the more traditional aspects of African culture, such as Candomblé. State, cultural, and tourist agencies, black intellectuals, and even some clergy now refer to Candomblé as cultura negra or cultura afro-baiana. Young Afro-Brazilians have become more secularized; as a whole, they seem less religious than their parents. Some who have embraced the black movements have begun to examine Candomblé under a new ethnic light. They use Candomblé diacritically, more as a symbol of blackness than for its religious properties.[15]

In my own theoretical analysis of the blocos afro and the influence of Candomblé, some of the young drummers I interacted with were not active members of the religion per se. However, some were from communities that regarded Candomblé musicians as icons of popular music. For many blocos afro, I believe that the appropriation of Afrocentric musical ideas, the "Afro" sound, and Candomblé religion are part of a holistic knowledge and awareness (that I previously discussed) of how African culture has enriched Brazilian society. I believe that for many young members of blocos afro, this knowledge that is manifested through drumming enhances a better understanding and appreciation of Afro-Brazilian historical background, ancestry, racial makeup, and identity within the Brazilian landscape. Thus, for many blocos afro, drumming as in Candomblé religion mediates an active engagement between musicians and locals (the audience). Moreover, drumming in the blocos afro is part of a black aesthetic (along with singing and dancing) that continues to give Brazil a distinct character.

Drumming and the innovation of hybrid styles such as samba-reggae are part of a "musico-aesthetic" that for many blocos afro, inform a new black identity and at the same time connect them with other African and African diasporic areas. Thus, the "Afro" sound is a reconnection to and reinvention of African aesthetic roots. I believe that the incorporation of Candomblé religious elements and African roots are also examples of musical choice, preference, and freedom that has informed new and innovative musical ideas of the blocos afro.

During a 1990s interview Billy Esmeraldo Santos Anquimimo, the social director of Olodum, expressed the importance of Candomblé and African roots as integral parts of Afro-Brazilian identity and popular music production:

> We try to put in the minds of the people that we have to fight, not in blood, but just to help ourselves. We try to encourage our brothers to be proud as black people. One thing we try to do is keep alive the culture and religion, try to develop our old teaching[s] which many black people had. The other influence is music, the beat comes from Candomblé, from samba, all those things come from Africa.[16]

For many blocos afro members I spoke with, the sacred (Candomblé religion) has given a type of spice/emotionalism to secular social movements, popular music, and cultural identity. Moreover, sacred themes, imagery, and symbols from Candomblé religion are also appropriated as part of the aesthetic valorization of many blocos afro organizations in their expressions of black identity in Brazil. Carnival organizations as Ilê Aiyê and Olodum and others have also appropriated Candomblé imagery and symbols to promote a sense of baianidade ("Bahianness") and African ethnic pride. Thus, for many young Afro-Brazilians, group names—such as Olodum, a term that stems from Olódùmarè, the name of supreme being in Candomblé religion, and Ilê Aiyê, a Yoruba term that can be translated "house of life"—have significant value as cultural expressions and as outward acknowledgment of symbols and imagery handed down from African heritage.

Many that I spoke with often reinvented, appropriated, and secularized the sacred term *axé* as metaphor and symbol to indicate Afro-Brazilian (secular) black power/pride. Similar to the symbolism of the black power movement in the United States, with shouts of "black power" during musical performances and in daily interaction, many young drummers in the blocos afro often greeted each other and locals with the expression of axé to indicate an Afrocentric and symbolic meaning of power, pride, and celebration of physical features, dark skin color, and Afro-Brazilian black identity.

The sacred and secular are often integrated in the drumming and musical performances of blocos afro organizations when they offer prayers and songs dedicated to the orixás. Similar to the afoxés, before performances some blocos afro may observe rituals such as the Padê offering of special prayers, liquids, and foods to the orixá Exú for a successful performance. And, like individual artists, some blocos afro have composed and performed songs conveying a "musico-aesthetics" of place, religion, and Afro-Brazilian culture. Many of these songs are thematic of imagery and symbols that also situate the orixás in the secular world, assisting people dealing with problems they experience in everyday life. Some of the songs also praise the orixás as spiritual icons assisting in liberating black people to racial equality and success. For example, in the song "Rainha do

Mar" (1992), composed by Wilson Jatiassu and recorded by Banda Mel, the lyrics make reference to Yemanjá, who is imagined as the queen of the sea ("Rainha do mar") and imagined as the energy of light, of moonlight, and of the world of black people ("energia da luz do lugar do mundo do negro"). The song also includes prayerlike expression of liberation (libertação), peace, and happiness of the people ("o povo precisa de paz e felicidade").

"Beija-flor" (1992), a song composed by Moby and recorded by Banda Mel, also makes reference to Yemanjá. In the lyrics there are references to waves of the sea ("sobre as ondas do mar") and washing the soul with Yemanjá ("Eu vou lavar a alma com Yemanjá"). Several songs recorded by Timbalada make reference to Candomblé and the orixás. For example, "Canto Pro Mar" (1998) and "Mãe Oya" (1998) make reference to the West African deity Oya, who is praised as a great mother.[17] In "Toque de Timbaleiro" (1998), another song recorded by Timbalada, the lyrics make reference to timbal drummers who entertain people around the country of Brazil with rhythm that was created in Bahia ("Toque de Timbaleiro sacudindo o mundo inteiro foi criado na Bahia"). The song also makes reference to a connection between the sacred and secular with orixás, the force of ijexá, Candomblé, reggae, and magic ("Saudando os Orixás com a força ijexá, Candomblé, reggae, magia").[18]

Other examples of blocos afro songs that appropriate imagery and symbolism to convey a sense of the sacred in Candomblé religion include several songs recorded by Olodum about Yemanjá, such as "Canto da Yemanjá" and "Yemanjá, Amor do Mar" on the album *Da Atlântida a Bahia* (1994); in the song "As Forças de Olorum," Banda Reflexu's includes lyrics about the supreme deity in Candomblé; and the song "Caminho" (2003) by Ilê Aiyê has references to Umbanda and Candomblé religions in Brazil.[19]

The Beats Go On

In Salvador the drum is a powerful instrument that continues to energize the creativity of many young drummers. Axé and the African roots of Brazilian popular music are also embedded in the vitality of drumming that is expressed through the many blocos afro organizations. For many blocos afro, drums are part of a heritage that links them to historical memory, artistic innovation, religious, local, national, social, and black identity, and African and African diasporic areas. The organizations represent a type of regionalism in drum music that reflects rhythmic experimentation in the city of Salvador that continues to lead the way in popular music innovation of the northeastern region of Brazil that has influenced many contemporary popular music styles.

Like Candomblé musicians and afoxés, the blocos afro drummers have "percussive/performative power" and display an array of aesthetics, technical facility, and interpretive expressions to convey different types of emotions and sensational feelings to audiences. Moreover, their performances create spaces for social relationships on many levels between musicians who share similar training experiences, performance practices and etiquette, backgrounds, and politics. They also facilitate critiques of one another's music and talents in the community.

Similar to Candomblé musicians and afoxés, the blocos afro are also part of a greater musical space of diverse African and African diasporic areas where drumming symbolizes community, power, and celebration. One of my most memorable experiences with Afro-drumming traditions was when I observed the many talented drummers in the West African region. Of the many drummers, an organization called Komii An Bii stood out. The young drummers of this organization were all from low-income neighborhoods, but they were rich in musical innovation and exhibited high levels of technical facility and artistry in drumming. Komii An Bii is a local drum and dance ensemble organized in 1992 by a few musicians in Accra, Ghana. The group had approximately twenty-nine members that included male drummers and an additional corps of both young male and female dancers. Like members of blocos afro and afoxés, some members of Komii An Bii had experience with sacred drumming in particular shrines of their communities. Moreover, the organizational makeup of Komii An Bii was similar to many blocos afro organizations in Brazil. Its primary emphasis was to provide musical training and convey a sense of ethnic pride for lower-class youth in the communities.

Similar to the drum talent scouting that I observed in Salvador, members of Komii An Bii occasionally went through local neighborhoods to recruit young drummers and dancers. One of the most important events for recruitment was an intense weekly rehearsal on Saturday afternoons, which was open to the public. The rehearsals were essentially social gatherings that attracted locals from the community who engaged in dancing. During the rehearsals the musicians and dancers created social spaces and dialogues about their performances as well as the current events in the community.

When I returned to Salvador in 2002, some of the young drummers that I had met in 1998 were now grown. Some had gone on to pursue other interests while others had become more experienced with the sociopolitical platforms of the Negritude movement and remained in their organizations as senior members with the responsibility of training a new corps of young energetic drummers in new popular music styles. Some of the drummers were integrating styles such as rap in their drum performances.

Many of the mature drummers continued to appropriate themes, symbols, and imagery from Candomblé religion in their sociopolitical platforms for the betterment of Afro-Brazilian communities. Although some of the blocos afro had experienced changes in personnel, what remained constant was the enthusiasm and admiration for drumming that continued to influence the "secular impulses" of audiences—both locals and tourists—as they danced to the beats of different drummers.

6 | Say It Loud! I'm Black and I'm Proud

Popular Music and Axé Embodiment in Bahian Carnival/Ijexá

In many African and African diasporic areas, local, regional, and national identities are expressed through a sacred/secular connection of celebrations. During celebrations, people of different sociocultural and sociopolitical backgrounds come together. Unified by the excitement of spectacular pageantry, creative play, and costuming and masking, in many celebrations the sacred/secular is connected. Local, regional, and national identities may center on celebrating ancestral spirits, patron saints, local customs, folklore, or traditions belonging to a particular city, state, region, or ethnic group. Popular music is often a major expressive vehicle for individuals and groups that participate in these types of celebrations. Many aspects of the sacred/secular celebratory behaviors that I have described are very much part of the Afro-Brazilian experience in Brazil and other African diasporic areas where West African àsé continues to be nurtured.

In many West African communities, Gelede and Egúngún are examples of àsé sacred/secular celebrations where people celebrate ancestral spirits through artistic expressions and active participation in singing, drumming, dancing, and masking.[1] In many African diasporic areas people of African heritage have reinvented aspects of àsé sacred/secular celebrations in conjunction with the pre-Lenten celebrations of Carnival. Cities with a large Catholic influence often host pre-Lenten celebrations such as Carnival and Mardi Gras. In areas such as Cuba, Haiti, Brazil, Trinidad, and New Orleans, these celebrations feature secular music, dance, parades, masquerading, drinking, and merriment. They are followed by the sacred prayerful Ash Wednesday and Lent, a period of sacrifice involving giving up a personal vice, and finally the observance of the death and resurrection of Jesus.[2]

In Brazil many cities host annual Carnival celebrations that contribute to the distinctiveness of the country. Bahian Carnival in Salvador is a celebration that highly influenced my research on axé, its African roots, and the sacred/secular connections in Brazilian popular music and Afro-Brazilian identity. In the literature Bahian Carnival has been referred to as the "face of the city" that offers a social space (or public forum) where Afro-Brazilians annually celebrate their local/ethnic identity.[3] In this chapter I examine Bahian Carnival as a distinctive social and political space for expressing a sense of baianidade (local/ethnic identity) and African heritage, and also a venue for appropriating various popular music styles as powerful symbols of struggle, resistance, and hope. I also examine how axé, sacred themes, imagery, and symbols from Candomblé religion are embodied, secularized, altered, and negotiated in Bahian Carnival.

I decided to designate this chapter with the title of James Brown's popular song, "Say It Loud, I'm Black and I'm Proud" (1969) because it seems an appropriate way to describe how many young Afro-Brazilians in Salvador have responded to displays of ethnic and African identity during Bahian Carnival. Moreover, with influences from African and African diasporic areas, pan-Africanism, and black pride, since the mid-1970s many young Afro-Brazilians have continued to reinvent and reinterpret African sacred/secular identity through music performances, dance, and costumes during Bahian Carnival. Many popular music songs that they sing often serve as sources of hope and inspiration. Bahian Carnival is a major venue where songs such as "Que Bloco É Esse" (1975) by Ilê Aiyê and Olodum's renditions of "Faraó Divindade do Egito" (1987), "Madagascar Olodum" (1987), "Protesto do Olodum" (1988), "Revolta Olodum" (1990), and "Baianidade Nagô" (1992) have presented positive affirmations of black physical features, awareness of social inequality, and validation of historical heritages.

For many consumers Carnival is often associated with Rio de Janeiro, where the celebrations are comprised of spectacular pageantry that features competitive musical performances of escolas de samba and parades of thousands of energetic drummers, vocalists, and dancers. Such a celebration involves a great deal of preparation, including finding an appropriate Carnival theme that may be based on a political or historical issue or may even be a tribute to a particular person. Preparation also involves the selection of costumes, design of floats, rehearsals, and the selection of appropriate sambas (*samba enredo*), all based on the annual theme.

Roberto Da Matta, who focused on the popular Carnival in Rio de Janeiro, posits that Carnival celebrations in Brazil provide Brazilians with new avenues for social relations among people of diverse social and racial backgrounds. Social hierarchies that operate throughout the year are dissolved during the Carnival season. During the collective celebration of Carnival, individuals temporarily lose or suppress their social, racial, and sexual identities and simply become Brazilian.[4] When considering the many facets of Bahian Carnival, I do not fully agree with Da Matta's theoretical notions. Da Matta seems to offer a generalized view of Brazilian Carnival celebrations without regard to the unique qualities of

Carnival celebrations in different areas of Brazil. Da Matta seems to infer a celebration of a cohesive Brazilian identity that justifies a myth of racial democracy and equality for people of different colors. But Bahian Carnival is a celebration where racial identity is more pronounced with a focus on blackness and African heritage.

The popularity of Bahian Carnival is beginning to rival that of the commercial Carnival celebration in Rio de Janeiro. There are some similarities between the two. For example, similar to the escolas de samba in Rio, the many blocos afro organizations that participate in Bahian Carnival play a vital role in the energy of the celebrations. Bahian Carnival also incorporates themes, creative play, pageantry, and in a great way is an event where individuals may temporarily lose or suppress their social, racial, and sexual identities. Thus, with the incorporation of themes, pageantry, and the responses of some individuals that participate in the celebrations, some of Da Matta's theoretical notions may apply to facets of Bahian Carnival.

But, what distinguishes Bahian Carnival from Da Matta's theoretical notions is that during the celebration, many young Afro-Brazilians place more emphasis on the affirmation of black identity. I believe that, instead of simply becoming Brazilian, many locals in Salvador attempt to become more Afro-Brazilian—with emphasis on an Afrocentric identity and celebration.

As I discussed in the introduction of this book, for many young Afro-Brazilians that I met during my research, part of being Brazilian was acquiring more knowledge about their African ancestry and understanding the intricacies of Afro-Brazilian cultural identity. I referred to this as holistic knowledge that many young Afro-Brazilians attempted to integrate in their experiences of identifying themselves in the Brazilian landscape with an acute awareness of how African culture has enriched the society. Although many had not traveled to the African continent and experienced African culture firsthand, they attempted to reinvent and reinterpret African cultural traditions through various expressions of religion, music, and dance. Bahian Carnival culminates many of these experiences and is one of the ways in which young Afro-Brazilians reinvent and reinterpret African cultural traditions and create a sense of black identity in Brazil.

Axé and the African roots of Brazilian popular music are also embodied in Bahian Carnival. In Bahian Carnival young Afro-Brazilians continue to secularize Candomblé drumming, sacred themes, imagery, and symbols in public affirmation of their black identity. Also, many sacred rituals (e.g., prayers and special food offerings to the ancestral spirits) that are observed in the private sanctum of Candomblé are appropriated by many young Afro-Brazilians in the secular celebrations of Bahian Carnival.

Bahian Carnival and Brazilian Popular Music

Bahian Carnival is an integral part of the Brazilian popular music industry and technological innovation. During the celebrations some of Salvador's finest musicians perform, attracting massive crowds. Some musicians even attain professional status in the national and international markets. Performances by artists such as Daniela Mercury, Margareth Menezes, Carlinhos Brown, and blocos afro and afoxé organizations continue to draw massive crowds that inspire young musicians. Many performances are a testing ground for aspiring musicians and their songs are often recorded for annual compilations of Bahian Carnival music. For aspiring musicians, successful performances may generate a fan-based group of consumers.

Bahian Carnival is a celebration where there is "power and appeal of the drum," symbolic of community, rhythm, dance, and celebration. Bahian Carnival accommodates drums of different colors, shapes, and sizes that are played by both young and old drummers. The drums continue to inform musical experimentation and innovation. During processions they are interspersed in the various popular music styles with electronic instruments, the voice, trumpets, bells, rattles, and many others. The drums also inform the expressions of Negritude and the display of African heritage.

Bahian Carnival is also a celebration of innovation. No one could have predicted how much impact the innovation of the trios elétrico vehicles would have on Bahian Carnival celebrations and the expression of Negritude when in the 1950s two musicians, Dodô and Osmar, began performing an amplified version of the frevo on electric guitar and electrified cavaquinho while riding in the bed of a 1929 Ford pickup truck. The following year, they added an additional instrumentalist to their ensemble, thus creating the popular trio elétrico format. In 1969 Caetano Veloso expanded on the electronic instrumentation format with a vocal performance of his Carnival song "Atrás do Trio Elétrico" ("Behind the Trio Elétrico"), which portrayed Salvador as a place of happiness and pleasure.

During Bahian Carnival the trio elétrico has been one of the major formats for performing popular music that glorifies African heritage. The trio elétrico made it possible in the 1980s for Badauê, the politically charged afoxé, to sing loudly the songs of Negritude, and for Moraes Moreira to incorporate the sacred ijexá rhythm from Candomblé with various styles of secular popular music.

I have just presented descriptions of Bahian Carnival as a commercial event. But in essence Bahian Carnival is steeped in historicity and memory of repression of Afro-Brazilian culture; and similar to Candomblé religion, it has emerged within the constructs of racial identity in Brazil. In a country that has often denied its own racism, Bahian Carnival is also a time of the year when many young

Afro-Brazilians use popular music and dance to articulate their local, social, and ethnic identities by using African heritage as a point of reference. In many of the celebrations young Afro-Brazilians in Carnival organizations of the blocos afro and afoxés become more "vocal" as they often assign meaning to many popular music styles as a type of "musico-political" signification of racial identity.[5] Moreover, ijexá and the African nações are powerful symbols of Bahian Carnival, which is sometimes referred to as "Carnival Ijexá."[6]

The Bahian Carnival Complex

Bahian Carnival is a complex celebration that culminates the musical preparation of many local bands, blocos afro, and afoxés that have spent an extensive amount of time selecting appropriate popular musical repertoire based on a designated annual theme for the Carnival season. Most groups choose Carnival songs based on specific criteria such as appropriate instrumentation, lyrical content (e.g., Negritude songs), stylistic and musical appeal, and public response. This is one of the major reasons why local organizations perform their new repertoire in the months and weeks before Carnival in events such as the weekly festa da benção (blessing party) that attracts large numbers of people.

Preparation for Bahian Carnival involves not only rehearsals and special performances, but also selecting appropriate costumes and attire. Although corporations and local businesses often sponsor trio elétricos and musicians, most participants are required to purchase their own costumes for Carnival. Many of the smaller organizations require members to purchase special T-shirts bearing their logo. Depending on the quality and design, T-shirts may range in price from approximately $8 to $12 (in U.S. dollars).[7]

In addition to T-shirts, some of the larger organizations (e.g., Filhos de Gandhi and Olodum) may require members to purchase an entire costume comprised of clothing, headdresses, and ribbons. Several members of Filhos de Gandhi told me it took them approximately one year to save up enough funds to purchase their blue socks, robes, beads, musical instruments, and ribbons. Some members found skilled tailors and seamstresses in their neighborhoods who could make their garments. Some locals were also skilled at making the turbans representative of the Filhos de Gandhi persona.

Bahian Carnival is an event where participants (both locals and tourists) that desire to join in parading with their favorite blocos can pay a nominal fee and will be given a uniform called abadás that may consist of a T-shirt and shorts bearing the logos of the appropriate bloco and/or company sponsorship. Those who have paid the appropriate fees are allowed to participate in the processions with their favorite blocos inside the *cordão*, a rope that is carried by security personal to maintain a sense of decorum while parading and also to keep unwanted stragglers from disturbing the processions. Carnival participants who are not part of the blocos are situated outside of the cordão, congregate around the trio elétrico vehicles, and are often called *pipoca* (popcorn), participating by dancing during the performances. The symbolism of hot sizzling popcorn seems an appropriate designation: many young people's choreographic motions including jumping up and down.

The Celebration of African Heritage in Bahian Carnival

Bahian Carnival is distinguished from other Carnival celebrations in Brazil because of the emphasis on "blackness" and African heritage. The celebration of African heritage, Candomblé, the various afoxés, blocos afro, and styles of popular music all have become integral parts of the celebrations. Carnival provides a space where Afro-Brazilians can also become more "African." During the celebrations many Afro-Brazilians masquerade as Africans, adorned in costumes that represent their interpretations of African heritage. To dramatize the event some participants may even dress as African chiefs, with chains and shackles on their bare upper bodies. The African attire often heightens the experience of music and dance.

The African presence in Bahian Carnival has an extensive history involving various and often competing factors: elitist ideologies, community-based Carnival organizations, technological innovations, and popular music. Over different periods of time the celebration of African heritage has involved criticism and suppression by local authorities, an acute awareness of black experience outside of Brazil, and adopting and reworking various styles of imported popular music.

The history of Carnival in Bahia is similar to that in other Brazilian cities. In the early part of the nineteenth century Salvador had a mixture of pre-Lenten celebrations, including a series of masked balls hosted by the upper classes in elegant hotels. The lower classes often participated in street celebrations that involved music, dance, and revelry. The local authorities were highly critical of these types of celebrations and eventually banned and replaced them in the mid-nineteenth century with the Carnival celebration. The first Carnival celebration involved a presentation of floats and bands that performed polkas and operatic overtures. The upper class participated, dressing in European-style costumes.

Celebration of African heritage in Bahian Carnival began after the abolition of slavery in 1888, when the afoxés began performing sacred Candomblé music at secular public celebrations that included an exotic display of African themes such of honoring ancestral spirits and African royalty. Like Candomblé religion, celebrating African heritage in Bahian Carnival was grounded in cultural memory of participating in communal festivals honoring the ancestral spirits such as in West African Gelede and Egúngún celebrations. In Salvador this type of celebratory behavior was another reinventing of traditional African aesthetics of processions, pageantry, music, and dance.

In the early part of the twentieth century the authorities banned and suppressed African aesthetic displays during Bahian Carnival.[8] The banning and suppression of African-type displays were part of a greater concern that related to dealing with the African presence and issues of blackness. A major concern for elites and intellectuals was questioning whether Brazil had become "Africanized." Particularly in Salvador, where the population of Africans greatly outnumbered the white elite, African culture became a concern. During celebrations such as Bahian Carnival, with glorification of African heritage celebrated in public displays by the afoxés was in conflict with the sociopolitical norms of white elitism in Brazilian society.

Parading as Africans (outside of Africa) did not mediate class distinctions within Brazilian culture, nor was it regarded as a point of national pride or an emblem of brasilidade (Brazilianness). Exotic displays of African themes did not fit into an ideological scheme that related to elitist notions of what was supposed to be "authentically" Brazilian, the product of African and European miscegenation. The suppression of African displays during Bahian Carnival also related to elitist ideologies of tastefulness—that is, sacred music, dance, drumming from Candomblé in the public space (and in the vicinity of celebrations where the elites engaged in secular polkas, operatic overtures, masked balls, and dressing in European-style costumes) was often regarded as inappropriate.

Despite suppression by local authorities, the afoxés continued to be part of Bahian Carnival, but as a folkloric presentation of African culture. The Filhos de Gandhi in 1949 brought to Bahian Carnival a sense of exoticism with their inclusion of imagery and symbolism of a non-Brazilian, Mahatma Gandhi, as an inspiration for the organization during their processions. This was followed by the Mercadores de Bagda (Merchants of Baghdad) in the 1950s, a Carnival organization formed mostly by employees of the Brazilian oil company Petrobrás that appropriated exotic images from the Orient. Members of this organization formed a new middle class in Salvador; participating in Bahian Carnival was one way of celebrating their status and success in the community. Members dressed as merchants and caliphs with bright turbans, necklaces, and bracelets. Some even rode on horseback. The musical repertoire consisted of sambas performed by an ensemble of woodwinds and various percussion players.

In the late 1960s some Afro-Brazilians participated in the blocos de índios and dressed in a Hollywood version of Native American costumes wearing white and red pants, red headdresses, and white stripes of face paint. Local authorities considered members of the blocos de índios violent and aggressive and made them frequent victims of repression, brutality, and incarceration.

For many Afro-Brazilians, masquerading in Native American garb did not contribute to expressions of black identity; they needed to find a unique expression that clearly represented the young Afro-Brazilian in Bahian Carnival. This involved becoming aware of black experience outside of Brazil, adopting and reworking various styles of imported popular music, and a graphic return to displaying African heritage in Carnival celebrations.

Saying It Loud in Bahian Carnival

In the 1970s, with the growing interest in the social and cultural politics associated with pan-Africanism, black pride, and Negritude, the importation of soul, funk, reggae, merengue, salsa, and soca, young Afro-Brazilians entered into a dialogue with the experience and artistic creativity of other black communities. Songs such as James Brown's "Say It Loud, I'm Black and I'm Proud" (1969) and Aretha Franklin's "Respect" (1967) were regarded as more than aesthetic valorization.

For many these songs were symbolic of the hope and economic success for black performers that Afro-Brazilians wanted to translate into their own culture. Edmilson Lemos, forty-four, who had had extensive performance experience in the United States (Los Angeles), was very positive about how the Negritude movement, soul, funk, reggae, soca, and other popular styles influenced his career and many young Afro-Brazilian musicians. As a popular musician Lemos had many opportunities to perform during Bahian Carnival, and experienced the popular music firsthand. He stated that when he first heard soul music in the early 1970s some people in his neighborhood had tapes and records from the United States. At that time he did not understand most of the song lyrics. But he really enjoyed the instrumentation, rhythms, and performances by the musicians. Lemos expressed that African American popular music performers like James Brown were admired by Afro-Brazilians as role models of successful and talented black people.

Bahian Carnival is part of a diasporic dialogue and an active engagement where young people in other areas have also responded with various popular music styles in similar celebrations of Carnival to affirm racial/ethnic identity. For example, similar to Afro-Brazilians, soul music also provided a new and appealing voice with a powerful message for young Trinidadians. In Carnival celebrations in the 1970s and 1980s, to compete with African American and Jamaican music, young musicians in Trinidad created their own electronic music and called it soca or "soul calypso," using multitrack recording technology and electronic instruments such as drum machines and synthesizers.[9] Like soul and reggae music among African American and Afro-Brazilian youths, soca appealed to young people in Trinidad. It was a symbol of hope for social progress and prosperity that allowed young Trinidadians to sing loudly and advocate for social progress and prosperity in their communities.

Similar to youths in other areas, Bahian Carnival has become a celebration where Afro-Brazilians include styles of funk, soul, reggae, and soca to sing loudly about their African heritage. When Ilê Aiyê first paraded in the 1975 Bahian Carnival celebrations, it was a historical moment for the advocacy of "blackness." Their participation was a symbolic affirmation that being a dark-skinned Afro-Brazilian was something positive. For the first time, having hair textures and facial and physical features different from white Brazilians was regarded with pride and respect. Moreover, Ilê Aiyê's 1975 performance of Paulinho Camafeu's song "Que Bloco É Esse" ("What Group is That") was a symbolic critique of traditional images of blacks and mulattos. After this many bloco afro Carnival songs began to "say it loud" with personal ("I am") and collective ("We are") affirmations of black pride. In addition, with Olodum's 1987 premiere of "Faraó Divindade do Egito" ("Pharaoh Divinity of Egypt"), the voice-and-drum performance of samba-reggae at Bahian Carnival not only represented new musical innovations in popular music from Salvador but also symbolically represented blackness and ethnic diversity.

For almost twenty years axé music has dominated popular music performance in Bahian Carnival. With axé music, Bahian Carnival has become a venue for music experimentation and fusion of local and imported styles. Daniela Mercury, Margareth Menezes, Carlinhos Brown, Ivete Sangalo, and groups as Olodum, Timbalada, Ara Ketu, Banda Eva, and É o Tchan draw massive crowds during Carnival celebrations. In axé music many artists continue to "say it loud" with personal and collective affirmations of black pride and baianidade.

Axé Embodiment: Sacred Themes, Images, and Symbols of Candomblé Religion in Bahian Carnival

In Salvador most locals are aware that Bahian Carnival leads to the Lenten season in the Roman Catholic calendar, and some regard the event as a way of preparing for the redemptive Lenten season, during which they observe a special period of sacrifice to commemorate the death and resurrection of Jesus. Bahian Carnival is also the culmination of a festival season that normally lasts from mid-October through early February and that often combines observances with rituals from Catholicism and Candomblé as symbolic of worship, prayers to Catholic saints, and food offerings as an appeasement of the orixás. Catholic masses are given by many local churches a few days before Bahian Carnival, to offer prayers for a successful season and protection of the community. Many of the pre-festivities that celebrate the orixás are regarded as a time to be prayerful, thankful, and to generate positive types of axé energy (e.g., financial success, happiness, hope, talent) for the Carnival season. Local Carnival organizations may participate in an observance of a Candomblé Padê ritual, offering of special foods and liquids as an appeasement to the orixás for a successful Carnival season.

During Bahian Carnival musical performances may include songs with lyrics focusing on Candomblé and the orixás—often secularizing Candomblé themes, imagery, and symbolism. For example, in the song "Festa" (2002), pop artist Ivete Sangalo provides lyrics that convey a sense of a sacred/secular connection between Carnival, popular music, Candomblé, and the excitement of the celebrations with lyrics like "Festa no Gueto . . . [festival/party in the ghetto] . . . Vem gente de toda, tem raça de toda fé . . . [People of all colors, races and faith] . . . Guitarras de rock 'n' roll, batuque de Candomblé vai lá [rock 'n' roll guitars, batuque (drumming) of Candomblé are there]."

The popular song "Dandalunda," composed by Carlinhos Brown and performed by Margareth Menezes, was one of the most successful songs of the 2003 Bahian Carnival celebration. In Candomblé religion Dandalunda is a deity syncretized with the orixá Yemanjá where practitioners blend religious attributes of the ancestral spirits of West African and Congo-Angola heritages. The song lyrics refer to the sacred terreiros of Candomblé religion, Dona (Lady) Oxum, dancing Oxóssi, and the pureness of Iansã.[10] The song also situates the orixás in the secular world as many people experience the orixás' engaging in dancing.

Axé Axé: Salvador, "Capital da Alegria"

The themes of Bahian Carnival often center on peace, love, and hope. I was fortunate to experience the entire sacred/secular celebration associated with Bahian Carnival in 1999, when racial solidarity was very much part of the year's theme. Prior to Carnival I was able to attend special services at the Rosário dos Pretos Church and at another Catholic congregation, Our Lady of the Immaculate Conception of the Beach (also known as Conceição da Paria) where masses and prayers were offered for the protection of locals and congregants as they participated in Carnival celebrations.

One of the songs that appealed to me during the special masses at Rosários dos Pretos Church was "Ó que Coisa Bonita." Especially during the advent of Bahian Carnival the lyrics seemed to convey a sense of brotherhood, community, black identity, and the power of axé outside of Candomblé religion in the context of spirituality, faith, and energy associated with Jesus. This song also seemed to culminate the pre-Lenten season into the observance of Ash Wednesday:

Ó que coisa bonita!
[Oh what a beautiful thing!]
Deus Pai Libertador,

[God Father Liberator,]
Criar negra cor.
[To create black color.]
Ó que coisa bonita!
[Oh what a beautiful thing!]
Jesus é nosso irmão,
[Jesus is our brother,]
sem separação
[without separation]
Ó que coisa bonita!
[Oh what a beautiful thing!]
Ó Espírito, a fé, a força, o axé
[The Spirit, faith, force, axé]
Ó que coisa bonita!
[Oh what a beautiful thing!][11]

"Ó que coisa bonita" has a highly syncopated rhythmic structure and instrumentation of bells, drums, tambourines, and guitars. The song was arranged in a two-part harmonic structure that could be sung as a round by the choir and congregation. An instrumental interlude was followed by the choir singing a verse before the congregation was signaled to join in the singing. As the congregation joined in they were encouraged to clap or sway to the rhythmic accompaniment.

After the masses there were processions of Catholics and practitioners of Candomblé, who carried large banners, flowers, replicas of saints, and the insignias of orixás. During the processions participants continued to sing "Ó que coisa bonita" in the background, their voices overlaid with the drumming of the blocos afro while other participants engaged in dancing.

The 1999 Bahian Carnival celebration was a special event because it commemorated the 450th anniversary of the establishment of Salvador as the first capital city of Brazil. The festival celebrated the history that has made Brazil a unique source of cultural, religious, and musical richness. Throughout my stay in Salvador, I saw countless advertisements, billboards, and media coverage about this anniversary celebration. The Carnival theme for the year was "Salvador 450 Anos: Capital da Alegria" ("Salvador 450 Years: City of Happiness"). This inclusive theme emphasized the multiracial histories and cultural contacts that distinguish Brazil.

Because the 1999 Bahian Carnival was an important landmark in Brazilian history, local and state government agencies actively supported the festivities. The beautifications of the city and of local monuments were prime targets for sponsorship by some of these agencies. Renovations of streets, hotels, and historical buildings were completed in time for Carnival. The historic Pelourinho district was decorated with graphic displays that represented important artifacts from Brazilian history, such as the first vessel to transport the Portuguese to the area. Replicas of Native Americans, afoxés, and baianas were also featured.

The 1999 Carnival was also the fiftieth anniversary of the founding of the afoxé Filhos de Gandhi. Their theme for the year was "50 Anos de Axé/Paz" ("50 years of axé and peace)." Each member of the group wore blue and white ribbons inscribed with the theme. Several also carried banners bearing the images of international civil rights activists and musicians who had contributed to world peace, including Martin Luther King, the Dalai Lama, John Lennon, Desmond Tutu, and Henry David Thoreau.

International popular music legends Gilberto Gil and Caetano Veloso participated as official members of Filhos de Gandhi. One of the highlights was seeing Gil and Veloso with open arms, offering signs of peace and axé to the large crowds of spectators as they rode on top of the organization's trio elétrico vehicle. An orchestra of approximately one hundred musicians accompanied Gil and Veloso on the vehicle. The amplified sounds of this orchestra were interspersed with fanfare medleys from a corps of additional musicians playing valveless trumpets in procession with thousands of members who danced to the ijexá rhythm.

Many of the trio elétrico vehicles were portable stages where popular musicians could perform for crowds of Carnival participants. Equipped with Hollywood-type billboard lighting featuring the names of the performers, these vehicles were massive, some as high as three stories. During performances, popular musicians riding on top of the trio elétricos seemed to tower over the city and the crowds.

Many of these vehicles were equipped with bandstands that accommodated ensembles of instrumentalists playing saxophones, trumpets, electronic keyboards and synthesizers, and drum sets. They also accommodated additional singers and dancers. Some musicians engaged in a call-and-response dialogue with the gathered crowds, which often sang and danced to the vibrant sounds of the trios elétricos and traveled with them along the Carnival route.

Bahian Carnival 1999 was a public celebration where the sacred imagery and symbols of Candomblé were secularized by participants who adorned themselves in the costumes of baianas or orixás. Some locals also regarded the imagery of the terreiro and axé as a symbolic affirmation and expression of ethnic identity, brotherhood/sisterhood, and community affiliation. In the celebrations the axé of the orixás was often dramatized through visual and artistic displays of dress, music, dance, and iconography of certain orixás (e.g., Yemanjá, Iansã, Oxum, Xangô, Oxalá, Ogum, Oxóssi, and Exú). Some of the trio elétrico vehicles also displayed iconic images of sacred objects (e.g., bows and arrows, swords,

Participants of Bahian Carnival 1999 following a trio elétrico in Salvador.

fans) associated with particular orixás. For example, several female singers dressed as the orixá Oxum, in golden gowns with thin veils over their faces attached to gold-beaded crowns. They had heavy bracelets on their arms and held Oxum's abebe fan. As the vehicles progressed slowly along the Carnival route, the popular tunes resounded with lyrics referring to African heritage and the spiritual qualities of many of the orixás.

Bahian Carnival 1999 was a celebration that stimulated creative impulses and musical experimentation. During the performances the musicians were actively engaged in displaying an array of aesthetics, technical facility, emotions, and sensational feelings to massive crowds. The hands and bodies of the musicians were catalysts for producing high energy levels in the Carnival participants. In addition to the more popular Afrocentric blocos—Olodum, Timbalada, Ilê Aiyê, Filhos de Gandhi—some of the others also displayed a sense of black pride by wearing African attire and identifying themselves with such names as 100% Negro, AmorAxé, Engenheiros do Axé, Nação Ijexá, Babalorixás, Filhos de Oxum, Chocolate, and Ibeji.

Some of the larger blocos often included a corps of dancers situated in front of the drummers. The dancers wore an assortment of elaborate costumes, including African attire and Native American headdresses. The dancers seemed to enhance the creativity of the musicians; they took turns responding to each other as onlookers filled in with handclaps and shouts. When the drummers played samba-reggae or the ijexá rhythm, the choreography included angular shuffling, and complex hip and arms movements.

The processions lasted for many hours, offering a continuous cycle of blocos afro, afoxés, and trio elétricos performing their renditions of Bahian Carnival music. The processions were also symbolic expressions of community, solidarity, affirmation, and innovation, and gave meaning to the musical performances. In the processions, musicians attempted to heat up the crowds, demonstrating their most proficient musical skills.

Local music groups had several opportunities to participate in the processions, performing on scheduled days. They often began performing at approximately 4:00 in afternoon in the Pelourinho district where they performed for a few hours, then began to follow one of the Carnival routes, which normally flowed from streets near the Praça da Sé area to Palco de Ondina, and vice versa.

The Carnival route was approximately ten miles in circumference and was structured so that the musicians could proceed down different streets, allowing the many spectators to enjoy different performances each day. For example, one day a bloco afro such as Olodum began its procession near Praça da Sé, followed a route on Avenue Carlos Gomes, and ended up at Palco de Ondina. A few days later, in a second procession, Olodum began performing at Palco de Ondina and followed a route on Avenue Sete to the Praça de Sé area. But no matter the route, each group progressed very slowly, so the processions normally lasted for several hours and usually late into the night. The smaller groups generally performed in the early evening, while the more popular blocos afro (Olodum, Timbalada, and Ilê Aiyê) performed later at night. By that time, crowds along the Carnival routes usually numbered in the thousands.

At Carnival the local and global were constantly in motion. The experience I had with Bahian Carnival was very positive and memorable. I truly appreciated how Salvador was a city of happiness and musical diversity. What was most fascinating about my experience was seeing the constant movements of the groups as they paraded through the streets. I believe that the sound of axé music, ijexá, and samba-reggae presented a sense of pride in Afro-Brazilian culture as both locals and tourists joined in the processions.

There was much variety in Bahian Carnival and spaces for the "creative play" of masquerading, frivolity, and dramatization. While many participants dramatized their African heritage, other blocos participated in the festivities strictly as recreational entertainment. Some Carnival organizations participated in creative play by cross-dressing. For example, the local all-male group As Muquiranas traditionally dressed in female garments. Members of this organization paraded in makeup, colorful wigs, bikini tops, skirts, and high heels. Their trio elétrico band members also dressed in similar garments. Other men heightened the sense of frivolity by wearing colorful fluorescent phallic devices strapped to their outer garments. Some of the local men dressed as baianas, in laced white garments. While other groups affiliated with the blocos de índios—Apaches do Tororó and Commanches do Pelô—portrayed a Hollywood image of Native Americans, carrying tomahawks, peace pipes, and wearing elaborate headdresses and strips of tape to mark their faces.

Dancing to the Music in the Streets

In Bahian Carnival performances on the trio elétrico vehicles, there were often innovative exchanges between the musicians, the dancers, and the massive crowds. During Carnival 1999 some of the most innovative movements by young males in the crowds were combative moves while they were dancing that seemed to be fist-fighting; but some of the locals stated that this style of dancing had become popular especially with young males in the Pelourinho district.

My experience with Bahian Carnival 1999 is one I will never forget. For many people Bahian Carnival was a celebration that allowed them to translate their experiences of life into music. In popular songs musicians conveyed an aesthetic, spirit, and beauty of Salvador as being a place rich in heritage and culture, with lyrics that made reference to "festa na gueto" ("party in the ghetto"), "o toque do afoxé ("rhythm of the afoxé"), and "felicidade" ("happiness in the city"). This was also part of local/ethnic identity.

The different aspects of Carnival music—rhythm, dance, and textures of sound—stimulated in participants a type of creative play. Participants were stimulated to re-create sound with their bodies and imitate it with their voices in call-and-response dialogues that often overlapped the complex rhythms and instruments of the many blocos afro and afoxé organizations. Moreover, when Carnival commenced many neighborhoods streets, churches, and municipal buildings' steps were used as dance floors where massive crowds gathered to enjoy the music. The continuous sounds of vibrant drumming energized the Carnival crowds.

During my stay in Salvador, I was constantly aware of the plight of the poor and homeless, both educated and uneducated. However, during the Carnival season, the disadvantaged were less visible than at any other time of the year. Although some locals and tourists chose to view the festivities from hotel balconies, apartments, and condominiums, many participated by "dancing in the streets." During this time, different social classes were difficult to distinguish, as the crowds seemed to be concentrated mainly on dancing and enjoying the music.

When some of the larger blocos afro such as Olodum and Ilê Aiyê performed, the crowds were so large that participants barely had room to move. Perhaps because it was the year of the 450th celebration of Salvador, the crowds really seemed to be aware of the significance of celebrating Salvador's historical roots. The celebrations of Bahian Carnival 1999 were well structured, with detailed information regarding performances published in *Guia do Carnaval da Bahia*.[12]

I stood in the midst of the massive crowds feeling the kinetic energy of the people, each of whom in some way enhanced the excitement and appeal of Carnival. The popular musicians seemed to be competing for the crowd's reaction, trying to heat up the immense crowds to make them active participants in the music process. Although there was drinking and reveling, most of the crowds that I experienced seemed to be mainly focused on the energy and enjoyment of the music. The performances along the Carnival routes were well choreographed and seemed to flow from one to another. The local groups, some of which had waited for over a year to perform at Carnival, performed with obvious cultural pride.

During Bahian Carnival 1999 there was an African diasporic connection in that some tourists had come to Salvador to commemorate and celebrate their African heritage. I met several African Americans from the United States who had traveled to Salvador as part of a yearlong pilgrimage. They were attempting to travel many of the slave routes from Africa to parts of the African diaspora in order to experience and commemorate the lives and deaths of the displaced Africans. A few days after Carnival ended, members of this group participated in a special observance near the Pelourinho district, marching in procession and carrying banners as they said special prayers and performed special songs.[13]

Axé Consumerism and Tourism

Carnival has a major influence on the Bahian economy, bringing in government sponsorship, commercialization, media coverage, and mass-market consumerism. Bahian Carnival attracts tourists from North America, Europe, and other geographic areas. Thus, a major goal of the local municipalities is to make the city of Salvador appealing to tourists. Moreover, because of tourism, areas such as the Pelourinho district often receive governmental sponsorship for historical landmark renovations, road construction, hotel and restaurant expansions, and increased local entertainment.

Bahian Carnival is a time of the year when axé is marketed and when some blocos afro organizations identify themselves as axé (e.g., Arca do Axé, Axé Baba). Also, during the celebrations there are entrepreneurial opportunities with products that are often marketed as Axé (e.g., T-shirts, trinkets, music). Some local merchants and vendors are able to earn approximately a year's salary by selling merchandise of beverages, souvenirs, and audio/video recordings. Carnival has also become an axé business enterprise where enticing advertising and marketing strategies are integrated for attracting an international audience. The festivities are marketed on websites and advertised on billboards sponsored by companies such as Axé Chevrolet, which announce Carnival celebrations with greetings and blessings of axé. For example, the Bahian Carnival 1999 celebration was advertised by Banco General Motors, one of the largest business conglomerates in Salvador, as "Na Bahia de Todos os Santos dos Orixás e do axé, os seguros Banco GM oferecem a maior proteção." ("In Bahia All Saints Bay of the Orixás and axé, Banco GM insurance [coverage] offers the best protection.") This advertisement was posted on billboards and on official Carnival informational brochures. For the Bahian Carnival celebration of 2008 there were several websites with enticing advertisements such as: "Carnival in Bahia is it, baby! That is of course, if parties and crowds are your thing. Nowhere else comes close. Carnival Bahia is not nubile women in feathers high up on floaters à la Carnival Rio. It's YOU out there on the streets doing it 'til you drop."[14]

The marketing of Bahian Carnival, popular music, and dance often includes strategies that center on sexuality. With the graphic displays of thinly clad men and women on the cover of compact disc packages, Bahian Carnival music is often mass-produced and sold on the international market as the annual *Axé Bahia* series. Also, as Bahian Carnival has become increasingly popular and successful, Salvador has experienced an increase in what some of the locals described as "sex tourism." That is, some tourists come not only to enjoy the landscape and pageantry but also to pursue what locals described as "sexual adventures with hot black Brazilians." Many young girls and boys are exploited and become objects for tourists who enjoy themselves for a few days, only to return home after Carnival is over. Many popular musicians are aware of the problems faced by young Afro-Brazilians and use their status to advocate against sexual exploitation and AIDS awareness. For example, Carlinhos Brown has spoken out against sexual exploitation during Bahian Carnival: "We want Carnival without children in prostitution, without violence to [families], without sexual abuse, sexual harassment of our sisters who end up having less opportunity than me, than men have with music."[15]

One of Brazil's most successful popular musicians, Daniela Mercury has used her status to advocate for human rights and social and health campaigns in Brazil. Because of her outspoken advocacy on issues of sexual exploitation and transmitted diseases, in November 2005 Mercury was dropped from a Christmas concert to be held at the Vatican in Rome, which alleged that her position was against the moral doctrine of the Catholic church. The allegations stemmed in part from her participation in a campaign to fight AIDS and other sexually transmitted diseases during Carnival celebrations in Brazil.

Mercury was also alleged to have appeared in TV ads promoting the distribution of free condoms and encouraging people to use them. The 2005 Vatican concert was intended to raise funds for foreign missions of the Jesuit order. The religious officials who cancelled her performance expressed concerns that Mercury would publicly promote the use of condoms while at the Vatican.[16]

Let Them Be Black!

I use this subheading because I believe that Bahian Carnival has now become a celebration where "blackness" and black creativity are marketable commodities of exotic Bahian culture. From the various popular music styles, drumming of the blocos afro and afoxés, the abadás, visual and artistic displays of African heritage, to the appropriation of Candomblé scared themes, images, and symbols, Bahian Carnival attracts a consuming public. This public is important to the reception of Bahian Carnival and popular music on local, national, and international levels.

Locals expressed an array of opinions about Bahian Carnival, the significance of African heritage displays, and the appropriation of Candomblé themes, images, and symbols. Most people I spoke with thought of Bahian Carnival as a time of the year when they could celebrate and enjoy the festivities with their families; others expressed a concern that, although Carnival was a time when young Afro-Brazilians could collectively express a sense of their African heritage, the excitement of the festivities had a way of averting attention from the social problems at hand. The reasoning was that because of the massive crowds, businesses attempting to earn a profit, and the excitement of music and dance, some participants simply choose to enjoy the festivities without becoming politically involved. Thus, if a bloco afro organization participates in the processions by carrying a banner that reads "Mais igualdade racial de gente de cor" ("More equality for people of color"), the crowds may or may not fully comprehend the significance of the message being conveyed because of Bahian Carnival's party atmosphere.

Josué Cassiano, forty-two, was an employee affiliated with one of the local tour agencies in the Pelourinho district. He believed that Bahian Carnival may actually be an aversion from the reality of poverty and low-income status experienced by Afro-Brazilians in Salvador. He remarked:

> Bahian Carnival is an important event in Salvador. Every year I actively participate in the events with my family. But I believe that Bahian Carnival gets our minds off of the problems at hand. There are many blacks in Salvador that need some kind of education and skill. Instead of spending all that money revitalizing the city for Carnival, why not invest some of it in helping young Afro-Brazilians learn some kind of skill? Instead of repression, I believe that the local government now supports Afro-Brazilian participation and the blocos afro

in festivities such as Bahian Carnival because this type of support is another tactic to get people's mind off of their problems so they will not have the time to actively revolt and protest.[17]

Practitioners of Candomblé with whom I spoke had varying responses about the appropriation of sacred themes, imagery, and symbols in Bahian Carnival. For example, Luiz Murisoea, seventy-five, the pai de santo at the Ilê Oxum terreiro, believed that similar to Candomblé religion, Bahian Carnival had become a major tourist attraction and that this has caused many local businesses to realize the value in displaying African heritage in the celebration. Thus, if they appropriate axé and sacred images from Candomblé, many local businesses see this as capitalizing on the "richness of Afro-Brazilian culture."[18]

Some older practitioners expressed criticisms that the ijexá sacred rhythm has been taken out of the sanctity of Candomblé religion and secularized in Carnival songs and dances by popular musicians. On the other hand, several Candomblé musicians and younger practitioners whom I became acquainted with felt that ijexá was the music of Bahian Carnival and part of the city's celebration. In their opinion, participating in Bahian Carnival had nothing to do with their acts of devotion to Candomblé. During Bahian Carnival 1999 I encountered several Candomblé musicians who also were members of local bands that performed with the trio elétricos, blocos afro, and afoxés. Like other participants, they wanted to enjoy the celebrations and the popular music.

Nivaldo Dario Nascimento, thirty-five, used Bahian Carnival as a time when he could earn extra money by performing popular music. Nascimento was one of the Candomblé musicians that I observed performing popular music on a trio elétrico vehicle. He was very interested in his African heritage. As part of his ethnic identity he often wore African-style caps and dashikis. But Nascimento felt that Bahian Carnival was not a time for him to be politically involved protesting against racism in Brazil. For Nascimento, Bahian Carnival was a professional "gig" where he was normally hired as an entertainer to perform popular music. During Carnival, his major concern was performing for the massive crowds.

Letting the Good Times Roll

In Bahian Carnival there is what I refer to as "axé imagination," where locals and businesses often conjure up positive images of the sacred themes, images, and symbols from Candomblé religion that are often secularized, negotiated, and altered for consumer consumption, popular music production, dance innovation, and the celebration of black identity. Thus, the celebrations contribute much to what I describe as the spread of axé and the African roots of Brazilian popular music and Afro-Brazilian culture. For many popular musicians Bahian Carnival is more than a celebration; it is part of their professional careers in the popular music industry, where they continually attempt to produce innovative popular music for a consuming public. Bahian Carnival is a time when the city of Salvador displays high energy levels and happiness through artistic expressions of popular music, dance, and drumming.

Carnival is also a celebration when many young Afro-Brazilians choose to "make some noise" and express loudly a sense of baianidade and African heritage. The sacred/secular are connected in Bahian Carnival celebrations. Candomblé religion (the sacred) and popular music (the secular) often become connected in displays of local/ethnic identity that Afro-Brazilians regard openly as powerful symbols of struggle, resistance, and hope. The celebratory spirit sacred/secular influences of Bahian Carnival also connect Salvador with other African diasporic areas where people of African descent continue to experience their own sociopolitical challenges. In areas such as Cuba, Haiti, Trinidad, and New Orleans, people of African descent continue to be active participants in Carnival celebrations. Similar to the Afro-Brazilian community in Salvador, in some of these areas people of African decent have experienced artistic repression and suppression of African-type displays in public spaces.

This chapter began with a title designation of James Brown's popular song, "Say It Loud, I'm Black and I'm Proud," and will conclude with the point that in Bahian Carnival there are many ways of "making noise" and to say things loudly through vocal, drum, popular music, dance, and visual and artistic expressions. Popular musicians sing loudly atop the trio elétrico vehicles and compel the massive crowds to enjoy the festivities. The many blocos afro and afoxé organizations drum in rhythmic cadences that often reflect a sense of pride and the true spirit of their Afro-Brazilian heritage. Together they all contribute to the vibrancy of axé and the African roots of Bahian Carnival and Brazilian popular music.

7 | Stylizing Axé as Brazilian Popular Music

Axé music reflects musical diversity. The ingredients of axé music are mixed and range from samba to ijexá, frevo, carimbó, reggae, funk, soul, rap, merengue, and soca. In this chapter I examine axé as an innovative style of Brazilian popular music. When one examines axé music as an innovative popular style, one must acknowledge that it did not just suddenly appear on international charts, but was gradually accepted by the commercial industry, media, and consuming public as an innovative style of Afro-Brazilian popular music.

Axé music was developed over a period of time by young Afro-Brazilians who were involved with the Negritude movement and also embraced aspects of Candomblé religion, music, and imagery as symbols of blackness. Many of these young Afro-Brazilians were experimenting with imported popular music, and traditional samba had to share space with new and innovative styles. The new sound of the blocos afro, musical experimentation of trio elétricos, Bahian Carnival, and more access to advanced technology, local and regional markets, and young fans all contributed to the emergence of axé music.

Creating New and Innovative Styles: Labels of Popular Music

When musicians create a song, they make choices such as what types of instruments to use, how to play them, how fast the tempo should go, and how the beat is realized. When similar choices are made from song to song, they produce style. Style is comprehensive; it is the sum of the shared features that are immediately apparent as well as those that take time to unfold. Style also occurs at different levels: we can talk about the style of an individual song, the style of a performer, the style of several performances with similar sound, the style of a generation, and even the style of an era.

Many styles are also regarded as labels.[1] For example, when the label *samba-reggae* is used to describe popular music, people often associate it with particular performers, blocos afro, and with sounds of vibrant drumming with vocals, and fast explosive rhythms. Labels such as samba-reggae, jazz, rock and roll, rap, soul, and funk are shorthand for style. They enable people to communicate in a word or two pertinent information about the sound of a particular performance or group of performances or era.

In both Western and non-Western societies, when new and innovative styles and labels of popular music are introduced, they often receive an array of responses and criticisms from artists, local media, and communities. Moreover, new and innovative rhythms, lyrics, and artists often are judged by the standards of the more accepted popular music styles in the community. New and innovative styles are often surrounded by controversy—older versus younger generation, aesthetic preference, and positive/negative effects on the young. This may result in debates by the local media and communities, who may spend a great amount of time attempting to find ways of describing, categorizing, and labeling the new and innovative styles. On the other hand, because of the debates, criticisms, and controversy, young people may be more drawn to the new and innovative styles. This is evident with styles and labels such as bossa nova, jazz, rock and roll, trends (e.g., Beatlemania, Tropicália), and artists (e.g., Caetano Veloso, Gilberto Gil, Elvis Presley, Madonna, Public Enemy, Kanye West, Luiz Caldas).

The initial responses and criticisms of what has been categorized and labeled axé music are similar to other popular styles. For example, there were different types of reactions when bossa nova, an altered style of samba, emerged in Rio de Janeiro in the late 1950s and 1960s. Bossa nova appealed to the white middle and upper class sectors of society. This new style expanded the stylistic and musical vocabulary of traditional samba with more subdued tempi, rhythmic swinging motion (balanço), and with textures of strumming guitars and vocals; it also integrated the dynamic melodies, harmony, rhythm, syncopation, and other stylistic influences from American cool jazz.

In the 1960s the enormous success of bossa nova brought Brazilian music into an international dialogue. Thus, besides receiving recording contracts, Brazilian musicians such as Antonio Carlos Jobim were given opportunities to perform concert engagements of the new music in places such as the United States, where the increasingly popular style was promoted by the media and popularized in American culture as a dance craze. Moreover, the style attracted some of the best American jazz musicians—Charlie Byrd, John Coltrane, Stan Getz, Chet Baker, Ella Fitzgerald, Sarah Vaughn and many others who recorded bossa nova albums. Some musicians also experimented with incorporating bossa nova with other styles of popular music, such as funk and soul. For example, in 1962, after an extensive tour of Brazil with the Dizzy Gillespie Orchestra, Quincy Jones composed and recorded the album *Big Band Bossa Nova*, which included "Soul Bossa Nova," a composition that many years later would become the theme song of the 1997 film *Austin Powers: International Man of Mystery*.

Although a success, bossa nova also sparked some criticism within the Brazilian society. A prime example is in the 1960s, when music historian José Ramos Tinhorão argued that bossa nova composers were influenced by American jazz, and were producing music alienated from its traditional samba roots.[2] However, there were also positive responses to the style by the younger generation. After the coup that in 1964 brought a military regime to power in Brazil, many young people began to use popular music as a vehicle for protest, a mechanism for the advocacy of social change, and an instrument for young urban Brazilians to experiment with musical styles. For these young people bossa nova gradually developed into a social protest movement made up of their peers—high school and college students. In addition for some innovative artists, bossa nova stimulated a type of regional interest in rhythmic and melodic motifs and an acute awareness of social problems (e.g., poverty, unemployment) that existed in Brazil.

In Brazil more heads turned in the mid-1960s when popular music began to be modernized with electronic instruments and through the invasion of international popular styles. Groups of young whites wanted to embrace rock music from England and the United States. Especially through the innovations of the Jovem Guarda (Young Guard) and their "iê iê iê" Beatles-influenced style, youth rock movement and the popularity of the singer Roberto Carlos swept through the mass media.

The region of Bahia did not remain silent: in 1967 Caetano Veloso and Gilberto Gil introduced their new and innovative "som universal" (universal sound), the musical style that combined Brazilian themes and Afro-Brazilian rhythms with electric instrumentation. As prime innovators of the Tropicália movement, Gil and Veloso opened the way for musical and poetic experimentation and diversification in Brazilian popular music. Although short-lived (1967–69), Tropicália left a legacy in Brazilian popular music where an entire arts movement—music, theater, poetry, and the visual arts—was used as a mechanism to convey sentiments to the middle classes about the social problems that existed in Brazil.

Bossa nova, Jovem Guarda, and Tropicália are only a few examples of styles that have taken Brazilian popular music in different directions and generated an array of responses and criticisms. Individual songs, performers, and sounds all have contributed to the popularization of these styles. These styles have been critically judged by the standards of popular music such as traditional samba.

The emergence of axé music stems from change in musical preferences as young Afro-Brazilians in the urban areas of Rio de Janeiro, São Paulo, and Salvador began to respond in positive ways to imported black popular music. By the 1970s Afro-Brazilians were critical of rock music and regarded the samba as linked with the commercialism of the dominant white society. For young Afro-Brazilians finding meaning in popular music of their own choice, styles that could be manipulated in terms of textures, lyrics, instrumentation, and rhythms to accommodate local tastes was a primary interest. The more modern popular music styles of soul, funk, reggae, merengue, and soca became favored by a new generation of music connoisseurs, young Afro-Brazilians who were becoming more politically active in their communities than their parents had been.

The response to imported popular music by the older generation was often negative; Brazilian intellectuals who had historically served as spokesmen for the minority community were critical. They perceived the attraction to imported popular music as a threat to the white, elite definition of both "Brazilianness" and Afro-Brazilian cultural practices.[3] The musicians' choice of imported styles can be said to have challenged the internal systems of political representation in Brazil. Afro-Brazilians' deviation from samba, the channel of musical expression that was most accepted by the elites, was an expression of dissatisfaction with the status quo. Celebrations such as Bahian Carnival became a major venue to create popular music that would eventually give to rise to axé music.

The label *axé* to denote a popular music style in Afro-Brazilian culture has some similarities with designations of jazz or rock and roll in African American culture where the actual performers are not credited with the designation/naming of the style in popular culture.[4] Such designations/labels were often associated with negative stereotypes of black music and cultural expressions pervasive in the Jim Crow South. Criticism came from communities, local churches, and the media about negative influences that these styles contributed to the moral decay of young people in American society. One only needs to examine the responses given to early jazz musicians and rock legends such as Chuck Berry and Elvis Presley. Presley generated both positive and negative responses with his sexually suggestive gyrating hip movements. Popularization and acceptance of these styles within mainstream American culture gradually rose after talented and charismatic white musicians began to perform them.

When the term axé was first applied to music by the journalist Hagamenon Brito in the mid-1980s, it was used as a derogatory designation for new, hybrid, and innovative black dance music that was pervasive in Salvador.[5] This designation was a type of "race record" labeling of a new style of popular music being generated in Bahian Carnival. The popularity of axé music is often associated with Daniela Mercury, the talented and charismatic performer regarded as the "queen" of axé music. Mercury is a white Brazilian whom the media in the past has described as "the blackest white woman in Bahia," because she sings and dances like a black Bahian woman.[6]

Mercury is one of the most talented axé musicians and both blacks and whites have responded favorably to her performances. One could argue that this kind of royal designation is similar to the reception given to the talented and charismatic "kings" of swing (Benny Goodman), rock and roll (Elvis Presley), and musicians associated with the 1960s British Invasion (e.g., Beatles, Rolling Stones), who enjoyed fame and commercial success performing African American music. The difference is that Mercury acknowledges she is part of the Afro-Brazilian heritage in axé music and this is often reflected in many of the songs she performs and composes.

Mercury had performed as a singer for the trio elétrico associated with the bloco Eva.[7] Her album *Daniela Mercury* (1991), featured the song "Swing da Cor" ("Swing of Color") on which she is accompanied by rhythmic samba-reggae. This album was a huge success and brought samba-reggae to the forefront in Brazil. Mercury's 1992 recording of "O Canto da Cidade" ("The Song of the City"), a song co-written by Tote Gira, expresses pride in the African heritage that gave axé music its popularity in Brazil. This is one of the songs most successfully to capture the true spirit of Bahian Carnival.

Although Mercury is a white Brazilian, the song captures her "blackness" and African heritage within. In the song Mercury conjures up a romanticized, idyllic image of Salvador's African heritage, and suggests that Mercury is part of this heritage and the same color as the city. But the song acknowledges that in the midst of the city are the ghetto, the street, and the faith of the people. As she walks around the city she hears the sounds of Africa in the music of the afoxés:

A cor desse cidade sou eu
[I am the color of this city]
O canto desse cidade é meu
[The song of this city is mine]
O gueto, a rua, a fé
[The ghetto, street, faith]
Eu vou andando a pé
[I am walking]
Pela cidade bonita
[Through the beautiful city]
O toque do afoxé
[The rhythm of the afoxé]
É a força
[and its rhythm]
De onde vem?
[Where does it come from?]
Ningúem explica
[Nobody explains]
Elá é bonita . . .
[It is beautiful . . .]
Eu sou o primeiro que canta
[I am the first to sing]

Eu sou o carnival
[I am the carnival]
A cor dessa cidade sou eu
[I am the color of the city]
O canto dessa cidade é meu
[The song of this city is mine]

Axé Music

The marketing and labeling of axé music is linked with the popularity of hybrid rhythms and samba-reggae style of the blocos afro. Many individual performers and groups have contributed to the stylization of axé music.[8] Like other styles, axé music has evolved over time at different levels; each individual song helped define the style. This began before Daniela Mercury's popularization of axé music. In the mid-1980s Luiz Caldas had heads turning with his experimentation of salsa, rock, and samba in his album *Magia* (1985), which basically initiated the style that would later become known as axé music. This album included the historic song "Fricote," the first to use the fricote rhythm (also called deboche), which Caldas invented by combining elements from ijexá and reggae. This song was a forerunner of axé music. "Fricote" has been criticized for portraying black women as sexual objects. The lyrics include double entendres and suggest sexual promiscuity between black men and women. In the song, a black woman (*nega*) is approached by a black man (*nego*), who shouts and grabs the woman in an effort to put lipstick (a phallic symbol) on her buchecha (a word meaning "cheek" that can also refer to female genitalia).

Since the recording of "Fricote" many songs have contributed to the stylization of axé music. With the popularity of the blocos afro, samba-reggae, and the commercial success of Mercury, many Afro-Brazilian artists have taken advantage of performing and creating the new and innovative music for public consumption and have changed the axé designation from a negative one to a positive one.

Some members of large blocos have formed smaller bands in the axé popular music industry. This can be seen with the popularity of Ivete Sangalo and Banda Eva and Ara Ketu. Banda Eva continues to be a major attraction at Bahian Carnival and has propelled axé music onto the national and international music scenes. Lead vocalist Ivete Sangalo, whose sultry voice epitomizes the sensual, has become an international star and an icon in the new generation of axé musicians.[9] In her performances on the trio elétricos, Sangalo often draws from an eclectic mix of popular styles that include MPB [música popular brasileira], blues, and soul.

Ara Ketu also continues to be a major blocos afro in Bahian Carnival, but in the 1980s transformed into a smaller band known as Banda Ara Ketu. One of the first groups to add electronic instruments to axé music, Banda Ara Ketu had established themselves with successful tours outside of the country before they achieved popularity in Brazil.

There are a variety of songs and artists that have contributed to the popularization of axé music. Over the years of conducting research on Brazilian popular music, some of my favorite songs include:

1985	Fricote	Luiz Caldas
1986	Eu sou Negão	Gerônimo
1987	Faraó Divinidade do Egito	Olodum
1988	Protesto do Olodum	Olodum
1989	Beijo no Boca	Banda Beijo
1990	Revolta Olodum	Olodum
1990	Elegibô	Margareth Menezes
1991	Prefixo de Verão	Banda Mel
1992	O Canto da Cidade	Daniela Mercury
1993	Doce Obsessão	Cheiro de Amor
1994	Requebra	Olodum
1995	Avisa Lá	Olodum
1996	Bom Demais	Ara Ketu
1997	Rapunzel	Daniela Mercury
1998	A Latinha	Timbalada
1999	Juliana	Pierre Onasis
2000	Cabelo Raspadinho	Chiclete com Banana
2001	Bate-Lata	Banda Beijo
2002	Festa	Ivete Sangalo
2003	Dandalunda	Margareth Menezes
2004	Maimbê Danda	Daniela Mercury

Many of these songs represent innovative artists and groups who have contributed to the emergence of axé music. Many were highly received by the consuming public and contributed to the popularity of axé music in the commercial market. Moreover, there is a "global spreading" of axé music in that some of the songs are continually rerecorded on commercial compilations that can be purchased not only in music stores in Brazil but in many other geographic areas and via websites. Many other songs and artists could have been listed, such as "Kizomba, Festa da Raça ("Kizomba, Celebration of the Race") and "Canto do Cor" ("Song of Color") by Banda Reflexu's, one of the first groups to record blocos afro songs in the samba-reggae style with electronic instruments; and As Meninas, a female ensemble that recorded several versions of the popular "Xibom Bombom" (1999), a major hit in the late 1990s.

Axé music has not been exclusive to the younger generation of performers but has attracted more established international Brazilian artists as well. For example, Caetano Veloso has performed axé music with Timbalada in the samba-reggae driven "Margarida Perfumada" (1998). Gal Costa, who has had an extensive professional career including participation in the Tropicália movement of the 1960s, has continued to reinvent her artistic style in Brazilian popular music. Costa's album *Aquele Frevo Axé* (1999) is an example of her varied interests in performing a variety of popular music styles. Costa's sentimental and rich vocal style has qualities similar to Roberta Flack, one of the prime artists of black romantic music in the United States during the 1970s and 1980s. Like Flack, in performance Costa conveys many types of emotions in songs that exhibit her extensive vocal range, texture, and smoothness of performance quality.

For many artists the axé music market has proved successful in the popular music industry that is geared to a consuming public. Axé music has distinguished the city of Salvador in the forefront of a competitive industry of Brazilian popular music and in the international music market.

Musical Innovation in Axé Music

When musicians enter the international market, their music is often shaped by new kinds of non-local forces. To attract an international audience they are pressured to comply with the international sound embodied in the use of Euro-American scales, tuning, and harmony, as well as the use of electronic instruments and accessible dance rhythms, all of which are seen as standard. In addition, to make their recordings more marketable the musicians must write about subjects that are accessible to a wide audience while at the same time featuring elements unique to their own culture.[10] International axé artists as Daniela Mercury, Margareth Menezes, and many others have complied with many of these standards, including tunings, harmonization, the use of electronic instruments, and dance rhythms. But at the same time, they express the unique aspects of their cultural background.

I do not believe that there is one standard or a generalized style for axé music because the musicians continue to perform, experiment, and record musical arrangements for small and large band ensembles often employing a variety of techniques that seem to evoke different moods and sentiments in listeners. The songs are not written in the same key, tempi, chord progressions, and instrumentation. Even when musicians incorporate the samba-reggae rhythmic structure as a backdrop in their compositions, there is variety. Some may choose to incorporate only voice and drum; others may include a funk sound and add electronic instrumentation on top of the samba-reggae base to create a mix of textures.[11] This not only involves musical and aesthetic preferences but marketability—choosing what they believe is fashionable and will attract a consuming audience. However, in this axé mixture of keys, tempi, chord progressions, and instrumentation, there is still an Afro-Brazilian sound through vocal quality, textures, and rhythms. I do not believe that axé musicians who incorporate elements from imported styles—soul, funk, reggae, soca—desire completely to lose identification with their local traditions; instead, I believe younger musicians are emerging who desire to extend their palette (knowledge of local traditions) with other techniques and styles that appeal to them, to compete successfully in an international market.

Some arrangements in axé music incorporate the most sophisticated recording technologies featuring instrumentation consisting of saxophones, trumpets, electronic keyboards, synthesizers, and digital programming. Some musicians may compose an arrangement that incorporates instrumental vamps, transitional bridges between sections, rifflike trumpet melodies, syncopated electric funk bass passages, vocal and instrumental improvisation, and background singers.

Axé music has opened the doors of opportunity (and a commercial market) for many performers. Margareth Menezes is a popular musician who has heightened innovation in axé music. Even before Daniela Mercury became legendary in Brazil for her renditions of axé music, Menezes was performing samba-reggae atop trio elétricos vehicles. Her career received a boost in the international music industry when she was invited by David Byrne (the former leader of the rock group Talking Heads) to accompany him on a world tour. The release of her first album, *Elegibô (A History of Ifá)* (1990), brought her international fame.[12]

Many of the songs Menezes performs especially during Bahian Carnival have become hits in the commercial market on album compilations. Menezes's album compilations feature a fusion of popular music styles—samba-reggae, afoxé, and funk—and some convey sociopolitical implications about issues relating to poverty, love, and racial inequality in Brazil. For example, *Elegibô* includes the song "Tenda do Amor" ("Test of Love"), an electronic afoxé intended to be a declaration of sexual and racial pride. Her rendition of "Negra Melodia" ("Black Melody"), sung in both Portuguese and English, is a mixture of reggae and samba that reflects the Brazilian black consciousness movement and the influences of the 1970s Jamaican Rastafarian movement and singer Bob Marley. "Tudo À Toa" ("All for Nothing") is a samba-funk with lyrics that express disgust with the living conditions in Brazilian urban slums.[13]

"Kindala" (1991) is a samba-funk song that Menezes dedicates to the hope and yearning for life brought to Brazil by the African people.[14] This song incorporates influences from African American funk and seems to follow neatly into a quadruple (4/4) rhythmic pattern with heavy emphasis placed on the syncopated accentuation of a deep and complex bass guitar line. The opening passages of the song incorporate traditional Brazilian-sounding instruments, but as the song progresses, syncopated backbeats played by percussion instruments support the funk-bass line and an instrumental trumpet vamp. The harmonic structure is supported with a series of trumpet and electronic keyboard riffs that give the music a mix of samba and funk feel.

In axé music, while some performers use the basic rhythmic and vocal structure of samba-reggae, others embellish this structure with electronic instruments and background singers. For example, the song "Margarida Perfumada" (1998) incorporates the heavy pulsation of drums playing interlocking parts. Tension is built as the drummers intersperse their rhythms with the melodic line sung by Caetano Veloso and the background singers.

The recent Margareth Menezes song "Dandalunda" (2003) shows a different stylistic treatment in axé music. This song employs a variety of vocal techniques, electronic instruments, and percussion to create highly energized and fast-paced dance music that follows a samba-reggae rhythmic scheme performed by an ensemble of drummers. But in key changes, chord progressions, tempi, and performers, this song sounds very different from "Margarida Perfumada." In this song there is a sequence and ostinato melodic line played on an electric bass as a countermelody against the vocal and drum parts.

The variety of axé music can also be seen in song topics and lyrics that include love, Carnival, community solidarity, racial equality, dance, sexuality, African history, black pride, humanity, and Afro-Brazilian spirituality in Candomblé religion. For example, Daniela Mercury's popular song "Sol da Liberdade" (2000) provides music and lyrics that seem to praise music and people from Brazil:

Sob o sol da liberdade
[Under the sun of freedom]
Liberdade em que se dança . . .
[Freedom in which one dances . . .]
Em teu samba retumbante
[In you resounding samba]
Brava gente Brasileira
[Brave Brazilian people]
Gente boa que se preze . . .
[Good people who are highly valued . . .]
Onde reina o samba-reggae
[Where samba-reggae reigns]

Axé performers enhance the music with their own personal artistry. For example, Margareth Menezes's intonation, vocal range, texture, and phrasing are far removed from those of Daniela Mercury or Ivete Sangalo both of whom have their special ways of performing and interpreting axé music. Even when large or small ensembles perform samba-reggae rhythms, the performers make them unique. I believe these musical, stylistic, and aesthetic differences are what attract fan-based audiences for the musicians.

Stylizing Axé Music with Carlinhos Brown

One musician who has taken advantage of advanced technology to produce some of the most compelling recordings in axé music is Carlinhos Brown. During my initial research in Brazil (1998–99) Brown was among the few international musicians whom I had a chance to observe in performances and to share in his involvement with the Afro-Brazilian community. Brown is a musician able to "think out of the box" and innovate new styles in Brazilian popular music. Part of his charisma is his great sense of musicality to produce music that is at the cutting edge of innovation. From my own observations of Brown I describe his musical talent as similar to Antonio Carlos Jobim, Herbie Hancock, or Keith Jarrett, where his skills allow him an extensive palette to experiment with an array of styles—classical, samba, reggae, bossa nova, funk, jazz, techno—from which he carefully selects the rhythms, voicings, harmonies, and chords he feels appropriate to convey his musical ideas.

As the major innovator of Timbalada, Brown often participates in the activities and processions with the blocos afro. Moreover, in his work, he attempts to avoid racial protest and explicit appeals to pan-Africanism. Instead, he places more emphasis on instilling a sense of pride in young Afro-Brazilians and the expressive cultures of a globalized black youth without making references to specific struggles of black communities in Brazil and abroad. He does acknowledge how popular music from African diasporic areas has continued to influence his music.

Brown's work with Timbalada helped him develop as a serious musician, composer, and innovative user of electric guitars, horns, keyboards, vocal/lyrical hooks, and melodic drum arrangements. Brown stated about the importance of the drum in his experience as an Afro-Brazilian: "Timbalada was a benchmark of hearing for me. . . . I needed to know not only the road but to let loose all the ancestrality that I love and the gift of the drum that was given to me."[15]

Luiz Caldas, Daniela Mercury, Margareth Menezes, Marisa Monte, Maria Bethânia, Gal Costa, and Caetano Veloso are among the artists who have recorded songs by Carlinhos Brown. *Alfagamabetízado* (*AlphaGammaBeta-ized*) (1996), Brown's first solo album recorded in Salvador, Paris, and Rio de Janeiro and produced by Wally Badarou and Arto Lindsay, diverges from his percussive work with Timbalada by including soft ballads, colorful orchestration, and an array of musical instruments (e.g., acoustic guitar, cello, violin, congas, djembes, and accordion). Musically, *Alfagamabetízado* combines axé music with northeastern rhythms, 1970s-type funk, bossa nova, and jazz-fusion sonorities.

Omelete Man (1998) is an example of axé music, hybridization, eclecticism, and world fusion music. Brown is pictured on its cover as a Pan-like creature playing a flute. This album was influenced by Afro-Beat, bossa nova, música romântica, samba-reggae, and African American funk and rap. Brown experiments with sound using many techniques. For example, the songs "Irará" and "Tribal United Dance" feature what sounds like Native American chanting, high-pitched ululations, and poetic rapping on top of funk-type bass lines played on an assortment of electronic instruments topped off with a petition to the orixá Xangô. Brown also sings two songs, "Water My Girl" and "Soul By Soul," in Portuguese and English. Along with all of these musical ingredients, Brown also uses an array of instrumentation including cuíca, surdos, mandolin, Hammond B3 organ, violins, violas, cellos, and West African talking drums.

The processes of globalization, fusion, appropriation, and hybridity are synonymous with Carlinhos Brown as he continually reinvents himself in Brazilian popular music. He is not afraid to experiment with new sounds and continually brings Brazilian popular music into an age of technology and electronic mixes (e.g., funky, high-tech, and trio elétrico). This type of innovation can be seen in contemporary songs such as "Já sei namorar" from *Os Tribalistas* (2002), a compilation he recorded with Arnaldo Antunes and Marisa Monte, and *Candyall Beat* (2004), recorded with Argentinean musician DJ Dero.

Brown's success and notoriety in axé music has allowed him to explore other ventures and mediums. For example, *El Milagro de Candeal* (*The Miracle in Candeal*) is a 2005 documentary (in Portuguese with English subtitles) that premiered in New York City at the 13th African diaspora Film Festival. The film attempts to connect Afro-Brazilian heritage with the African diaspora. Directed by Fernando Trueba, a Spaniard whose previous work includes the documentary *Calle 54*, *The Miracle in Candeal* focuses on the neighborhood of Candeal Pequeno in Salvador and the vital role that Carlinhos Brown has played in its revitalization and in the education of young Afro-Brazilians through music. Candeal Pequeno was a neighborhood that experienced high crime and poverty rates. When Brown arrived with his sponsorship, fame, and success as an international artist in axé music, he assisted in establishing a music school, health clinic, computer centers, and with reconstructing sewage lines and a water treatment plant. Brown also played a crucial role in setting up a state-of-the-art recording studio where musicians from many parts of Brazil now have opportunities to record their music.

The film also documents musical exchanges between Cuba and Brazil—in particular between the cities of Havana and Salvador, which share historical, cultural, and musical similarities. This encounter begins when pianist Bebo Valdes, the father of jazz pianist Jesus "Chucho" Valdes, attempts to search for his African roots in the "black" city of Salvador. Upon arrival Valdes meets a local musician, Mateus, who initially acts as tour guide. Mateus becomes enthralled with Valdes's stories of exile in Stockholm, Sweden, for forty years.

Mateus expresses his belief that all Africans in the Americas are exiles. He later invites Valdes to witness a "miracle" in the Candeal community. While visiting Candeal, Valdes meets Carlinhos Brown and observes young Afro-Brazilians in music lessons and at rehearsals. Valdes is then invited to participate in jam sessions with Brown and the young musicians. He also performs with Caetano Veloso, Gilberto Gil, and Marisa Monte. The film ends with a performance by Brown and the bloco Timbalada.

During the times that I observed Carlinhos Brown in concert and at his work in the community, I could see how much he was admired by Afro-Brazilians. Many locals described him as a hero and someone who cared about the well-being of his friends and family. Moreover, his work with many individual artists and Timbalada has influenced many people to dance to the rhythms of his music.

Axé Dance

Some axé musicians have experimented with popular dance and stylized choreographic movements from samba, carimbó, salsa, merengue, and the lambada in what is known as axé dance. Depending on the songs, axé dance movements are varied and can require a vast amount of youthful energy. Axé dance can be as simple as mimicking a game of jump rope (Dança da Cordinha) or the movements of animals (turtles), or as complex as trying to combine movements of samba, lambada, forró, and hip-hop.

Since the 1990s, the group, É o Tchan (formerly known as Gera Samba) has promoted new innovations in commercial dance music on the international market and in Bahian Carnival. They developed a variety of samba known as *axé pagode* that became very popular during the late 1990s.[16] Pagode lyrics and choreography often associate being black and Bahian with sexual innuendo and sensual dancing.

É o Tchan normally includes black males and white female dancers, one blonde and the other brunette. This group celebrates the negão (the big black guy), the lourinha (blondie), and the moreninha (little brunette). The music and choreography of groups such as É o Tchan has made it the norm for many young people, particularly during Bahian Carnival, to display their sensuality in public. É o Tchan's repertoire includes axé and pagode songs such as "Dança do Pôe Pôe," "A Dança do Bumbum" (fancy dance), and "Pega no Ganjá." The dances include various types of pelvic thrusts, swift derrière bumps and shaking, circular and angular foot movements, jumps, and leaps. In performance, the group dances suggestively and the female members wear revealing garments such as cutoff short-shorts and tank tops. During Bahian Carnival 1999, many young females attending the celebrations wore this type of attire.

In axé music and dance performances there is a sense of creative play, in that musicians often perform songs geared mainly for interaction with live audiences. During these performances musicians encourage the audience to sing and dance. In this way audience members become active agents and part of the performance. They often "heat up" the performers and vice versa through intensified manipulation of rhythmic and tempi changes. For example, during my initial field research in Salvador, "Marcha Re" (1999) by Terra Samba was one of the most popular axé songs I constantly heard played on the airwaves and in live performances. This song involves sensual dancing that I previously discussed where the dancers' (both males and females) choreographic movements basically center on the derrière area. As the tempo of the song increases the musicians often encourage the dancers to increase their choreographic movements.

Another song I heard played frequently was "A Dança do Bumbum," first recorded by É o Tchan in the mid-1990s. As the song was performed the musicians often improvised on the lyrics and often made reference to members of the group (e.g., the lourinha/"blondie") as they encouraged the audience to dance and shake their derrières ("Agora mexe . . . mexe, mexe lourinha . . .") ("Now shake, shake, shake blondie"). In live performances of this song there was much creative play, sensual dancing, and audience interaction as the musicians continued to manipulate the lyrics, rhythms, and tempi. I often experienced this type of musical intensity among the young people in Salvador as they danced to axé music.

Local Perspectives: Songs of the City

The popular music industry and the consuming public often tend to associate certain styles and genres with particular musicians (e.g., Bob Marley—reggae, Aretha Franklin and James Brown—soul, Caetano Veloso and Gilberto Gil— tropicália, Daniela Mercury and Carlinhos Brown—axé music). Because of the success of many axé artists, some of the local amateur musicians attempted to redefine their local styles to make them appeal to an international audience. Moreover, as the market in Brazil has grown and diversified, competition has driven local musicians to seek new means of self-promotion inside Brazil as well as in the international market.

In several neighborhoods of Salvador (especially in the Pelourinho district), many Afro-Brazilians that I spoke with had no knowledge about the origins of the term axé in popular music and whether this usage could be attributed to one person or was introduced to the public by the local media. Some explained that they mainly became aware of axé music as a designation on commercial labels located in music stores in their neighborhoods. To these Afro-Brazilians axé music was something new and "happening" in popular music, and this was partly because Salvador continually attracted many popular musicians and styles.

The labeling of axé as a popular style made many young people take note of a new and emerging style, especially when the music was made available in local stores. Some also explained that they were excited about the sounds of samba-reggae in Bahian Carnival, and by what Olodum was doing musically in the Pelourinho district. Furthermore, they believed that this type of music would eventually lead to something new and innovative in their communities. But it all seemed to come full circle when Carlinhos Brown, with Timbalada, began working in the Candeal Pequeno community and young people realized that something innovative was happening with popular music in Salvador. Moreover, popular musicians (such as Brown) who often hosted clinics to work with young musicians were regarded as a valuable source in achieving professional goals in axé music.

In Salvador, axé music has become an important movement of cultural affirmation that links Afro-Brazilians to a communitywide sharing of black pride and Negritude. Like the hip-hop generation in the United States, for some young people axé music is synonymous with youth culture, which has the power to electrify and energize people. Afro-Brazilian youths identify their affiliation with axé not only through the music they listen to but also through the clothes they wear. Axé music is significant not just as a new trend in popular music but also as an iconic symbol of struggle, resistance, and black pride among local youth groups in cities such as Salvador, Rio de Janeiro, and São Paulo. I must also emphasize that there are many young white Brazilian fans as well who contribute to the local, national, and international marketing of axé music.

In the streets and neighborhoods of Salvador—Pelourinho, Pernambues, and Liberdade—young Afro-Brazilians explained that using axé to refer to a style of popular music is something that should be regarded as positive. Axé was a term they all were familiar with from Candomblé religion. Although many were not active practitioners, they were aware of the sacred importance of spiritual axé in Candomblé and its African heritage. In the secular sense axé was used as a designation for a popular music style that made people take note of the music and musicians. Furthermore, it allowed musicians to leverage their knowledge of many popular music styles.

Some local musicians made interesting comments about why people should not be offended by the use of axé to denote a popular music style. Most of these musicians were not active participants in Candomblé religion per se. One reference was made about how the sacred and secular seemed to complement each other during the weekly attractions on Tuesday nights during the festa da ben-ção (blessing party), when Catholic masses given at several churches were fol-lowed by samba-reggae and axé music performances.

Another comment made reference to local churches in the Pelourinho dis-trict that held services where church musicians performed what sounded like popular music. Although the songs made reference to Jesus, the rhythms per-formed by the musicians often sounded like popular music and included a con-temporary sound with electronic instruments (e.g., keyboards and guitars). But many congregants did not seem to be offended and often participated by sway-ing, clapping, or even dancing while the music was being performed. These young critics were referring to songs such as "Ó que coisa bonita" (previously discussed in chapter 6), which is often performed at the Rosário dos Pretos church and during Sunday services and some of the local pre-Carnival festivals in the city.

Although performing axé music professionally was a major goal, several lo-cal musicians described how difficult it is to pursue careers in the popular music industry. Thus, finding talented musicians, sponsorship, management, perfor-mance venues, media coverage, rehearsal time and space, and conflicts with par-ents in pursuing music careers were some of the challenges they faced as per-formers. Another problem was finding performance opportunities outside of Salvador. In many instances this would involve attaining the appropriate funds to purchase travel visas and adjusting to language and cultural barriers.

For Lula Almeida, who had established a successful performing career in popular music, beginning his career outside of Salvador was a challenge. How-ever, he was very confident in his talent and believed that he would succeed as a popular musician. When I interviewed Almeida he had already established himself as a performing musician in Los Angeles. He expressed that when he initially arrived in Los Angeles the city was very different than Salvador and he had to make many types of adjustments. But Almeida was so determined to suc-ceed that one of his first objectives was to connect with his friends from Salva-dor who had previously relocated to the area.

Almeida described that part of his initial task was also finding appropri-ate clubs where he could perform axé music and also learn more about the pop-lar styles that the Los Angeles crowd enjoyed. Initially he did not have much access to electronic instruments and decided that he would perform more samba-reggae type songs in a traditional voice and drum format. He believed that the crowds where he performed (e.g., Zabumba, Café Dansa) enjoyed the music. He was later hired to perform weekly concerts in Los Angeles. He was also able to form Afro-Brazil, a group that performs a variety of popular styles. It took sev-eral years before Almeida felt comfortable performing axé music in Los Angeles and experimenting with various popular styles. But he believed that his talent in performing axé music helped him succeed in Los Angeles and gain respect as a professional musician from his family and friends in Salvador.[17]

The New Millennium: Axé, a Musical Style of Change

Several years have passed since I spoke with the local musicians in Salvador about the influence of axé music in their communities. In a more recent experience, outside of Salvador, I had an opportunity to discuss with other musicians in the popular music industry their opinions about axé music. One of the musicians I interviewed was pop singer Izzy Gordon, an intelligent, beautiful, and talented performer who I respectfully call the incredible "Ms. G." Ms. G. is from São Paulo and from a family of noted musicians. She is the daughter of jazz musician Dave Gordon and niece of the legendary singer and bossa nova composer Dolores Duran.

Ms. G. considered performing as a pop singer an easy task because her training in popular music began when she was very young. She described that throughout her childhood she grew up listening to jazz and bossa nova. Her home was a constant rehearsal and performance space where musicians such as Rita Lee, Jair Rodrigues, Marisa Gata Mansa, and many others would gather to perform with her father in jam sessions. In many of these sessions the musicians would basically take cues from each other and produce some of the most innovative music. For Ms. G. what was appealing about the jam sessions was that the musicians would play many types of music and this helped her to expand her knowledge of popular music.

Ms. G. described that her favorite composers include both Brazilian and American musicians such as Dolores Duran, Djavan, Chico Buarque de Hollanda, Antonio Carlos Jobim, Cole Porter, Duke Ellington, Quincy Jones, Bono, and Stevie Wonder. She attempts to incorporate an extensive amount of "herself" during her performances—that is, to create music that moves individuals in a positive way. Ms. G. believed she accomplished this goal in a recent concert in São Paulo where Quincy Jones and Bono were among the attendees who praised her performance as something new and energetic in Brazilian popular music.

As a professional singer Ms. G. draws her inspiration and techniques from many styles of popular music—MPB, disco, soul, jazz, bossa nova, and blues. Favorite female singers that have influenced her career include both Brazilian and African American singers such as Elis Regina, Marisa Gata Mansa, Ella Fitzgerald, and Sarah Vaughan. She has attempted to develop a style that truly reflects her coming of age and maturity in popular music. Ms. G. has a current album, *Aos Mestres com Carinho Homenagem a Dolores Duran* (*To the Masters with*

Pop singer Izzy Gordon
with legendary composer
Quincy Jones in São Paulo.

Izzy Gordon with pop icon
Bono in São Paulo.

Affection: Homage to Dolores Duran) (2005), that is a compilation of contemporary versions of songs composed by her aunt, Dolores Duran, and a rendition of the famous standard "My Funny Valentine."[18]

During my conversations with Ms. G. she offered some comments about the influence of axé music in Brazil:

> Although I am not an axé music performer, I am aware of how important the style has become in Brazilian popular music. Axé is music of change and a new era in Brazilian popular music. Whether people like it or not, the style has made many people [musicians] think about popular music. Axé is the music of black people of Bahia. Yes, when I first heard axé music it was very different than what I had been performing. To me the rhythms were like "Afro beats," rhythms from Africa. Also some of the instruments that I heard in some re-cordings of axé music sounded like congas and bongos. Together this was an interesting music mix. Axé music really was a style that musically put Bahia on the popular music charts. In the past years axé music has grown a lot and now played in the big cities like São Paulo and Rio de Janeiro where more and more young people are enjoying the style. Now there are many types of axé music—axé Bahia, axé Carioca, and axé Paulista. This is good because more people are listening to the music and local clubs tend to play music that they know will at-tract young crowds. For many local clubs in Rio and São Paulo, axé music has become a crowd pleaser.[19]

I also had opportunity to explore responses and criticisms about axé music from a contingent of young white Brazilian students from Salvador, São Paulo, and Rio de Janeiro who were studying in an international program in the United States at the University of Kansas (Lawrence). These students ranged in age from eighteen to twenty-four and specialized in a variety of academic majors, from graphic design to journalism, on graduate and undergraduate levels. Some were recruited to the program via scholarships in the athletic department (e.g., volley-ball). The university has an organization known as the Brazilian Student As-sociation or BRASA, composed of approximately forty Brazilian natives, non-Brazilian students of Portuguese, Latin American studies, and members of the local community who are interested in Brazilian culture.

During the academic year BRASA sponsors social and cultural activities including A Mesa Brazil (The Brazilian Table), a weekly dialogue and meeting covering various topics on Brazilian culture; A Semana Brasileira (The Brazilian Week), a weeklong series of lectures and presentations on Brazilian music and culture; Micareta (Carnival Out of Season), a fall party; and a Carnival celebra-tion in the spring. Like the annual celebrations in Rio de Janeiro and Salvador, the Carnival parties at Kansas are based on a particular theme. These celebra-tions are held at Abe and Jakes, a Lawrence club, and draw hundreds of partici-pants. During the celebrations, BRASA sponsors samba and axé dance work-shops for students and local community participants.

The Brazilian students at the University of Kansas expressed that they were not practitioners of Candomblé religion. They were aware that the term *axé* is somehow related to Afro-Brazilian religion, but they most often used it as a salutation. Most of the students expressed that it took time for axé music as a popular style to be accepted by young people in their communities, because the music was so different. Most people were accustomed to hearing the samba. For many young people outside of Salvador the music was abstract, something they had to get used to. Similar to Ms. G.'s response, the Brazilian students expressed that axé music was associated with blacks from Bahia. Jana Correa, one of the spokespersons for the BRASA organization, described axé music:

> Axé music is a mix of lambada with Brazilian samba. It also has some Afro-Brazilian influences. This is what makes axé music unique. This kind of music has its own identity because of the unique movements and joy of the lyrics. They are not very metaphoric or fancy. They are simple and clear and that is why axé music is so popular nowadays. Also, its rhythm makes it impossible not to swing! In my home city of Rio, axé music was the target of a lot of prejudice in the past decade, being called "black music of the northeast." A lot of people did not really take the music serious. Nowadays, however, the opinions about axé music have changed in Rio. "Micaretas" [out-of-season Carnival parties] and even nightclubs play axé music all the time. It is very popular among "cariocas," or the ones born in Rio de Janeiro, and it has conquered a special place among the young population.[20]

Most of the other Brazilian students described axé music as simply dance music for young people. Moreover, similar to the responses that I received years earlier in Salvador, the Brazilian students in Kansas also associated it with particular artists and groups such as Luiz Caldas, Daniela Mercury, Margareth Menezes, Carlinhos Brown, É o Tchan, Banda Eva, and Ivete Sangalo.

Axé Music and African/African Diasporic Connections

Axé music is part of artistic creativity that links contemporary Afro-Brazilian popular musical production in Salvador with the African and African diasporic areas. In the song "Alegria da Cidade" (1990), composed by Lazzo/Jorge Portugal and recorded by Margareth Menezes, the lyrics of the song refer to an "I am"/ "We are" connection with Bahia, popular music, and blacks who occupy space in a large black community (gueto):

A minha pele ébano é
[My ebony skin is]
A minha alma nua
[My naked soul]
Espalhando a luz do sol

[Spreading the light of the sun]
Espalhando a luz da lua
[Spreading the light of the moon]
Minha pele é linguagem . . .
[My skin is a language . . .]
No coração da America eu sou o jazz, o rock . . .
[In the heart of America I am jazz, I am rock . . .]
Na beleza do afoxé ou no balanço no reggae
[In the beauty of the afoxé or the swinging in reggae]
Eu sou o sol da Jamaica
[I am the sun of Jamaica]
Eu sou cor da Bahia . . .
[I am the color of Bahia . . .]
Liberdade, Curuzu, Harlem, Palmares, Soweto
Nosso céu é todo blue e mundo é um grande gueto
[Our sky is all blue and the world is a large ghetto][21]

Axé music joins other styles—samba, soul, funk, reggae, rumba, calypso, soca, highlife, jùjú, and Afro-Beat—in the continuing cycle of Afrocentric music production. Moreover, similar to the emergence of African-influenced religions, popular music styles in many African and African diasporic areas have often come into contact with musical and stylistic influences that are appropriated from other cultures. Because of this, the music has often undergone different processes of fusion resulting in the creation of syncretic and hybrid rhythms. Rhythmic innovation in popular music is another legacy Brazil shares with other African and African diasporic areas where musicians have attempted to merge various rhythms to create syncretic and hybrid styles. This type of creativity is evident in axé music, where musicians have experimented with both local and imported styles.

The rhythms of samba-reggae first developed by the blocos afro were very important in the emergence of the popular music that became categorized and labeled as axé. Samba-reggae was in many ways a catalyst for musicians "thinking out of the box," away from the duple rhythmic structures of samba music and dance. Several popular musicians I interviewed explained that samba-reggae gave to axé music a freedom to experiment with the various rhythms using an assortment of traditional Brazilian instruments—drums, rattles, whistles, bells, and tambourines—that could be combined with keyboard synthesizers and electric basses. Moreover, in their music they could draw elements from many styles to combine with popular sounds from African American music—jazz, soul, funk, rap, and rhythm and blues. This type of experimentation allowed musicians to create the ultimate fusion and hybrid popular music styles.

In many styles of Afro-Brazilian popular music, the raw sound of drumming has continually been a major feature in the music, where drummers perform vibrant rhythms with high levels of technical facility. This is an especially accurate observation in live performances I observed throughout my time in Brazil. In national and international markets, axé musicians now have access to high-tech recording and commercial opportunities with the mass production of annual compilations such as the *Axé Bahia* series. This has ushered in an age of technology in the recording studios, where the sound of raw drumming from actual musicians can sometimes be replaced by digital and electronic drum set programming devices.

Depending on the artist, in a recording studio a single voice or instrument can be electronically manipulated to imitate the sound quality of backup singers or instrumental ensembles. Moreover, depending on the artist, percussive sounds of cuícas, bells, complicated drum parts, or even backbeats may not necessarily require actual musicians but in some instances can be digitally programmed with assistance of engineers and editors. This is not a criticism of any axé musician that may take advantage of such technological innovation. But if one chooses, advancement in technology can possibly offer axé musicians more opportunities in commercial markets to reach a wider audience.

The Future of Axé Music

Axé and the African roots of Brazilian popular music are also embedded not only in the style of music known as axé but also in the many artists that continue to energize the style. Axé music is a compound term indicative of commercial consciousness and group secularization. With the emergence of axé music in Bahian Carnival and the popular music industry, the term axé, a holy concept that stems from African religious heritage, has been turned into a marketing label. In Afro-Brazilian religions axé mediates between the sacred and secular worlds and is encapsulated as power, spirituality, and creative energy. But even more important than this power is its importance in the history of the Candomblé religion and Afro-Brazilian identity in Brazil, where West African àsé was essential for survival and the continuation of African culture.

Within the sacred contexts of the Candomblé sanctum, practitioners revere a Supreme Creator and the orixás. They are guided by their belief in the essence of axé as the manifestation of blessings of protection and survival, prosperity, fruitful harvest, harmony with nature, good fortune, wisdom, and talent—all the tools people need to live and function in the secular/human world. Practitioners of Candomblé now face the secularization of axé as a label to designate a style of Brazilian popular music.

In many ways there is a sacred/secular connection with axé music and the spiritual axé of the Candomblé religion. Some axé musicians compose songs with lyrics that capture the spiritual qualities of a particular orixá, and the songs are often geared for entertainment outside of the Candomblé sanctum. Also, in axé music musicians make reference to Candomblé religion and communicating with the spiritual world as a way of conveying a sense of religiosity, Afro-Brazilian identity, pride, cultural traditions, and Afro-Brazilian history to popular music consumers.

In a secular sense, axé is an appropriation and commercial strategy for labeling a contemporary Afro-Brazilian popular music style. There are good and bad aspects of this type of labeling. Although in popular culture axé music is secular, some people may still regard this type of music as having spiritual/sacred qualities to influence good fortune and prosperity. The axé music industry has created a type of "global spreading," an outlet for the production, consumption, and distribution of Afro-Brazilian popular music. The production of axé music provides outlets for many types of creative impulses in music and dance. Some musicians create the music to attract a secular audience but also to reap the rewards of their success.

Although the musicians play an important role in the popularization of axé music, I believe that the audience (the fans) have "consumer power" and contribute much to the popularity, dissemination, and longevity of axé music. Many of these fans are part of what I would describe as a musical community; they keep axé music vibrant by attending the concerts and festivals and by purchasing the albums. The success of axé music can also be credited to the international market itself, including the record producers, technology, and promotional world/concert tours.

Axé music provides high levels of excitement and enjoyment to a "now" generation of popular music consumers made up of both black and white audiences. In Brazil many young people are now drawn to axé music because it is a dance craze, but just as many are drawn to the cultural movement it represents. Thus, some associate the style with an "aesthetic power" that is encoded through dance, dress, and sound. Also, for some young people, axé music is used to express local, social, and ethnic identity. In its many years of development, axé music has been nurtured and has matured. Similar to other popular styles, axé music is not static and may in the future influence the creation of other innovative styles of Brazilian popular music for a newer generation of young consuming fans.

Epilogue

Afro-Brazilian identity is multidimensional and a product of old and new sociocultural/sociopolitical experiences. When I began my research I was interested in understanding this multidimensionality and the significance of "blackness"—how people of African descent have continued to reinvent and reinterpret African religious, music, and dance traditions in contemporary Brazilian culture. I soon realized that the black experience in Brazil was not self-contained but somehow extended to other areas. This extension of the black experience (in Brazil and other areas) was grounded in the heritage of West African àsé.

My research took me to many areas where I experienced the richness of Afrocentric religious and artistic traditions. In the black experience in Brazil and other African diasporic areas, the sacred often informs the secular and vice versa. This stems from the heritage of African religiosity, a tradition that influenced the sacred/secular aspects of communal life (e.g., worship, education, politics, harvesting, communal welfare, artistic innovation). Religiosity also influenced music production—rhythms, timbres, textures, nuances, vocal/instrumental styles, and dances—that energized a connective flow of the sacred/secular worlds. I believe that popular musicians such as Carlinhos Brown, Gilberto Gil, Bob Marley, Ray Charles, James Brown, Aretha Franklin, B. B. King, Fela Kuti, and many others mediate a connective flow of the sacred/secular "African worlds" in the black experiences of many areas. Understanding these experiences was "holistic knowledge" that enriched my inquiries of racial identity, sacred Candomblé religion, and secular popular music in Afro-Brazilian culture. Moreover, my experience crystallized the value of religion and popular music and also demonstrated how Afro-Brazilians are unique but linked with other African and African diasporic areas where the power and creative energy of West African àsé continue to be spread and nurtured in various ways.

Axé and the African roots of Brazilian popular music are embedded in a sacred/secular connection of religion, individual artists, Carnival organizations, music, musical instruments, drumming, dance, imagery, symbols, festive celebrations, and the richness of Afro-Brazilian culture. With its many influences, the popularity of axé is similar to a spice, a major ingredient that has given Afro-Brazilian culture its dynamic flavor.

When Africans were transported into Brazil as slaves, the power and creative energy of West African àsé began to spread, connecting the sacred and secular worlds. In Brazil this resulted in the emergence of Candomblé, a religion that has affected society on many levels. Those who practice Candomblé make lifelong commitments to serve the orixás. Candomblé shapes the way people live their lives, affecting the eating of certain foods, the wearing of special colors associated with particular orixás, and celebration of the orixás on special days of the week. Candomblé religious practices are passed down from one generation to the next. Young people learn the rituals, music, and dance associated with each orixá at an early age and eventually become the new leaders, musicians, and initiates in the Candomblé community.

In the sacred setting of the sanctum, Candomblé music is a life-giving source for communicating with the spiritual world. Moreover, the drum and drummers are catalysts for the spread of axé and blessings bestowed from the spiritual world. In the secular setting of the public space, when celebrations and festivals are pervaded with Candomblé iconography, the popular culture becomes connected in sacred/secular expressions. Candomblé themes, images, symbols, and music have been appropriated, secularized, and reinvented by popular musicians, many of whom continue to both seek blessings of sacred axé and perform in secular venues.

In a world of instantly available global communication, traditional religious and musical values are often challenged. Candomblé practitioners are confronted with difficult issues such as tourism, commercialism, and secularization of sacred rituals and music. Because Candomblé continues to be an important tradition in Brazilian culture, people in many cities use Candomblé images and symbols in all types of public celebrations. On many secular occasions it is not unusual to find people making special offerings to the orixás and dancing to Candomblé music.

Axé has gone beyond the Candomblé sanctum to become a driving force that inspires people in their daily lives and interactions. The term has been appropriated as part of local/ethnic identity, African heritage, social and political agendas, commercialism, and popular music. In Brazilian culture, the various types of appropriations of axé are ways that the sacred has become connected with the secular-consuming world outside of the Candomblé sanctum. Thus, one often hears references to Candomblé, the orixás, and axé in popular songs. The fact that axé confers luck, hope, peace, and prosperity is a major reason why Candomblé is exploited in popular culture.

In the new millennium Afro-Brazilians continue to struggle for racial equality and economic opportunity. They also use their musical talents as prospects for a brighter future. Perhaps this is the essence of the West African àsé heritage that is manifested as "axé" in the Afro-Brazilian community, to make positive things happen in the secular world. For many Afro-Brazilians the sacred (axé) has often given meaning and depth (success, survival, artistic innovation, and prosperity) to the secular experiences of everyday life.

Candomblé ceremonies normally end by celebrating Oxalá, father of all the orixás and ancestral guardian associated with peace, hope, and prosperity. In many festivals in Salvador, Filhos de Gandhi, the most prominent of the afoxé organizations, marches in processions in their symbolic turbans and white-and-blue attire carrying banners displaying the images of iconic leaders such as Zumbi, Mahatma Gandhi, and Martin Luther King, performing the ijexá rhythm derived from Candomblé. With polyrhythmic layers of atabaques, trumpets, whistles, and shakers, the music sounds like an orchestra. In the background, members of Filhos de Gandhi often wave and motion to the crowds with the blessings of axé. This book will also end by offering blessings and the axé of peace, hope, and prosperity to all.

Axé!

Notes

Introduction

1. The pronunciation of the term *axé* sounds similar to ah-shay or ah-shah.

2. More than a mere square, the Largo do Pelourinho is a place of remembrance, reflection, and celebration. During the colonial period the Pelourinho was indicative of and symbolic as the "whipping post," a place where Africans were dehumanized, tortured, and sold at auction as property to the highest bidder. Today the Largo do Pelourinho is also a place of cultural preservation, with sites such as the Casa de Jorge Amado, a museum and library that contains the books of one of Brazil's most famous novelists, and the Museu da Cidade (city museum) whose goal is to preserve the African heritage by exhibiting many artifacts from Candomblé.

3. The origin of the Palmares is uncertain, but it is estimated that it was organized in the mid-sixteenth century. The warrior and former slave known as Zumbi had a major role in the organization of the Palmares. He became the symbolic king of this quilombo community and took up arms against Brazilian enslavers. In November 1695 Zumbi was captured and decapitated and his head publicly exhibited. Even so, many Africans continued to resist slavery.

4. Crook 2005: 21.

5. See Rodrigues 1957 (1894). In this work Rodrigues explained that most Africans and mestiços were mentally deficient and should be exempt from any criminal responsibility. Also see Borges 1995: 63. Borges gives descriptive analysis of the research done by Rodrigues and other intellectuals on Afro-Brazilian culture.

6. See Needell 1995: 51–71. Needell provides a discussion on the personality of Gilberto Freyre and an analysis of *The Masters and The Slaves*.

7. See Borges 1995: 71–72.

8. Carvalho 1999: 261–95. Carvalho examines multiple black identities in Brazilian popular music.

9. See Telles (2004), Prandi 2004: 35–43, Carvalho 2003: 205–15 and 1995: 159–79, Godet and Souza (2001), Nascimento (2001) and (1992), Crook and Johnson (1999), Armstrong (2001a) and (1999), Lesser (1999), Ojo-Ade (1999), Bacelar 1999: 85–101 and (1989), Degler (1986), Ortiz (1985), Fontaine (1985), Haberly (1983), Skidmore (1994) and 1985: 11–24, Azevedo (1975), Pierson (1942), and Rodrigues (1935).

10. See Covin (2006), Hanchard (1999) and (1994), Crook and Johnson (1999), Andrews (1991), and Fernandes (1989).

11. Pitanga 1999: 38.

12. Grasse 2003: 106.

13. These ethnic groups are also associated with the Candomblé religion.

14. Some Afro-Brazilians associated with the Nagô identify themselves as Quêto, Kétou, or Kétu, which refer to Yoruba-speaking nation-states in Benin and Nigeria. Also see Parrinder 1947: 122–29 and (1961) and Garcia 1935: 21–27. Some scholars believe that, because they came from contiguous territories in Africa, many Africans shared closely related languages and could easily communicate among themselves.

Among slaves there came a gradual use of an African language known as Nagô, a term that has several grammatical forms: Nagot (French) and Nagote (feminine). The use of Nagô intensified the slaves' isolation from the white world and retarded the process of acculturation, and was one of the major reasons for the retention and preservation of African culture in Brazil.

15. In Afro-Brazilian culture the Gêge people are also known as JeJe. See Matory 2005 [Appendix B] and 1999b: 57–80, and Rodrigues (1988[1905]). According to Matory, the term *JeJe* first appeared in Brazilian documents in 1739. He also cites Nina Rodrigues as one of the early scholars that attempted to establish an etymology of the term Ewe, the name of a dialect spoken in Togo and southwestern Ghana, as the origin of the term JeJe. However, the word JeJe may have also originated from the Geng, or Gen, which describes the dialect of the Mina people of Togo and southwestern Benin.

16. Some of the scholarly sources that examine the nações and their significance to the emergence of Candomblé include Póvoas (1989), Mattoso 1988: 69–88, Santos (1976), and Lima (1971).

17. Harding 2000: 45–46, Béhague 1984: 222, and Omari (1984).

18. Personal interviews with Luz 1999, Valde 1998, Silva 1998, and Santos 1998.

19. See Matory (2005), Clarke (1983), and Landes (1947). Similar to women's roles in Africa, in Brazil women became responsible for cooking the sacred foods, caring for the altars, ornamenting the houses of worship on special holidays, and taking care of the instruction of the women and children.

20. Rowe and Schelling 1991: 122–27.

21. See Mariani 1994: 83. Mariani notes that in Angola the substitution of dancers was indicated throughout the umbigada that the Africans called semba. There were two forms, the stamping of the foot in front of the person chosen for the umbigada (semba). In Congo the invitation was made with the stamping of the feet or a quick greeting.

22. Some scholars may have relegated Afro-Brazilian cultural studies to the realm of folklore because of available publishing opportunities in folkloric journals. Early studies that fit this pattern include Carneiro (1940), Landes (1940), Ramos (1935), and Aimes (1905).

23. Also see Verger (2002 [1981]). Another important work by Pierre Verger includes his comparative study of the Yoruba orixás.

24. See Melville J. and Frances S. Herskovits, *Folk Music of Brazil: Afro-Bahian Religious Songs: Songs of African Cult Groups* (1941–42), Library of Congress/Archive of Folk Song LP AFS L13. This is a compilation of songs for the orixás of Candomblé.

25. Also see Bastide (1978).

26. See Gerard Béhague, *Afro-Brazilian Religious Music: Candomblé Songs for Salvador, Bahia (Cantigas de Candomblé)* (1977), Lyrichord LP LLST 7315. All the selections in this compilation were recorded in actual Candomblé ceremonies in Brazil by Béhague between 1967 and 1975.

27. Contemporary Portuguese and English sources on Afro-Brazilian culture and Candomblé include studies by Matory (2005), Johnson (2002), Silva (2000), Harding (2000), Voeks (1997), Braga 1999: 201–12 and (1998), Prandi (1996), Santos (1995), Wafer (1991), Pinto 1991: 70–87, Santos (1976), and Lima (1971).

28. See studies by Guilbault 1997: 31–44, Mitchell (1996), Straw (1995), Stokes (1994), and Williams and Chrisman (1993).

29. Several studies examine the historical, sociocultural, and musicological dimensions and reinvention of African traditions in African diasporic areas. See works by Feldman (2006), Hagedorn (2001), Vélez (2000), Matory 1999a: 72–103, Kubik (1999), Simmons 1999: 158–69, Browning (1998), Small (1998), Palmer 1998: 22–25, Southern (1997), Mukuna 1997: 239–48, Averill (1997), Fleurant (1996), Cesaire (1995), Cornelius (1989), Murphy (1994), Conniff and Davis (1994), Wilcken and Augustin (1992), Waterman 1990: 367–79, Meadows 1993: 189–207, Brandon (1993), Holloway (1990), Knight and Bilby 1993: 243–75, Anderson (1990), Maultsby 1990: 185–210, Gates (1988), Stuckey (1987), Mason (1985), González-Wippler (1985) and (1973), Deren (1983 [1953]), Raboteau (1978), Levine (1977), Neal (1971), Herskovits (1958 [1941]), and Waterman 1952: 207–18.

30. See Morris 1999: 187–200, Kirshenblatt-Gimblett 1995: 367–80, and Hanson 1989: 987–99. Also see Firth 2000: 305–22 and Dugany 1996: 176–92.

31. Studies that focus on globalization, musical borrowing and appropriation, fusion, and hybridization include Crook (2005), Monson (2000), Perrone and Dunn (2001), Roberts (1998), Sansone 1996: 197–219, and Canclini (1995).

32. See Peterson, Vásquez, and Williams 2001: 16. Also see Vásquez and Marquardt (2003), Appadurai (1997), Bhabha (1994), and Rex and Mason (1986).

33. See Matory (2005), Mann and Bay (2001), Asante (1988), Floyd 1999: 2, Thornton (1998), Gilroy (1993), Rawley (1981), and Curtin (1969) and 1976: 595–627.

34. See Loza (2003), Schechter (1999), Salman and Dam (1996), Sansone 1997: 457–92 and 1996: 197–219, Rowe and Schelling 1991: 122–27, Sulsbruck (1987), Klein (1986), and Pescatello (1975).

35. Abiodun 1994: 71 and Vega 1999: 47. Abiodun and Vega use the term "religio-aesthetic" to describe the survival and manifestations of West African àsé in the African diaspora.

36. See Terry (1934) and Stearns (1958). Also see Cavin 1975: 4–27, and Peretti (1997).

37. See Gillespie (1979). Also see Averill 1997: 58, which discusses the emergence of "Vodou-Jazz" in Haiti in the 1940s.

38. For a discussion on the blues, spirituality, and sacred/secular issues see Oakley (1997), Prévos (1996), Spencer (1993), Calt, (1994), Finn (1992), Cone (1991 [1972]), Epstein (1977), and Garon (1971).

39. Although first recorded in the 1950s, Waters's recording of "Got My Mojo Working" performed at the 1960 Newport Jazz Festival has become a classic. "Voodoo Chile" is from Hendrix's third album, *Electric Ladyland* (1968), Polydor B000R25XJ6.

40. B. B. King's incorporation of the phrase, "Let's Go To Church," is recorded in a popular song titled "I Like To Live The Love," featured on the album *Bobby Bland and B. B. King I Like To Live The Love* (1993), MCAD-20379.

Chapter 1. Sacred/Secular Influences:
The Reinvention of West African Àsé in Brazil

1. Elmina, also known as Fort São Jorge da Mina, was the first fort constructed by the Portuguese for trade and a place to house African slaves. This fort was the headquarters of the Portuguese in what was known as the Gold Coast until its conquest by the Dutch in the seventeenth century.

2. Several scholarly studies provide a detailed history and analysis of the Yoruba

people and cultural traditions. See Apter (1992), Smith (1976), Opefeyitimi 1975: 15–30, Bascom (1969), Johnson (1969), and Parrinder (1961) and 1947: 122–29. Also see Waterman 2000: 169. Waterman asserts that the Yoruba people were also known as "Yariba." This particular term appeared in written form in the 1700s in the Hausa-Fulani clerics' historical account of the Oyo kingdom.

3. Many of the philosophical concepts, beliefs, and practices observed in Yoruba religion are examined in Dolin 2001: 69–82, Drewal 1999: 143–74, Donkor (1997), Mbiti (1990), Karade (1994), and Lawson (1984). Also see Simpson (1980), Ikenga-Mueth 1982: 11–24, and McKenzie 1976: 189–207.

4. In Candomblé this form of ancestral masking is often referred to as Bàbá Egún.

5. See Adegbite 1988: 18–19. The Yoruba religion was founded in the city of Ife, which is believed to be the place where the creation of Earth began. Also see Greene 1996: 122–38 and Idowu (1963). In myth Olódùmarè is also imagined as being the creator and chief source of "spiritual power" that he bestows upon the ancestral spirits.

6. Walker 1990: 108–11.

7. See McKenzie 1976: 189–297 and Gleason (1971). Also see Lawson 1984: 55–58. In Yoruba religion the pantheon of òrìsàs is extensive and may include ancestral spirits that are specific to certain shrines and places of worship.

8. Other names for the trickster/guardian include Esu, Eshu, Legba, Esu-Elegbara, and Eshu-Ellegua.

9. Also see MacLean 1969: 37, Drewal 1992: 178, and Hock-Smith (1978). In past research some scholars have noted that mature women are often referred to as *àjé* and are recognized in their communities as awon ìyá wa (our mothers). Àjé has been translated in the literature as witchcraft or witch. Scholars have noted that, unlike the English connotation, a mature woman who is described as "witch" is not necessarily either antisocial or the personification of evil. Instead, she is regarded as an important member of the community and is shown respect, affection, and deference. In my own research in West Africa, the locals often referred to mature women as "mama" and "spiritual mama."

10. Also see DjeDje 2000: 159, McKenzie 1976: 190, and Lindon 1990: 206.

11. See Adegbite 1988: 15–26 and Thieme (1969) and 1940: 359–62. In Yoruba religion there are also musical myths that pervade about certain drums. For example, one myth is that the ancestral spirits created drums. These include the Ìgbìn created by Obàtálá, Ìpèsè by Òrúnmìlà, Bàtá by Èsù, Ògìda by Ògún, and Àgbá-Obalùfòn by Obalùfòn.

12. See Ajayi 1994: 183–202.

13. This album also features performances by Brazilian percussionist Airto Moriera and Mexican American guitarist Carlos Santana.

14. For a scholarly analysis of JùJú music and Afro-Beat see Tenaille (2002), Waterman (1992), Collins (1992), Stewart (1992), and Alaja-Browne 1989: 55–72.

15. Studies that examine Central African history, slave trade, and religion include Sweet (2003), Heywood (2002), MacGaffey (1986), and Vansina 1962: 369–90.

16. In Candomblé religion some practitioners often join mythologies and revere both Zambi (Central Africa) and Olódùmarè (West Africa) as Supreme Beings.

17. Sweet 2003: 140–54.

18. Ibid.

19. One of the earliest studies to include a discussion of syncretism in Afro-Brazilian religious culture is Rodrigues (1897). Rodrigues refers to the concealing of the African spirits behind the faces of the Catholic Saints as an "illusion of conversion." He stresses that although the Catholic priests attempted to convert the Africans by teaching them Catholic beliefs and practices, they received the "impression" that Africans had accepted a Catholic type of religiosity. For a discussion of syncretism in Afro-Brazilian culture see Greenfield and Droogers (2001).

20. Personal interview with Silva in 1998. Also see Ferretti 2001: 99–111. According to Ferretti, the word Caboclo is derived from the indigenous Tupi word kari'boka, which translates to "descended from the white man." Scholars are uncertain as to whether the term was part of Brazilian vernacular during the mid-eighteenth century.

21. Ferretti 2001: 99–111 and Santos (1995).

22. Chapter 2 of this book includes more discussion of the ijexá rhythm.

23. Cleuza, the leader of the Gantois, passed away sometime during my initial study of Candomblé. The daughter of Mãe Menininha, one of the most legendary leaders in Candomblé history, her death was widely covered by the local media.

24. Personal interviews with Silva in 1998 and Luz in 1999. Some scholarly sources that focus on the roles of women in early Candomblé religion include Wimberly 1998: 74–87, Clarke 1993: 97–113, Carneiro 1940: 271–78, and Landes (1947) and 1940: 261–70.

25. It should be noted that the prefixes of the terms *iyalorixá* and *babalorixá* stem from Yoruba terminology ìyá (mother) and baba (father).

26. Practitioners must undergo an extensive seven-year initiation period before they are allowed to organize their own terreiro.

27. See Béhague 1984: 247. In his study of Candomblé, Béhague provided some detail of a Gêge (Ewe/Fon) funeral rite, known as azeri, that is similar to the Yoruba axêaxê.

28. Personal interview with Marques in 1998.

29. Personal interview with Vincente in 2002.

30. Personal interviews with Luz in 1999 and Santos in 2002.

31. This particular ceremony occurred on October 22, 1998.

32. Personal interview with De Souza in 2002.

33. Pemba is a powder made from chalk, coconut palms, and two types of seeds, fava de oridō and nanoscada.

34. In my own experience this is perhaps an accurate myth. Initially conducting research in Salvador in 1998, I did leave a ceremony at approximately midnight, before all of the rituals had ended. While returning to my home in the Pelourinho district I was violently robbed by several young Afro-Brazilian males (nonpractitioners). Although this experience may seem negative, months later several of the young males who had participated in the robbery learned of my research on Candomblé religion and Afro-Brazilian culture, apologized for their actions, and welcomed me into the community.

35. Personal interviews with Santos and Cassiano in 2002. According to Santos and Cassiano, Marujo is similar to Exú, the trickster/guardian in the orixá pantheon. Martin's role as a mediator is similar to the spirits Da Roda and Xorokquê, who are

believed to control the trickery of Exú. Although Marujo has spiritual qualities that are similar to the Exú this particular spirit is not a possessor of axé. The practitioners of the Tera Jima terreiro only associate axé energy with the orixas.

36. Personal interview with Motta in 1998.

37. Béhague 2000: 276.

38. Some Portuguese and English sources that examine the major facets of Umbanda include Hale 2001: 213–29, Brown 1999: 213–36 and (1994), Trindade (1991), Brown and Brick 1987: 74–95, Concone (1987), Figger (1983), Nunes (1966), and Camargo (1961).

39. Personal interview with De Souza in 2002.

40. See Silverstein 1995: 141.

41. Fita ribbons are worn around the wrist in honor of Senhor do Bonfim, who is syncretized with the orixá Oxalá/Jesus Christ. When tying on the ribbon, one makes three wishes that are believed to come true in the two months or more that it takes the ribbon to fall off. One must allow the ribbon to fall off by natural wear and tear; cutting it off is said to bring bad luck.

42. Personal interview with Badaró in 1998.

43. Personal interview with Murisoea in 1998.

44. Personal interview with Pain in 1998.

45. Crook 2005: 29 and Carvalho 1994.

46. Personal interview with Silva in 1998.

Chapter 2. From the Sacred to the Secular: Popularizing Candomblé Rhythms

1. Early studies that focus on music in Candomblé religion include Pinto 1997: 11–33, 1991b: 70–87, and (1991a), Lavergne and Pessoa de Barros 1986: 25–39, Béhague 1984: 222–54 and 1977: 4–14, Oderigo 1975: 178–231, Merriam 1963: 98–135 and 1956: 53–67, and Herskovits 1944: 477–92.

2. Each terreiro has a unique way of communicating with and celebrating the orixás. In many terreiros that I observed, after the initiates danced and experienced spirit possession they often embraced each member of the audience as a sign of peace and love. In other terreiros, after the initiates danced and experienced spirit possession they ate the sacred foods of the orixás. In both instances, music was continuous.

3. Personal interview with Valde in 1998.

4. Personal interview with Pain in 1998. Although Pain offered an opinion about communicating with the spiritual world without music, he emphasized that his response in no way negated his devotion or dedication to the religion or the way that music is performed in the ceremonies.

5. Personal interview with Lúcia in 1998.

6. Personal interview with Roberto in 1998.

7. See Béhague 1984: 229–37 and Herskovits 1944: 485–86. Also see Shapiro 1995: 828–47.

8. Also see Lo-Bamijoko 1984: 7. The Candomblé term *ojá* may have originated from a similar term used in West African Nigerian culture. According to Lo-Bamijoko, a similar term "oja" is used in Nigeria among the Igbo people as the name given to

various types of flutelike instruments used in initiation, praise singing, and as talking instruments.

9. Most of the practitioners were uncertain as to a universal spelling or an identification of the ijexá rhythm. Other practitioners identified the rhythm as gexá, jexá, and Congo-Angola.

10. Also see Béhague 1984: 237–43. Béhague provided a detailed analysis of the xirê held in many terreiros in Salvador. He described the ceremony as a "generalized public ritual" open to all, including outsiders (both locals and tourists).

11. In many terreiros the amount of songs sung for an orixá ranged from approximately seven to twenty-one. Most of these songs are short and repetitive in length.

12. Some terreiros also incorporate Central African languages such as Kimbundu, but in the terreiros I observed most initiated practitioners used Yoruba in their ceremonial rituals.

13. See Music Example 1.

14. The etymology of the word afoxé has been researched by a few scholars. For example, Peter Fryer 2000: 24 believes that the word stems from the Yoruba *àfòse*, a term used to describe a priest who can foretell the future. In this sense this type of priest may be similar to that of the babalaô in many Yoruba communities that has a role of forecasting one's future through the process of Ifá divination. Also see Larry Crook 2005: 136–38. Crook explains that usage of afoxé may be recent, but the groups themselves have maintained a tradition that stretches back to the nineteenth century. He notes that, in the mid-1930s, Brazilian journalist and ethnographer Edison Carneiro suggested that afoxé was among secular dances performed in the Bahian Carnival. But Rodger Bastide (in Crook's translation) described the afoxé as a recreational manifestation of Candomblé during Carnival.

15. Moura 2001: 165–66.

16. Crook 1993: 92–94.

17. The Filhos de Gandhi recently received international exposure through film. *The Sons of Gandhi*, a 2005 documentary directed by Lino de Almeida, covers the creation and development of the Filhos de Gandhi and shows how the values of Mahatma Gandhi inspired them. In Portuguese with English subtitles, the documentary places special emphasis on how men of all ages in Afro-Brazilian communities struggle against racism and marginalization. In December 2005 this documentary premiered in the United States as part of the Special Brazil segment at the 13th annual African Diaspora Film Festival (ADFF) in New York.

18. Personal interview with De Souza in 2002.

19. The song "Filhos de Gandhi" is recorded on the album *Gil & Jorge* (1975), Polygram Records B000046KT.

20. Filhos de Gandhi also recorded an album titled *Afoxé* (1997) that is a compilation of devotional songs honoring several orixás and featuring the ijexá rhythm. This album was sponsored by the Fundação Cultural do Estado da Bahia.

21. Performances of Filhos de Gandhi may incorporate beaded types instruments of various sizes.

22. Cohen 2000: 19.

23. *Presents Candombless* (2005), Tratore Records 7898369063065.

24. Personal interview with Almeida in 1997.

25. Personal interview with Lemos in 1998.

26. Personal interview with Badaró in 1998.

27. See Tenser 2003: 110, Tarasti 1995: 304, Béhague 1994: 155, and Wright 1992: 35–37. Elements of Candomblé music have also been incorporated in art music. For example, the noted Brazilian composer Heitor Villa-Lobos (1887–1959), in *Canções típicas brasileiras* (*Typical Brazilian Songs*), a work composed in 1919, incorporated musical and stylistic elements from Candomblé, represented in a selection titled "Xangô." Also, in 1968 José Maceda (1917–2004), a Filipino musician and ethnomusicologist, spent a year studying Candomblé music and conducting research in terreiros of Salvador. He was so impressed with his experience that he performed Candomblé music in a classical music concert held at Universidade Federal da Bahia.

28. Balé Folclórico was founded in Salvador by Walson Botelho and Ninho Reis. The goal of the company is to present, in music and dance, the folklore and popular culture of Brazil. Their repertoire consists of music and dance from Candomblé, capoeira, and samba de roda.

Chapter 3. Axé Embodiment in Brazilian Popular Music: Sacred Themes, Imagery, and Symbols

1. See Wilder 1976: 1–2. Wilder presents a theoretical notion of "theopoetic" and sacred imagery that he believes can influence faith and confession.

2. There are several scholarly sources that examine the mythology and spiritual attributes of the orixás. See Verger 2002 [1981], Montes 2001: 334–45, Silva (1995), Barnes (1989), Gleason (1987) and (1971), Mason (1985), and Santos (1975).

3. See Patai 1988: 68–70. There are many theories surrounding the imagery of Yemanjá as a Marian figure. One such theory is that the fusion of Catholicism and Candomblé religion produced a "multifaced" Mary. Females in Salvador particularly have identified with the image of Mary as poor: her husband was a craftsman, they had no home in which to bear her child, and they migrated from place to place. Eventually this image was replaced with Yemanjá, who became the culmination of these experiences. She became the symbol of motherhood, and was also considered to be a great and divine being.

4. The orixá Omolú is also known by the names Obaluaiye, Xapanã, and Sappona.

5. The orixá Nana is also known as Nanan and Buruku.

6. Oxalá, the father of all the orixás, is also known by the names Oxaguian (syncretized with the adolescent Jesus Christ) and Oxalufon (syncretized with the mature Jesus Christ).

7. The Yoruba regard twins as spiritual children who can bring either double prosperity or double trouble to a family.

8. Personal interview with Azevedo in 1999.

9. Personal interview with Luz in 1999.

10. Here I refer to Bantu terms (kandombele, kandombile, kandomide, kulomba-ku-domba-a, and kò-dómb-éd-à) that make reference to prayer and veneration discussed in the introduction of this book.

11. For discussions about the origins of the terms *Candomblé* and *samba*, see Harding 2000: 45, Fryer 2000: 102–3, Mariani 1994: 86–88, Raphael 1990: 73–83, and Kubik 1979: 18.

12. See Moura (1983). Also see Guillermoprieto 1991: 22–29.

13. See Turner 1942: 55–67. Also see Mattoso 1988: 69–88.

14. The name jùjú was coined by mandolin player Tunde King in the late 1930s.

15. See Alaja-Browne 1989: 55–72. Also see Waterman 2000: 175–76, (1992), and 1990: 367–79.

16. Also see Carvalho 1999: 262–63. Carvalho has done extensive research on black identities in Brazil, and suggests that one of the goals of Brazilian popular music is to appeal to the commercial music industry, which tends to de-ritualize music from religious and ethnic communities by transforming ideas from sacred rituals into aesthetic elements. The lyrics of popular songs are most often secular, but can also have sacred qualities that express love, admiration of a specific deity, emotional states, desires, fantasies, and abstract ethical and philosophical issues.

17. See *Cidade do Salvador* (2002), Universal B00006LVPY. This album includes a song dedicated to the orixá Iansã. Also see *Gilberto Gil/Maria Bethânia/Caetano Veloso* (1995), Iris Music B000005SLF. This album includes a song about the orixá Yemanjá.

18. Many of Caymmi's songs are compiled in a seven- disc set, *Amor E Mar* (2001), EMI International.

19. Also see Perrone 1989: 62.

20. The song "A Deusa dos Orixás" is recorded in the album *Os Samba* (1989) and produced by David Byrne.

21. The bread of life is found in the New Testament, John 6:51.

22. "Embala Eu" ("Surround Me") is on *Yelé Brazil* (1994), Hemisphere Records.

23. "O Encanto do Gantois" is also on *Os Samba* (1989).

24. Personal interview with Luz in 1999.

25. Personal interview with Silva in 1998.

26. Personal interview with Ramos in 1998.

27. Personal Interview with Murisoea in 1998.

28. The song "Nação" is on *Com Vida* (1995), Hemisphere Records.

29. The song "Aldeia de Okarimbé" is on *Os Samba* (1989).

30. The television series *Tenda dos Milagres* is based on a novel by Jorge Amado.

31. "Santos Catolicos e Candomblé" is on *Trilhas: Maria Maria/Ultimo Trem* (2004), EMI International.

32. *Elegibô* (1990), Mango Records B000003QJX.

33. See Woodward 2000: 87–88.

34. "Sol da Liberdade" and "Dara" are on Mercury's *Sol da Liberdade* (2000), BMG International B00004TW4X.

35. De Silva 1989: 58–59 and Cone 1970: 56.

Chapter 4. The Sacred/Secular Popularity of Drums and Drummers

1. For studies that focus on the drum and drumming traditions in African and African diasporic areas, see Crook 2005: 112–27 and 1999: 219–223, Hagedorn (2001), Vélez (2000), Monson 2000: 329–52, Simmons 1999: 158–69, Fleurant (1996), Lindsay (1996), Kinni-Olusanyin 1994: 29–38, Dagan (1993), Wilcken and Augustin (1992), Adgebite 1988: 15–26, Béhague 1984: 222–54 and 1977: 4–14, Martins (1983), Nodal 1983: 157–77, Howard (1967), and Herskovits 1944: 477–92.

2. Performative power is a concept that Drewal (1992: 291) explains in her study of West African àsé as the power of accomplishment: the power to get things done, and the power to make things happen. In this chapter I use the term to describe the

accomplishments of the many musicians in Candomblé religion empowered with the creative energy of àsé/axé who through their performances continually make positive things happen in the sacred/secular experiences of devoted practitioners. For discussion of performative power and aché in Cuban Santería, see Hagedorn (2001: 212–14, 232).

3. Although in this discussion I am primarily using the art of drumming as the major part of a spiritual lexicon, singing, dancing, and spirit possession also enhance the musical vocabulary of the orixás.

4. Personal interview with Carlos in 1998.

5. Marques is a member of Ilê Oya Geí, a terreiro located in São Martins in Salvador.

6. Over a period of one year beginning in 1998 I conducted several interviews with Marques.

7. Also see Béhague 1984: 225–26. Béhague described the alabê as a master drummer who in most terreiros has seniority over the other musicians. Although the master musician has the responsibility to play the rum, during musical performances he may play any drum he wishes. This is also an accurate description of my observations of Candomblé music and musicians.

8. Personal interview with De Souza in 2002.

9. Personal interview with Nascimento in 1998.

10. Personal interview with Pain in 1998.

11. Marques was also a skilled dancer. In many of the lessons he would demonstrate the choreographic movements of the orixás to demonstrate how dance and the drum rhythms correspond.

12. Thomas 2000: 276, Gerstin 1998: 385–86, and Merriam 1964: 123–44.

13. Personal interview with Ramos in 1998.

14. Concerned that Candomblé music be preserved, in 1963 Murisoea decided to record songs from the Candomblé repertoires for a local cultural foundation in Salvador.

15. Personal interview with Carlos in 1998.

16. Personal interviews with Marques in 1998 and 1999.

17. Personal interview with Lemos in 1998.

18. Personal interviews with Junior and Rios in several segments in 1998, 1999, and 2002. Both musicians were exceptionally talented and their knowledge of Candomblé and popular music greatly benefited my research.

19. Personal interview with Junior in 1998.

20. Personal interview with Lúcia in 1998.

21. See Spencer 1989: 1–16. Theomusicology is a theologically informed discipline that attempts to examine sacred influences in secular music.

22. Ibid.

Chapter 5. Secular Impulses:
Dancing to the Beats of Different Drummers

1. Tirro 1993: 433. One of the major reasons Roach's performance was banned in South Africa was that the composition included the song "Tears for Johannesburg" that expressed sentiments about apartheid.

2. For academic studies that focus on Afro-Brazilian social movements, see

Garcia (2006), Covin (2006), Hanchard (1999) and (1994), Butler (1998), and Nogueira (1985).

3. Many academic studies have examined the sociocultural and musicological impacts of the blocos afro organizations in Afro-Brazilian culture. See Crook 2005: 217–99 and 1993: 90–108, Dunn 1992: 11–20, and Perrone 1992: 42–50.

4. The popularity of Ilê Aiyê was boosted by the album *Refavela* (1977), on which Gilberto Gil included the song "Ilê Aiyê." In 1999, Ilê Aiyê made its New York debut at the Damrosch Park Bandshell as part of Lincoln Center's Out of Doors concert series. For a review of Ilê Aiyê's New York concert, see Pareles (2000).

5. Lima 2001: 223–29, Crook 1993: 98, and Perrone 1992: 46.

6. Some of the most recent sources that focus on Olodum include Armstrong 2001: 177–91, Rodrigues 1999: 43–51 and 1996: 43–51, Schaeber 1997: 145–60, Dantas (1994), and Hayter-Hames 1992: 30–31.

7. For academic sources that focus on bloco Timbalada, see Lima 2001: 220–32 and 1997: 161–80. According to Lima, Candeal Pequeno was formerly the property of a wealthy family of free Africans who had come to the area to search for expatriated family members. Unsuccessful in their search, they acquired the land and organized a Candomblé terreiro dedicated to the orixá Ogum, the Yoruba deity of iron, represented by a stone brought from the coast of Africa. Practitioners residing in Candeal Pequeno identify themselves as direct descendents of this African family and continue to guard the stone.

8. Also see Hill 2004: 12–19.

9. See Vidigal 1996: 12–15. According to Vidigal, Bob Marley visited Rio de Janeiro in the 1980s, and suggested that samba and reggae were similar because they stemmed from African roots.

10. Caetano Veloso made the first reference to reggae music in a Brazilian song ("Nine Out of Ten," in the album *Transa*, 1972). He and Gilberto Gil, who had heard the emerging style while in exile in London, became the first nationally known artists to record, perform, and promote the style. In Salvador the first record completely dedicated to reggae was *Reggae da Saudade*, released in 1972 by Jorge Alfredo and Chico Evangelista.

11. For discussion of musical hybridity in Brazil, Africa, and African diasporic areas, see Crook 2005: 271–99, Erlmann 1996: 467–87, and Lipsitz (1994). These studies provide a celebratory reading of musical hybridity and artistic production by a vast range of artists who have united in a new kind of politics.

12. The texture and sound of switches used by Olodum in place of drumsticks are similar to the agidavis used by Candomblé musicians.

13. See Galinsky: 2002: 201, Crook 2001: 237–36, and McGowan and Pessanha 1998: 126.

14. Crook 2005: 281.

15. Sansone 2001: 136–60. Sansone was formerly the coordinator of a graduate program called S.A.M.B.A. (Sócio-Antropologia da Música Bahiana [Socio-Anthropology of Music in Bahia]). Sansone also worked with A Cor da Bahia (The Color of Bahia), a program for research on racial relations, culture, and black identity in Bahia. Together with a group of scholars from this program, Sansone and Jocélino Teles dos Santos coedited a volume of essays titled *Ritmos em trânsito* (*Rhythms in Transit*) (1997), which examines the influence of African American and Jamaican music in Brazil in different local contexts.

16. See full interview in Hayter-Hames 1992: 30.

17. Oya is a West African deity that many Afro-Brazilians regard as the orixá Iansã.

18. The songs "Canto Pro Mar" and "Toque de Timbaleiro" are both on the Timbalada album *Millennium* (1998), PolyGram 538-218-2. "Mãe Oya" is recorded on *Brazilian Collection A-Z* (1998), PolyGram B000060GK.

19. "Caminho" is recorded on Ilê Aiyê's album *Canto Negro* (2003), Warner Brasil B000CRTSZO.

Chapter 6. Say It Loud! I'm Black and I'm Proud: Popular Music and Axé Embodiment in Bahian Carnival/Ijexá

1. See Lawal (1996) and Drewal and Drewal (1983).

2. There are several studies that focus on celebrations and Carnival that relate to musical performance, black identity, creative play, cultural performances, and secular ritual. Some studies have also focused on Carnival with paradigms of class, gender, local, regional, and national identities, and conflicts. See Mason (1999), Nunley and McCarty (1999), Brown 1999: 149–57, Averill 1999: 126–91, (1997) and 1994: 217–47, Kinzer (1990), Guillermoprieto (1990), Lent (1990), Parker (1991), Moore and Myerhoff (1977), Hill (1972), Kertzer (1988), Napier (1986), Spitzer (1986), Crowley (1984), MacAloon (1984), Farber 1983: 33–34, and Turner and Turner 1982: 201–19.

3. Moura 2001: 161–76. In addition, other Portuguese and English academic sources examine the many facets of Bahian Carnival, popular music consumption, and ethnic identity; see Armstrong 2001: 177–91 and 1999: 139–58, Godi 1997: 73–96, Fischer 1996, Crook 1993: 90–108, Dunn 1992: 11–20, Perrone 1992: 42–50, Crowley (1984), and Risério (1981).

4. See Da Matta (1980).

5. Two recent documentaries directed by Bahian native Carolina Morares-Liu serve as educational and reference sources for exploring Bahian Carnival and the significant roles that the blocos afro and afoxés have played in revitalizing and politicizing the celebrations. In the short film *Bloco Afro and Afoxé: Afro-Brazilian Carnival as a Political and Religious Stage* (2003), Morares-Liu presents a descriptive analysis of the role that local community-based groups have played in the politics of re-Africanization in Bahian Carnival. Included in the film are segments featuring artists such as Gilberto Gil and Daniela Mercury. *The Festive Land: Carnaval in Bahia* (2001) examines the popularity of Bahian Carnival as an expressive showcase of the uniqueness of Bahia. In this film are musical performances, dances, expressions of Candomblé imagery and symbols, and scenes of people enjoying the celebrations.

6. See Risério (1981).

7. During my initial stay in Brazil in 1998–99, the Brazilian réis fluctuated several times from approximately $1.35 to $1.50 per U.S. dollar.

8. Fryer 2000: 23 and Dunn 1992: 13.

9. See Brown 1999: 156.

10. See Margareth Menezes, *Afropopbrasileiros* (2002), Universal B00006BC6D. This is a compilation of Brazilian fusion music. Included is the popular song "Dandalunda."

11. "Ó que coisa bonita" is a traditional song; the locals and church personnel I spoke with did not credit a composer and lyricist.

12. Emtursa, the local department of tourism, and some businesses provided sponsorship to publish the local Carnival guidebooks.

13. See Fountain (1998). The Interfaith Pilgrimage of the Middle Passage was carried out by approximately fifty people comprised of blacks, whites, and Asians from various religious, political, and social organizations across the United States.

14. See www.bahia-online.net.

15. See Terrell 2004: 29.

16. News releases of Daniela Mercury's criticism by the Catholic church can be found on several newswires and websites such as CNN International, Associated Press, and Reuters.

17. Personal interviews with Cassiano in 1998 and 1999.

18. Personal interviews with Murisoea in 1998 and 1999.

Chapter 7. Stylizing Axé as Brazilian Popular Music

1. See Campbell and Brody 1999: 7–8.

2. Tinhorão 1991: 230.

3. Hanchard: 1994: 114 and Magaldi 1999: 316.

4. Numerous academic studies examine the origins of jazz and rock and roll in African American culture. See Porter (1997), Gioia (1997), Kamen 1972: 5–16, Eisen (1969), and Longstreet (1965).

5. See Filho and Herschmann 2003: 352. Also see Guerreiro 2000: 1136. Filho and Herschmann note that some popular musicians have been openly critical about axé music. For example, they cite Dori Caymmi as having commented that axé music was rubbish and a backward step of one hundred years in terms of Brazilian music. Moreover, his father, Dorival Caymmi, the popular musician many regard as the father of Bahian music, also commented that what was being produced in Bahia was not really Brazilian music.

6. See Carvalho 1999: 285–87.

7. For a discussion of Daniela Mercury see Gilman 1997: 40–43.

8. See Guerreiro 2000: 137. According to Guerreiro, in Salvador axé musicians were often referred to as *axezeiros*. Also see Filho and Herschmann 2003: 257n4.

9. Some recent sources that focus on Sangalo's role as an axé music performer include Weinoldt 1998: 45–47 and Gomes 2004: 27.

10. Guibault 1993: 37, 150. Also cited in Firth 2000: 312–13.

11. Academic studies on funk music in Brazil include Sansone 2001: 136–60, Hershmann (1997), Veiga, 1996: 88–92, Yúdice 1997: 24–29, and Vianna (1988). In Brazil the term "funk" began to be used in the 1970s to refer to contemporary black popular music imported from the United States. Also see Risério 1999: 249–59 and (1981). In Salvador funk was understood to mean imported, electronically mixed dance music from the United States and Europe. In the lower-income communities of Rio de Janeiro, which boasted one of the largest funk scenes, the music was Brazilianized mainly through dancing sessions.

12. Margareth Menezes is one of the innovators of axé music who has influenced a new generation of Afro-Brazilian music. For a source that discusses Menezes' talents as performer, see Pessanha 1991: 46.

13. See Margareth Menezes, *Elegibô* (1990), Mango B000003QJX.

14. *Kindala* (1991), Mango B000003QKV.

15. See Terrell 2004: 29. Also see Gilman 1996: 41–44.

16. See Galinsky 1996: 120–49. Pagode is another style of samba that developed in Rio de Janeiro in the mid-1970s and became a major musical movement in the 1980s. The innovators of pagode samba include a group of musicians associated with the Carnival bloco Cacique de Ramos, who started performing samba in informal sessions for pagode parties. During these performances, the musicians began to add new stylistic features such as new percussive hand-drumming techniques instead of drumsticks, and the use of the banjo instead of the cavaquinho. In addition, the musicians incorporated new percussion instruments such as the tan tan, a type of drum that was smaller in size, lighter in sound, and more portable that the traditional surdo bass drum.

17. Personal interviews with Almeida in 1997.

18. Aos Mestres com Carinho: Homenagem a Dolores Duran (2005), Trama B000BEZ002.

19. Personal interview with Izzy Gordon in July 2006. Sincere gratitude goes to Ms. Jana Correa, whose assistance and dedication made this interview possible.

20. Interview with Jana Correa and members of BRASA in October 2005.

21. "Alegria da Cidade" is recorded on Menezes' *Elegibô* (1990).

Glossary

adarrum—A rapid rhythm used to summon all the orixás simultaneously.

adjá—A bell used to summon orixás.

afoxé—An Afro-Bahian Carnival group that dances and performs music derived from Candomblé ritual music.

agidavis—Drumsticks.

agogô—A musical instrument similar to a cowbell, consisting of one or two bells of different sizes, played with a metal stick.

aiyé—In Yoruba mythology, the tangible world of the living.

alabê—Chief/master drummer.

àsé—A spiritual power and energy that is said to exist in West African Yoruba religion.

atabaques—A corps of drums (rum, rumpi, lê) used in Candomblé.

avaninha—A processional rhythm performed in Candomblé ceremonies.

Axé Opô Afonjá—One of the oldest Candomblé terreiros (houses of worship) in Salvador.

Axêaxê—A ceremonial rite given in honor of the deceased.

axé—A spiritual power and energy said to exist in Candomblé religion. Also, a style of popular music in Brazil.

axogun—A protector of a Candomblé terreiro (house of worship).

babalaô—In the Yoruba religion of West Africa, a person who mediates between humans and the spiritual world.

babalorixá—A leader of a Candomblé terreiro (house of worship), also known as "saint father" or pai de santo.

baiano, **baiana**—Afro-Brazilians in Salvador.

balanganda—Silver charm worn by many Afro-Brazilian women in Salvador.

bàtá—A drum believed to have been created by the orixá Exú.

batuque—An Afro-Brazilian music and secular dance form observed as early as the eighteenth century. Also, a generic name for Afro-Brazilian drumming and dances; a type of Afro-Brazilian religion; and a type of drum used in jongo.

blocos afro—Community-based Carnival organizations from Salvador.

bossa nova—An urban middle class musical genre that emerged in Rio de Janeiro in the late 1950s.

bravum—A processional rhythm performed in Candomblé ceremonies.

Caboclo—Native American spirits that are celebrated in Candomblé ceremonies.

Candomblé—An Afro-Brazilian religion based on the worship of a Supreme Being known as Olódùmarè, who rules through lesser deities known as orixás.

capoeira—An Afro-Brazilian martial art/dance brought by Bantu slaves from Angola.

carimbó—An Afro-Brazilian song and circle dance from Pará, dating from the nineteenth century. Couples take turns soloing in the center of the circle.

carnival ijexá—Performances based on Candomblé rhythms during Carnival in Salvador.

cavaquinho—A small guitarlike instrument used in Brazilian popular and folk music.

charutos—Cigars used as healing agents in Caboclo ceremonies and in the manifestations of Native American spirits.

Congo-Angola—An ethnic group of Central African ancestry in Salvador.

contra-rum—A medium-sized drum used in many Angolan Candomblé terreiros (houses of worship).

cuíca—A small friction drum that is constructed with a thin stick inside attached to the drumhead. In performance a drummer normally rubs the stick with a moistened cloth while applying pressure to the drumhead to produce squeaking sounds.

despacho—A special offering made to the orixá Exú.

Didá—An Afro-Brazilian female percussion organization in Salvador.

Egúngún—In Yoruba ceremonies, masked dancers who are believed to be the reincarnation of ancestors.

entoto—A square or star-shaped stone marker placed in the middle of the floor in most Candomblé terreiros (houses of worship).

Exú—The trickster/guardian orixá who is often linked with the devil.

figa—A good luck charm constructed to resemble a clenched fist.

filha de santo—A female initiate in Candomblé.

filho de santo—A male initiate in Candomblé.

Filhos de Gandhi (Sons of Gandhi)—A popular all-male Carnival organization in Salvador.

fita—A ribbon worn around the wrist as a symbol of good luck.

fricote—A song form that combines popular music elements from ijexá and reggae.

gan—A single-bell agogô.

Gantois—One of the oldest Candomblé terreiros (houses of worship) in Salvador.

Gêge—Ethnic groups of West African Ewe/Fon ancestry in Salvador. The Gêge are also known as JeJe.

girô—A Caboclo healing ceremony.

grave—The low tones produced by the rum.

Iansã—The orixá associated with St. Barbara. Also known as Oya.

Ijexá—In Salvador, an ethnic group of Yoruba ancestry with roots in present-day southeast Benin. Also, ijexá is a rhythm used in Candomblé ceremonies for the orixás Oxum, Yemanjá, and Oxalá.

Ilê Aiyê—One of the most famous Carnival organizations in Salvador.

Ilê—A Yoruba word meaning "house."

initiates—Sons and daughters of a Candomblé terreiro (house of worship) who are trained by the leaders.

irmandades—Special Afro-Brazilian religious organizations.

ìyá 'lù—A Yoruba term that denotes "mother or master drum."

iyalorixá—A priestess of a Candomblé terreiro (house of worship). Also called "saint mother" or mãe de santo.

jogo dos búzios—A game of casting cowry shells to determine one's future.

jùjú—A popular music genre that emerged in Lagos, Nigeria, in the 1930s.

kandombele, kandombile, kandomide, kulomba-ku-domba-a—Bantu terms that mean "to pray."

Ketu—In Salvador, an ethnic group of Yoruba ancestry with roots in present-day southwest Nigeria.

Kò-dómb-éd-à—A Bantu term meaning "to ask the intercession of."

lambada—A sexy dance for couples influenced by merengue, maxixe, and forró dances.

lê—The smallest drum in a set of atabaques.

Legba—Another name of the orixá Exú.

mãe de santo—"Saint mother," also known as iyalorixá.

mãe pequeno—"Little mother," also known as iakekerê.

Martin—The Caboclo trickster spirit who possesses participants in a drunken manner.

Marujo—A spiritual agent whose primary role is to control the trickery of Martin, the Caboclo trickster spirit.

merengue—A song and dance genre that originated in the Dominican Republic in the nineteenth century.

mulatto—People of African and European descent.

nações de Candomblés—The ethnic groups (nations) of Candomblé in Salvador.

Nações—African Nations.

Nagô—Ethnic groups of West African Yoruba, Ketu, and Ijexá ancestry in Salvador.

Nana—The orixá associated with St. Anna. Also known as Buruku.

Obá—A Yoruba word that means "king." Also a common greeting or exclamation in Brazilian Portuguese.

Obàtálá—A West African deity.

Ogan alabê—Elders in Candomblé religion who are also performing musicians.

Ogans—Civil protectors of Candomblé terreiros (houses of worship).

Ògún—A West African deity.

ojá abalá—A long red cloth used in many Candomblé ceremonies.

ojá—A cloth wrapped around sacred atabaques (drums).

Olodum—Carnival organization in Salvador.

Olódùmarè—The Supreme Being of the Candomblé religion.

Oríkì—Yoruba chants.

òrìsàs—Deities of the Yoruba religion.

Òrì—The root word of the term òrìsà/orixá that refers to the forces responsible for controlling one's being.

orixás—Afro-Brazilian deities (Portuguese spelling).

Òrúnmìlá—A West African deity.

orun—The spiritual world in Yoruba mythology.

Oxalá—The orixá associated with Jesus Christ.

Oxóssi—The orixá associated with St. Jorge.

Oxum—The orixá associated with Nossa Senhora das Candeias. Also known as Oxun.

Oxum-maré—The orixá associated with St. Bartolomeu.

padê—Special offerings given to the orixás.

pagode—A party or gathering where samba is performed. Also a popular type of samba that developed in Rio de Janeiro in the mid-1970s and became a major musical movement in the 1980s.

pandeiro—A musical instrument similar to a tambourine.

pai de santo—"Saint father," also known as babalorixá.

pai pequeno—"Little father," also known as babakekerê.

Pelourinho—Literally, "whipping post." The historic district of Salvador.

reais—Brazilian currency.

rum—The largest drum in a set of atabaques.

rumpi—The medium-sized drum in a set of atabaques.

samba-reggae—A mixture of samba and reggae developed in Salvador in the 1980s.

Sàngó—A West African deity. Also the name of the òrìsà religion in Trinidad.

shekere—A beaded gourd rattle.

surdo—A drum used in samba and played with stick.

tan tan—A small drum that is often used in pagode ensembles in place of the surdo.

tanoeiros—An atabaque maker.

terreiros—Candomblé houses of worship.

tias—Literally, "aunts." Women of Candomblé.

Tropicália/Tropicálismo—A popular music movement of the 1960s involving such artists as Caetano Veloso and Gilberto Gil.

Umbanda—An Afro-Brazilian religion developed in the twentieth century.

Xangô—The orixá associated with St. Jeronimo.

Yemanjá—The orixá associated with the Virgin Mary (Nossa Senhora da Conceição).

Bibliography

Abiodun, Rowland. 1994. "Understanding Yoruba Art and Aesthetics: The Concept of *Àsé.*" *African Arts* 27 (3): 68–102.

Adegbite, Ademola. 1988. "The Drum and Its Role in Yoruba Religion." *Journal of Religion in Africa* 8 (1): 15–26.

Aimes, Hubert H. S. 1905. "African Institutions in America." *Journal of American Folklore* 18 (68): 15–32.

Ajayi, Omofolabo Soyinka. 1994. "In Contest: The Dynamics of African Religious Dances." In *African Dance: An Artistic Historical and Philosophical Inquiry*, ed. Kariamu Welsh Asante. 183–202. Trenton, NJ: Africa World Press.

Alaja-Browne, Afolabi. 1989. "The Origin and Development of JùJú Music." *The Black Perspective in Music* 17 (1–2): 55–72.

Almeida, Lula. 1997. Personal interview with the author.

Anderson, Talmadge. 1990. *Black Studies: Theory, Method, and Cultural Perspectives.* Pullman: Washington State University Press.

Andrews, George Reid. 1991. *Blacks and Whites in São Paulo, 1888–1988.* Madison: University Press of Wisconsin.

Appadurai, Arjun. 1997. *Modernization at Large: Cultural Dimensions of Globalization.* Minneapolis: University of Minnesota Press.

Apter, Andrew. 1992. *Black Critics and Kings: The Hermeneutics of Power in Yoruba Society.* Chicago: University of Chicago Press.

Armstrong, Piers. 2001a. *Cultura Popular Na Bahia Estilística Cultural Pragmática.* Feira de Santana: UEFS.

———. 2001b. "Songs of Olodum Ethnicity, Activism, and Art in a Globalized Carnival Community." In *Brazilian Popular Music and Globalization*, ed. Charles A. Perrone and Christopher Dunn. 177–91. Gainesville: University Press of Florida.

———. 1999. *Third World Literary Fortunes: Brazilian Cultural Identity and Its International Reception*: Lewisburg, PA: Bucknell University Press; London: Associated University Press.

Asante, Molefi Kete. 1988. *Afrocentricity.* Trenton, NJ: Africa World Press.

Averill, Gage. 1999. "Caribbean Musics: Haiti and Trinidad and Tobago." In *Music in Latin American Culture Regional Traditions*, ed. John M. Schechter. 126–91. New York: Schirmer Books.

———. 1997. *A Day for the Hunter, a Day for the Prey: Popular Music and Power in Haiti.* Chicago: University of Chicago Press.

———. 1994. "*Anraje* to *Angaje*: Carnival Politics and Music in Haiti." *Ethnomusicology* 38 (2): 217–47.

Azevedo, Manoel Pedro. 1999. Personal interview with the author.

Azevedo, Thales de. 1975. *Democracia racial: ideological e realidade.* Petropolis, Brazil: Vozes.

Bacelar, Jeferson. 1999. "Blacks in Salvador, Brazil: Racial Paths." In *Black Brazil: Culture, Identity, and Social Mobilization*, ed. Larry Crook and Randal Johnson. 85–101. Los Angeles: UCLA Latin American Center Publications.

——. 1989. *Ser Negro em Salvador*. Salvador, Brazil: Yanamá.

Badaró, Luiz. 1998. Personal interview with the author.

Barnes, Sandra T. 1989. *Africa's Ogun: Old and New*. Bloomington: Indiana University Press.

Bascom, William R. 1969. *The Yoruba of Southwestern Nigeria*. New York: Holt, Reinhart and Winston.

Bastide, Roger. 1978. *The African Religions of Brazil: Toward a Sociology of the Interpenetration of Civilizations*. Trans. Helen Sebba. Baltimore: Johns Hopkins University Press.

——. 1958. *O Candomblé da Bahia (Rito Nagô)*. São Paulo: Companhia Editora Nacional.

Béhague, Gerard. 2000. "Afro-Brazilian Traditions." In *The Garland Handbook of Latin American Music*, ed. Dale A. Olsen and Daniel Sheehy, 272–87. New York and London: Garland.

——. 1994. *Heitor Villa-Lobos: The Search for Brazil's Musical Sound*. Austin: Institute of Latin American Studies.

——. 1984. "Patterns of Candomblé Music Performance: An Afro-Brazilian Religious Setting." In *Performance Practice: Ethnomusicological Perspective*, ed. Gerard Béhague. 222–54. Westport, CT: Greenwood Press.

——. 1977. "Some Liturgical Functions of Afro-Brazilian Religious Music in Salvador." *World of Music* 29 (3): 4–14.

Bhabha, Homi. 1994. *The Location of Culture*. New York: Routledge.

Borges, Dain. 1995. "The Recognition of Afro-Brazilian Symbols and Ideas, 1890–1940." *Luso–Brazilian Review* 32 (2): 59–78.

Braga, Júlio. 1999. "Candomblé in Bahia: Repression and Resistance." In *Black Brazil: Culture, Identity, and Social Mobilization*, ed. Larry Crook and Randal Johnson. 201–12. Los Angeles: UCLA Latin American Center Publications.

——. 1998. *Fuxico de Candomblé: Estudos afro-brasileiros*. Feira de Santana, Brazil: UEFS.

Brandon, George. 1993. *Santería from Africa to the New World: The Dead Sell Memories*. Bloomington: Indiana University Press.

BRASA. 2005. Personal interviews with the author.

Brown, Diana de G. 1999. "Power, Invention, and the Politics of Race: Umbanda Past and Future." In *Black Brazil: Culture, Identity, and Social Mobilization*, ed. Larry Crook and Randal Johnson. 213–36. Los Angeles: UCLA Latin American Center Publications.

——. 1994. *Umbanda: Religion and Politics in Urban Brazil*. New York: Columbia University Press.

Brown, Diana de G., and Mario Bick. 1987. "Religions, Class, and Context in Brazilian Umbanda." *American Ethnologist* 35: 74–95.

Brown, Ernest D. 1999. "Turn Up the Volume! The African Aesthetic in Trinidad's Carnival Music." In *Turn Up the Volume! A Celebration of African Music*, ed. Jacqueline Cogdell DjeDje. 149–57. Los Angeles: UCLA Fowler Museum of Cultural History.

Browning, Barbara. 1998. *Infectious Rhythm: Metaphors of Contagion and the Spread of African Culture*. New York and London: Routledge.

Butler, Kim. 1998. *Freedom Given, Freedom Won: Afro-Brazilians in Post Abolition São Paulo and Salvador*. New Brunswick, NJ: Rutgers University Press.

Calt, Stephen. 1994. *I'd Rather Be the Devil: Skip James and the Blues*. New York: Da Capo Press.

Camargo, Cândido Procópio Ferreirade. 1961. *Kardecismo e umbanda, uma interpretação sociológica*. São Paulo: Livraria Pioneira Editôra.

Campbell, Michael, and James Brody. 1999. *Rock and Roll: An Introduction*. Belmont, CA: Wadsworth Group/Thompson Learning.

Canclini, Néstor García. 1995. *Hybrid Cultures: Strategies for Entering and Exiting Modernity*. Minneapolis: University of Minneapolis Press.

Carlos, Antonio. 1998. Personal interview with the author.

Carneiro, Edison. 1940. "The Structure of African Cults in Bahia." *Journal of American Folklore* 53: 271–78.

——. 1936. *Religioes Negros Notas de etnografia religiosa Biblioteca de Divulgação Scientifica*, VII. Rio de Janeiro: Civilização Brasileira.

Carvalho, José Jorge de. 1999. "The Multiplicity of Black Identities in Brazilian Popular Music." In *Black Brazil: Culture, Identity, and Social Mobilization*, ed. Larry Crook and Randal Johnson. 261–95. Los Angeles: UCLA Latin American Center Publications.

——. 1994. "Black Music of All Colors: The Construction of Black Ethnicity in Ritual and Popular Genres of Afro-Brazilian Music." In *Music and Black Ethnicity: The Caribbean and South America*, ed. Gerard Béhague. 187–206. New Brunswick, NJ: Transaction Publishers.

Carvalho, Martha de Ulhôa. 2003. "Chiclete com Banana: Us and the Other in Brazilian Popular Music." In *Musical Cultures of Latin America: Global Effects, Past and Present, Selected Reports in Ethnomusicology*, Volume XI, ed. Steven Loza. 205–15. Los Angeles: Ethnomusicology Publications.

——.1995. "Tupi or Not Tupi MPB: Popular Music and Identity in Brazil." In *The Brazilian Puzzle: Culture on the Borderlands of the Western World*, ed. David J. Hess and Roberto A. Da Matta. 159–79. New York: Columbia University Press.

Cassiano, Josué. 1998, 1999, and 2002. Personal interviews with the author.

Cavin, Susan. 1975. "Missing Women on the Voodoo Trail to Jazz." *Journal of Jazz Studies* 1 (3): 4–27.

Caymmi, Dorival. 1947. *Cancioneiro da Bahia*. São Paulo: Livraria Martins Editôra.

Cesaire, Aime. 1995. "What Is Negritude to Me." In *African Presence in the Americas*, ed. Carlos Moore, Tanya R. Sanders, and Shawna Moore. 13–20. Trenton, NJ: African World Press.

Clarke, Peter B. 1983. "Why Women Are Priests and Teachers in Bahian Candomblé." In *Women as Teachers and Disciples in Traditional and New Religions*, ed. Elizabeth Puttick and Peter B. Clarke. 97–113. Queenstown, Ontario, Canada: Edwin Mellen.

Cohen, Aaron. 2000. "Jazz World: Drumming Up Support—Carlinhos Brown's Beat Lend Support to His Improvised Brazilian Neighborhood." *Down Beat* 67 (11): 18–20.

Collins, John. 1992. *West African Pop Roots*. Philadelphia: Temple University Press.

Concone, Maria Helena Villa Boas. 1987. *Umbanda: Uma religião brasileira*. São Paulo: Fac. De Filosofia, Letras e Ciências Humanas, U.S.P.

Cone, James H. 1991 [1972]. *The Spiritual and the Blues: An Interpretation*. Maryknoll, NY: Orbis.

——. 1970. *A Black Theology of Liberation*. New York: Lippincott.

Conniff, Michael L., and Thomas J. Davis. 1994. *Africans in the Americas: A History of the Black Diaspora*. New York: St. Martin's.

Cornelius, Steven. 1989. *The Convergence of Power: An Investigation into the Music Liturgy of Santería in New York City*. Ph.D. dissertation, University of California, Los Angeles.

Correa, Jana. 2005. Personal interview with the author.

Covin, David. 2006. *The Unified Black Movement in Brazil, 1978–2002*. London: McFarland.

Crook, Larry. 2005. *Brazilian Music: Northeastern Traditions and the Heartbeat of a Modern Nation*. Santa Barbara, CA: ABC-CLIO.

——. 2001. "Turned-Around Beat: *Maracatu de Baque Virado* and Chico Science." In *Brazilian Popular Music and Globalization*, ed. Charles A. Perrone and Christopher Dunn. 233–44. Gainesville: University Press of Florida.

——. 1999. "Northeastern Brazil." In *Music in Latin American Culture Regional Traditions*, ed. John M. Schechter. 192–235. New York: Schirmer Books.

——. 1993. "Black Consciousness, *samba reggae* and the Re-Africanization of Bahian Carnival Music in Brazil." *World of Music* 35 (2): 90–108.

Crook, Larry, and Randal Johnson, eds. 1999. *Black Brazil: Culture, Identity, and Social Mobilization*. Los Angeles: UCLA Latin American Center Publications.

Crowley, Daniel J. 1984. *African Myth and Black Reality in Bahian Carnival*, Monograph Series 25. Los Angeles: Museum of Cultural History, UCLA.

Curtin, Phillip. 1976. "Discussion: Measuring the Atlantic Slave Trade." *Journal of African History* 17 (2): 595–627.

——. 1969. *The Atlantic Slave Trade: A Census*. Madison: University of Wisconsin Press.

Dagan, Esther. 1993. *Drums: The Heartbeat of Africa*. Montréal: Galerie Armand Africa Art Publications.

Da Matta, Roberto A. 1980. *Carnavais, malandros e heróis: para uma sociologia do dilemma brasileiro*. Rio de Janeiro: Zahar Editores.

Dantas, Marcelo. 1994. *Olodum—de bloco afro a holding cultural*. Salvador, Brazil: Grupo Cultural Olodum/Casa Fundação de Jorge Amado.

Degler, Carl N. 1986. *Neither Black nor White: Slavery and Race Relations in Brazil and the U.S.* Madison: University of Wisconsin Press.

Deren, Maya. 1983 [1953]. *Divine Horsemen: The Living Gods of Haiti*. New Paltz, NY: Documentext McPherson.

De Silva, Earlston E. 1989. "The Theology of Black Power and Black Song: James Brown." In *Black Sacred Music: A Journal of Theomusicology. Special Issue of Theology of American Popular Music*, ed. Jon Michael Spencer. 3 (2): 57–67. Durham, NC: Duke University Press.

De Souza, Raymundo Nonato. 2002. Personal interview with the author.

DjeDje, Jacqueline Cogdell. 2000. "West Africa: An Introduction." In *The Garland Handbook of African Music*, ed. Ruth M. Stone. 140–68. New York: Garland.

Dolin, Kasey Qynn. 2001. "Yoruban Religious Survival in Brazilian Candomblé." *MACLAS Latin American Essays* 69 (14): 69–82.

Donkor, Anthony Ephirim. 1997. *African Spirituality: On Becoming Ancestors*. Trenton, NJ: African World Press.

Drewal, Henry John. 1999. "Art History, Agency, and Identity: Yoruba Transnational

Currents in Making of Black Brazil." In *Black Brazil: Culture, Identity, and Social Mobilization*, ed. Larry Crook and Randal Johnson. 143–74. Los Angeles: UCLA Latin American Center Publications.

Drewal, Margaret T. 1992. *Yoruba Ritual: Performers, Play, Agency*. Bloomington: Indiana University Press.

Drewal, Henry J., and Margaret T. Drewal. 1983. *Gelede: Art and Female Power among the Yoruba*. Bloomington: Indiana University Press.

Dugany, Jorge. 1996. "Rethinking the Popular: Caribbean Music and Identity." *Latin American Research Review* 17 (2): 176–92.

Dunn, Christopher. 1992. "Afro-Bahian Carnival: A Stage for Protest." *Afro-Hispanic Review* 11 (1–3): 11–20.

Eisen, Jonathan. 1969. *The Age of Rock: Sounds of the American Cultural Revolution*. New York: Vintage.

Epstein, Dena. 1977. *Sinful Tunes and Spirituals*. Urbana: University of Illinois Press.

Erlmann, Veit. 1996. "The Aesthetics of the Global Imagination: Reflections on World Music in the 1990s." *Public Culture* 8: 467–87.

Farber, Carole. 1983. "High, Healthy, and Happy: Ontario Mythology on Parade." In *The Celebration of Society: Perspectives on Contemporary Cultural Performance*, ed. Frank E. Manning. 33–50. Bowling Green, OH: Bowling Green University Popular Press.

Feldman, Heidi C. 2006. *Black Rhythms of Peru: Reviving African Musical Heritage in the Black Pacific*. Middletown, CT: Wesleyan University Press.

Fernandes, Florestan. 1989. *Significado do Protesto Negro*. São Paulo: Corez Editora/ Autores Associados.

———. 1958. *A integração do negro na sociedade de classes*. 2 vols. São Paulo: Dominus.

Ferretti, Mundicarmo M. R. 2001. "The Presence of Non-African Spirits in an Afro-Brazilian Religion: A Case of Afro-Amerindian Syncretism?" In *Reinventing Religious Syncretism and Transformation in Africa and the Americas*, ed. Sidney M. Greenfield and Andre Droogers. 99–111. Oxford and New York: Rowman and Littlefield.

Figger, Horst H. 1983. *Umbanda: religião, magia, possessão*. Teresópolis, Brazil: Jaguary Editores.

Filho, João Freire, and Micael Herschmann. 2003. "Debatable Tastes! Rethinking Hierarchical Distinctions in Brazilian Music." *Journal of Latin American Cultural Studies* 12 (3): 347–58.

Finn, Julio. 1992. *The Bluesman: The Musical Heritage of Black Men and Women in the Americas*. New York: Interlink.

Firth, Simon. 2000. "The Discourse of World Music." In *Western Music and Its Others: Difference, Representation, and Appropriation in Music*, ed. Georgina Born and David Hesmondhalgh. 305–22. Los Angeles and Berkeley: University of California Press.

Fischer, Tânia, ed. 1996. *O carnaval baiano: Negócios e oportunidades*. Brasília: SEBRAE.

Fleurant, Gerdès. 1996. *Dancing Spirits: Rhythms and Rituals of Haitian Vodun, The Rada Rite*. Westport, CT: Greenwood Press.

Floyd, Samuel A., Jr. 1999. "Black Music in the Circum-Caribbean." *American Music* 17 (1): 1–37.

Fontaine, Pierre-Michel. 1985. "Blacks and the Search for Power in Brazil." In *Race,*

Class, and Power in Brazil, ed. Pierre-Michel Fontaine. 56–72. Los Angeles: UCLA Center for Afro-American Studies.

Fountain, John W. 1998. "Taking the Long Road: A Walk on the Slave Road." *Washington Post:* B1, July 14.

Freire, Paulo. 1994. *Pedagogy of Hope (Pedagogia da Esperança).* Trans. Robert R. Barr. New York: Continuum.

———. 1970. *Pedagogy of the Oppressed (Pedagogia da oprimido).* Trans. Myra Bergman Ramos. New York: Herder and Herder.

Fryer, Peter. 2000. *Rhythms of Resistance: African Musical Heritage in Brazil.* Westport, CT: Wesleyan University Press.

Galinsky, Philip. 2002. "Music and Place in the Brazilian Popular Imagination: The Interplay of Local and Global in the Mangue Bit Movement of Recife, Pernambuco, Brazil." In *From Tejano to Tango: Latin American Popular Music,* ed. Walter Aaron Clark. 195–216. New York and London: Routledge.

———. 1996. "Co-option, Cultural Resistance, and Afro-Brazilian Identity: A History of the 'Pagode' Samba Movement in Rio de Janeiro." *Latin American Music Review* 17 (2): 120–49.

Garcia, Antonio dos Santos. 2006. *Mulheres da Cidade d' Oxum: relações de gênero, raça e classe e organização especial do movimento de barrio em Salvador.* Salvador, Brazil: Editora da UFBA.

Garcia, Rodolfo. 1935. "Vocabulario Nagô." In *Estudos Afro-Brasileiros,* vol. I, ed. E. Roquette Pinto. 21–27. Rio de Janeiro: Ariel Editôria Ltda.

Garon, Paul. 1971. *The Devil's Son-in-Law: The Story of Peetie Wheatstraw and His Songs.* London: Studio Vista.

Gates, Henry Louis, Jr. 1988. *The Signifying Monkey: A Theory of African-American Criticism.* New York: Oxford University Press.

Gerstin, Julian. 1998. "Reputation in a Musical Scene: The Everyday Context of Connection between Music, Identity, and Politics." *Ethnomusicology* 42 (2): 385–414.

Gillespie, Dizzy. 1979. *To Be or Not to Bop: Memoirs.* Garden City, NY: Doubleday.

Gilman, Bruce. 1996. "Carlinhos Brown: Planetary Minstrel." *Brazzil* [Sept.]: 41–44.

———. 1997. "Daniela Mercury: And Now the World." *Brazzil* [Jan.]: 40–43.

Gilroy, Paul. 1993. *The Black Atlantic: Modernity and Double Consciousness.* Cambridge: Harvard University Press.

Gioia, Ted. 1997. *The History of Jazz.* Oxford and New York: Oxford University Press.

Gleason, Judith. 1987. *Oya: In Praise of an African Goddess.* Boston and London: Shambhala.

———. 1971. *Orisha: The Yoruba Gods of Yorubaland.* New York: Atheneum.

Godi, Antonio J. V. dos Santos. 1997. "Música afro-carnavalesca: das multidões para o sucesso das massas elétricas." In *Ritmos em trânsito: Sócio-antropologia da música baiana,* ed. Livio Sansone and Jocélio Teles dos Santos. 73–96. São Paulo: Dynamis Editorial; Salvador, Brazil: Programa Cor da Bahia (UFBA) e Projeto S.A.M.B.A.

Godet, Rita Olivieri, and Lícia Soares Souza, eds. 2001. *Identidades e Representações na Cultura Brasileira.* João Pessoa: Editora Ideía.

Gomes, Tom. 2004. "Music: Latin-Sangalo Brazil's Queen of Song." *Billboard* 116: 27.

Gonzáles-Wippler, Migene. 1985. *Tales of the Orishas.* New York: Original Publications.

———. 1973. *Santería.* New York: Julian Press.

Gordon, Izzy. 2006. Personal interview with the author.

Grasse, Jonathan. 2003. "Perspectives on Brazilian Rap: MC Orpheu and *Pluralismo*." In *Musical Cultures of Latin America: Global Effects, Past and Present. Selected Reports in Ethnomusicology*, vol. XI, ed. Steven Loza. 101–10. Los Angeles: Ethnomusicology Publications.

Greene, Sandra E. 1996. "Religion, History, and the Supreme Gods of Africa: A Contribution to the Debate." *Journal of Religion in Africa* 26: 122–38.

Greenfield, Sidney M. 2001. "The Reinterpretation of Africa: Convergence and Syncretism in Brazilian Candomblé." In *Reinventing Religious Syncretism and Transformation in Africa and the Americas*, ed. Sidney M. Greenfield and André Droogers. 113–29. Oxford and New York: Rowman and Littlefield.

Guerreiro, Goli. 2000. *A Trama dos Tambores: A Música Afro-Pop de Salvador*. São Paulo: Editora 34.

Guilbault, Jocelyn. 1997. "Interpreting World Music: Challenging in Theory and Practice." *Popular Music* 16 (1): 31–44.

———. 1993. "On Redefining the Local through World Music." *World of Music* 35 (2): 33–47.

Guillermoprieto, Alma. 1991. *Samba*. New York: Vintage Departures.

Haberly, David T. 1983. *Three Sad Races: Racial Identity and National Consciousness in Brazilian Literature*. Cambridge: Cambridge University Press.

Hagedorn, Katherine J. 2001. *Divine Utterances: The Performance of Cuban Santeriá*. Washington: Smithsonian Institution Press.

Hale, Lindsay. 2001. "Mama Oxum: Reflections of Gender and Sexuality in Brazilian Umbanda." In *Òsun across the Waters: A Yoruba Goddess in Africa and the Americas*, ed. Joseph M. Murphy and Mei-Mei Sanford. 213–29. Bloomington: Indiana University Press.

Hanchard, Michael George. 1999. *Racial Politics in Contemporary Brazil*. Durham, NC: Duke University Press.

———. 1994. *Orpheus and Power: The Movimento Negro in Rio de Janeiro and São Paulo, Brazil, 1945–1988*. Princeton: Princeton University Press.

Hanson, Allan. 1989. "The Making of the Maori: Culture Invention and Its Logic." *American Anthropologist* 91 (4): 890–902.

Harding, Rachael E. 2000. *A Refuge in Thunder: Candomblé and Alternative Spaces of Blackness*. Bloomington: Indiana University Press.

Hayter-Hames, Jane. 1992. "Slaves to the Rhythm." *Folk Roots* 112: 30–31.

Hershmann, Micael, ed. 1997. *Abalando os anos 90: Funk e hip–hop: Globalização, violência e estilo cultural*. Rio de Janeiro: Rocco.

Herskovits, Melville J. 1958 [1941]. *Myth of the Negro Past*. Boston: Beacon.

———. 1944. "Drums and Drummers in Afro-Brazilian Cult Life." *Musical Quarterly* 30 (4): 477–92.

Heywood, Linda M., ed. 2002. *Central Africa and Cultural Transformation in the American Diaspora*. Cambridge: Cambridge University Press.

Hill, Errol. 1972. *The Trinidad Carnival: Mandate for a National Theatre*. Austin: University of Texas Press.

Hill, Julie. 2004. "The Magic of Escola Didá Social Reform for Women and Children in Brazil." *Percussive Notes* 42: 12–19.

Hock-Smith, Judith. 1978. "Radical Yoruba Female Sexuality: The Witch and the

Prostitute." In *Women in Ritual and Symbolic Roles*, ed. Judith Hock-Smith and A. Spring. 245–65. New York: Plenum.

Holloway, Joseph E., ed. 1990. *Africanisms in American Culture*. Bloomington: Indiana University Press.

Howard, Joseph H. 1967. *Drums in the Americas*. New York: Oak Publications.

Idowu, E. Bolji. 1963. *Olódùmarè God in Yoruba Belief*. New York: Praeger.

Ikenga-Mueth, Emefie. 1982. "Religious Concepts in West African Cosmologies: A Problem of Interpretation." *Journal of African History* 13 (1): 11–24.

Johnson, Christopher Paul. 2002. *Secrets, Gossip, and Gods: The Transformation of Brazilian Candomblé*. London and New York: Oxford University Press.

Johnson, Samuel. 1969 [1921]. *The History of the Yorubas: From Earliest Times to the Beginning of the British Protectorate*. London: Routledge and Kegan.

José, Ricardo. 1998. Personal interview with the author.

Junior, Arnoldo. 1998, 1999, and 2002. Personal interviews with the author.

Kamen, Henry. 1972. "The Roots of Jazz and Dance in Place Congo: A Reappraisal." *Yearbook for Inter–American Musical Research* 8: 5–16.

Karade, Baba Ifá. 1994. *The Handbook of Yoruba Religious Concepts*. York Beach, ME: Samuel Weiser.

Kertzer, David. I. 1988. *Ritual, Politics, and Power*. New Haven: Yale University Press.

King, Stephen. 1998. "International Reggae, Democratic Socialism, and the Secularization of the Rastafarian Movement, 1972–1980." *Popular Music and Society* 22 (3): 39–60.

Kinni-Olusanyin, Esilokun. 1994. "A Panoply of African Dance Dynamics." In *African Dance: An Artistic, Historical, and Philosophical Inquiry*, ed. Kariamu Welsh Asante. 29–38. Trenton, NJ: Africa World Press.

Kirshenblatt-Gimblett, Barbara. 1998. "Theorizing Heritage." *Ethnomusicology* 39 (3): 367–80.

Kinser, Samuel. 1990. *Carnival American Style: Mardi Gras at New Orleans and Mobile*. Chicago: University of Chicago Press.

Klein, Herbert S. 1986. *African Slavery in Latin America and the Caribbean*. Oxford: Oxford University Press.

Knight, Roderic, and Kenneth Bilby. 1993. "Music in Africa and the Caribbean." In *Africana Studies*, ed. Mario Azevedo. 243–75. Durham, NC: Carolina Academic Press.

Kubik, Gerhard. 1999. *Africa and the Blues*. Jackson: University Press of Mississippi.

———. 1979. *Angolan Traits in Black Music, Games and Dances: A Study of African Cultural Extension Overseas*. Lisbon: Junta de Investigações Científicas do Ultramar, Centro de Estudos de Antropologia Cultural.

Landes, Ruth. 1947. *The City of Women*. New York: Macmillan.

———. 1940. "Fetish Worship in Brazil." *Journal of American Folklore* 53: 261–70.

Lavergne, Barbara, and José Flavio Pessoa de Barros. 1986. "Chants sacrés et plantes liturgiques dans le Candomblé brésilien." *Cahiers du Monde Hispanique et Luso-Brésilien* 47: 25–29.

Lawal, Babatunde. 1996. *Gelede Spectacle: Art, Gender, and Social Harmony in an African Culture*. Seattle: University of Washington Press.

Lawson, E. Thomas. 1984. "The Yoruba and Their Religious Traditions." In *Religions of Africa Traditions in Transformation*. New York: Harper and Row.

Lemos, Edmilson. 1998. Personal interview with the author.

Lent, John, ed. 1990. *Caribbean Popular Culture*. Bowling Green, KY: Bowling Green University Popular Press.

Lesser, Jeffery. 1999. *Negotiating National Identity: Immigrants, Minorities, and the Struggle for Ethnicity in Brazil*. Durham, NC: Duke University Press.

Levine, Laurence W. 1977. *Black Culture and Black Consciousness: Afro-American Folk Thought from Slavery to Freedom*. Oxford: Oxford University Press.

Lima, Ari. 2001. "Black or *Brau* Music and Black Subjectivity in a Global Content." In *Brazilian Popular Music and Globalization*, ed. Charles A. Perrone and Christopher Dunn. 220–32. Gainesville: University Press of Florida.

———. 1997. "O fenômeno Timbalada: cultura musical afro-pop e juventude baiana Negro-mestiça." In *Ritmos em trânsito: sócio-antropologia da música baiana*, ed. Livio Sansone and Jocélino Teles dos Santos. 161–180. São Paulo: Dynamics Editorial; Salvador, Brazil: Programa A Cor da Bahia e projeto S.A.M.B.A.

Lima, Vivaldo da Costa. 1971. A família de santo nos Candomblés jeje-nagô da Bahia. Bahia: UFBA.

Lindon, Thomas. 1990. "*Oríkì Òrìsà*: The Yoruba Prayer of Praise." *Journal of African History* 2: 205–24.

Lindsay, Shawn. 1996. "Hand Drumming: An Essay in Practical Knowledge." In *Things as They Are: New Directions in Phenomenological Anthropology*, ed. Michael Jackson, 196–212. Bloomington: Indiana University Press.

Lipsitz, George. 1994. *Dangerous Crossroads: Popular Music, Postmodernism and the Poetics of Place*. London: Verso.

Lo-Bamijoko, Joy Nwosu. 1984. "Performance Practice in Nigerian Music." *The Black Perspective in Music* 12 (1): 3–20.

Longstreet, Stephen. 1965. *Sportin' House: A History of New Orleans Sinners and the Birth of Jazz*. Los Angeles: Sherbourne.

Loza, Steven, ed. 2003. *Musical Cultures of Latin America: Global Effects, Past and Present, Selected Topics in Ethnomusicology*, vol. XI. Los Angeles: Department of Ethnomusicology and Systematic Musicology.

Lúcia, Virgínia. 1998. Personal interview with the author.

Luz, Alícia dos Prazes. 1999. Personal interview with the author.

MacAloon, John J. 1984. *Rite, Drama, Festival, Spectacle: Rehearsals toward a Theory of Cultural Performance*. Philadelphia: Institute for the Study of Human Issues.

MacGaffey, Watt. 1986. *Religion and Society in Central Africa*. Chicago: University of Chicago Press.

MacLean, U. 1969. "Sickness Behavior among Yoruba (Ibadan)." In *Witchcraft and Healing, Seminar Proceedings, February 14–15*. 29–42. Edinburgh: Center for African Studies.

Magaldi, Cristina. 1999. "Adopting Imports: New Images and Alliances in Brazilian Popular Music of the 1990s." *Popular Music* 18 (3): 309–29.

Makuna, Kazadi. 1997. "Creative Practice of African Music: New Perspectives in the Scrutiny of Africanisms in the Diaspora." *Black Music Research* 17 (2): 239–48.

Mann, Kristin, and Edna G. Bay, eds. 2001. "Rethinking the African Diaspora: The Making of a Black Atlantic World in the Bight of Benin and Brazil." *Slavery and Abolition* Special Issue vol. 22 (1): 1–160.

Mariani, Myriam Evelyse. 1994. "African Influences in Brazilian Dance." In *African Dance: An Artistic, Historical and Philosophical Inquiry*, ed. Kariamu Welsh Asante. 79–97. Trenton, NJ: Africa World Press.

Marques, Arisvaldo. 1998 and 1999. Personal interviews with the author.

Martins, Bayo. 1983. *The Message of African Drumming*. Heidelberg: P Kivouvou Verlag-Editions Bantoues.

Mason, John. 1985. *Black Gods: Orisa Studies in the New World*. Brooklyn: Yoruba Theological Archministry.

Mason, Peter. 1999. *Bacchanal: The Carnival Culture of Trinidad*. Philadelphia: Temple University Press.

Matory, Lorand J. 2005. *Black Atlantic Religion: Tradition, Transnationalism, and Matriarchy in the Afro-Brazilian Candomblé*. Princeton: Princeton University Press.

———. 1999a. "The English Professors of Brazil: On the Diasporic Roots of the Yoruba Nation." *Comparative Studies in Society and History* 41: 72–103.

———. 1999b. "JeJe Repensando Nações e Transnacionalismo." *Mana: Estudos de Antropologia Social* 5 (1): 57–80.

Matta, Roberto Da. 1980. *Carnavais, malandros e heróis: Para uma sociologia do dilemma brasileiro*. Rio de Janeiro: Zahar Editor.

Mattoso, Katia M. de Queiros. 1988. "Slave, Free, and Freed Family Structures in Nineteenth-Century Salvador, Bahia." *Luso-Brazilian Review* 25 (1): 69–88.

Maultsby, Portia K. 1990. "Africanisms in African-American Music." In *Africanisms in American Culture*, ed. John E. Holloway. 185–210. Bloomington: Indiana University Press.

———. 1983. "Soul Music: Its Sociological and Political Significance in American Popular Culture." *Journal of Popular Culture* 17: 51–60.

Mbiti, John S. 1990 [1969]. *African Religions and Philosophy*. Portsmouth, NH: Heinemann.

McGowan, Chris, and Ricardo Pessanha. 1998. *The Brazilian Sound: Samba, Bossa Nova, and the Popular Music of Brazil*. 2nd ed. Philadelphia: Temple University Press.

McKenzie, P. R. 1976. "Yoruba Òrìsà Cults: Some Marginal Notes Concerning Their Cosmology and Concepts of Deity." *Journal of Religion in Africa* 8 (3): 189–207.

Meadows, Eddie S. 1993. "African-American Music." In *Africana Studies*, ed. Mario Azevedo. 277–98. Durham, NC: Carolina Academic Press.

Medeiros, José. 1957. *Candomblé*. Rio de Janeiro: Edições O Cruzeiro.

Merriam, Alan P. 1964. *The Anthropology of Music*. Evanston, IL: Northwestern University Press.

———. 1956. "Songs of the Ketu Cult of Bahia, Brazil." *African Music* 1 (3): 53–67.

———. 1963. "Songs of the Gêge and Jesha Cults of Bahia, Brazil." *Jahrbuch fur Musikalische Volks und Volkerkunde* 1: 98–135.

Mitchell, Tony. 1996. *Popular Music and Local Identity: Rock, Pop and Rap in Europe and Oceania*. London: Leicester University Press.

Monson, Ingrid, ed. 2000. *The African Diaspora: A Musical Perspective*. New York and London: Garland.

Montes, Maria Lúcia. 2001. "African Cosmologies in Brazilian Culture and Society." In *Brazil: Body and Soul*, ed. Edward J. Sullivan. 334–45. New York: Guggenheim Museum.

Moore, Sally F., and Barbara Meyerhoff, eds. 1977. *Secular Ritual*. Seattle: University of Washington Press.

Morris, Nancy. 1999. "Cultural Interaction in Latin America and Caribbean Music." *Latin American Music Review* 34 (1): 187–200.

Motta, Roberto. 1998. Personal interview with the author.

Moura, Milton Araújo. 2001. "World of Fantasy, Fantasy of the World: Geographic Space and Representation of Identity in the Carnival of Salvador, Bahia." In *Brazilian Popular Music and Globalization*, ed. Charles A. Perrone and Christopher Dunn. 161–76. Gainesville: University Press of Florida.

Moura, Roberto. 1983. *Tia Ciata e a pequena Africa no Rio de Janeiro*. Rio de Janeiro, RJ: FUNARTE, Instituto Nacional de Música, Divisão de Música Popular.

Murisoea, Luiz. 1998 and 1999. Personal interviews with the author.

Murphy, Joseph M. 1994. *Working the Spirit: Ceremonies of the African Diaspora*. Boston: Beacon.

———. 1988. *Santeriá: An African Religion in America*. Boston: Beacon.

Napier, A. David. 1986. *Masks, Transformation, and Paradox*. Berkeley: University of California Press.

Nascimento, Abdias do. 1992. *Africans in Brazil: A Pan-African Perspective*. Trenton, NJ: Africa World Press.

Nascimento, Abdias do, and Elisa Larkin Nascimento. 2001. "Dance of Deception: A Reading of Race Relations in Brazil." In *Beyond Racism: Race and Equality in Brazil, South Africa, and the United States*, ed. Charles Hamilton et al. 105–56. Boulder and London: Lynne Rienner.

Nascimento, Nivaldo Dario. 1998. Personal interview with the author.

Neal, Larry. 1971. "Some Reflections on the Black Aesthetic." In *The Black Aesthetic*, ed. Addison Gayle Jr. 13–16. Garden City, NY: Doubleday.

Needell, Jeffrey. 1995. "Identity, Race, Gender, and Modernity in the Origins of Gilberto Freyre's *Oeuvre*." *American Historical Review* 100 (1): 51–77.

Nodal, Robert. 1993. "The Social Evolution of the Afro-Cuban Drum." *Black Perspective in Music* 11 (2): 157–77.

Nogueira, Oracy. 1985. *Tanto Preto Quanto Branco: Estudos de Relações Racias*. São Paulo: Editoria LTDA.

Nunley, John M., and Cara McCarty. 1999. *Masks: Faces of Culture*. New York: Harry Abrams.

Nunes, Attila. 1966. *Antologia da umbanda*. Rio de Janeiro: Editôra Eco.

Oakley, Giles. 1997. *The Devil's Music: A History of the Blues*. 2nd ed. New York: Da Capo Press.

Oderigo, Nestor Ortiz. 1975. "La Musica de los Candomblés" and "Instrumentos Musicales de los Candomblés." In *Macumba Culturas Africanes en el Brasil*, ed. Nestor Ortiz Oderigo. 178–231. Buenos Aires: Editorial Plus Ultra.

Ojo-Ade, Femi. 1999. "Black Brazil: African Notes on a New Negritude." In *Black Brazil: Culture, Identity, and Social Mobilization*, ed. Larry Crook and Randal Johnson. 175–97. Los Angeles: UCLA Latin American Center Publications.

Omari, Mikelle Smith. 1984. *From the Inside to the Outside: The Art of Bahian Candomblé*. Museum of Cultural History, Monograph Series no. 24. Los Angeles: University of California Press.

Opefeyitimi, Ayo. 1975. "Ìwuré: Yorubaland." *Journal of Religion in Africa* 4 (1): 15–30.

Ortiz, Renato. 1985. *Cultura brasileira e identidade nacional*. São Paulo: Brasiliense.

Pain, Evaldo. 1998. Personal interview with the author.

Palmer, Colin. 1998. "Defining and Studying the Modern African Diaspora." *Perspectives* 36 (1): 22–25.

Pareles, Jon. 2000. "Soaring above the Beat: Pride in African Roots." *New York Times*: E5, Aug. 31.

Parker, Richard D. 1991. *Bodies, Pleasures, and Passions: Sexual Culture in Contemporary Brazil*. Boston: Beacon.

Parrinder, Edward Geoffrey. 1961. *West African Religion: A Study of the Beliefs and Practices of Akan, Ewe, Yoruba, Ibo, and Kindred Peoples*. London: Epworth.

———. 1947. "Yoruba-Speaking People in Dahomey." *Africa* 17 (2): 122–29.

Patai, Daphne. 1988. *Brazilian Women Speak: Contemporary Life Stories*. New Brunswick and London: Rutgers University Press.

Peretti, Burton W. 1997. *Jazz in American Culture*. Chicago: Ivan R. Dee.

Perrone, Charles A. 1992. "Axé, Ijexá, Olodum: The Rise of Afro- and African Popular Currents in Brazilian Popular Music." *Afro-Hispanic Review* 11 (1–3): 42–50.

———. 1989. *Masters of Contemporary Brazilian Song: MPB, 1965–1985*. Austin: University of Texas Press.

Perrone, Charles, and Christopher Dunn, eds. 2001. *Brazilian Popular Music and Globalization*. Gainesville: University Press of Florida.

Pescatello, Ann, ed. 1975. *The African in Latin America*. New York: University Press of America.

Pessanha, Ricardo. 1991. "Margareth Menezes: She's Not the Girl from Ipanema." *The Beat* 10 (2): 46.

Peterson, Anna L., Manuel A. Vásquez, and Phillip J. Williams. 2001. *Christianity, Social Change, and Globalization in the Americas*. New Brunswick, NJ: Rutgers University Press.

Pierson, Donald. 1942. *Negroes in Brazil: A Study of Race Contact at Bahia*. Chicago: University Press of Chicago.

Pinto, Tiago de Oliveira. 1997. "Healing Process as Musical Drama: The Ebó Ceremony in Bahian Candomblé of Brazil." *World of Music* 39 (1): 11–33.

———. 1991a. *Capoeira, Samba, Candomblé: Afro-Brasilianische Musik im Recôncavo (Bahia)*. Berlin: Reimer.

———. 1991b. "Making Ritual Drama: Dance, Music, and Representation in Brazilian Candomblé and Umbanda." *World of Music* 33 (1): 70–87.

Pitango, Antônio. 1999. "Where Are the Blacks?" In *Black Brazil Culture, Identity and Social Mobilization*, ed. Larry Crook and Randal Johnson. 31–42. Los Angeles: UCLA Latin American Center Publications.

Póvoas, Ruy do Carmo. 1989. *A Linguagem do Candomblé Níveis Sociolingüístico de Integração Afro-Portuguesa*. Rio de Janeiro: José Olympio Editora.

Prandi, Reginald. 2004. "Afro-Brazilian Identity and Memory." *Diogenes* 51 (201): 35–43.

———. 1996. *Herdeiras do axé: sociologia das religiões afro-brasileiras*. São Paulo: Hucitec.

Prévos, André J. M. 1996. "Religious Words in Blues Lyrics and Titles: A Study." In *Saints and Sinners: Religion, Blues and (D)evil in African-American Music and Literature*, ed. Robert Sacré. 313–30. Liège, Belgium: Societé Liègeoise de Musicologie, Etudes and Editions.

Porter, Lewis. 1997. *Jazz: A Century of Change*. New York: Schirmer.

Querino, Manuel. 1938. *Costumes Africanos no Brasil, Biblioteca de Divulgação Cientifica*, XV. Rio de Janeiro: Civilização Brasileira.

Raboteau, Albert. 1978. *Slave Religion: The "Invisible Institution" in the Antebellum South*. New York: Oxford University Press.

Ramos, Arthur. 1935. *O Folclore Negro do Brasil*. Rio de Janeiro: Civilização Brasileira S.A.

———. 1934. *O Negro Brasileiro*. São Paulo: Companhia Editora Nacional.

Ramos, Ludinho. 1998. Personal interview with the author.

Raphael, Alison. 1990. "From Popular Culture to Microenterprise: The History of Brazilian Samba Schools." *Latin American Music Review* 11 (1): 73–83.

Rawley, James A. 1981. *The Trans-Atlantic Slave Trade*. New York: W. W. Norton.

Rex, John, and David Mason, eds. 1986. *Theories of Race and Ethnic Relations*. Cambridge: Cambridge University Press.

Rios, Marcelo. 1998, 1999, and 2002. Personal interviews with the author.

Risério, Antônio. 1999. "Carnival: The Color of Change." In *Black Brazil: Culture, Identity, and Social Mobilization*, ed. Larry Crook and Randal Johnson. 249–59. Los Angeles: UCLA Latin American Center Publications.

———. 1981. *Carnaval ijexá: Notas sobre afoxés e blocos do novo carnaval afro-baiano*. Salvador, Brazil: Corrupio.

Roberto, Lazaro. 1998. Personal interview with the author.

Roberts, John Storm. 1998. *Black Music of Two Worlds: African, Caribbean, Latin, and African–American Traditions*. 2nd ed. New York: Schirmer.

Rodrigues, João Jorge Santos. 1999. "Olodum and the Black Struggle in Brazil." In *Black Brazil: Culture, Identity, and Social Mobilization*, ed. Larry Crook and Randal Johnson. 43–51. Los Angeles: UCLA Latin American Center Publications.

———. 1996. *Olodum, Estrada da paixão*. Salvador, Brazil: Fundação Casa Jorge Amado.

Rodrigues, Raimundo Nina. 1988 [1905]. *Os Africanos no Brasil*. 7th ed. Brasília: Universidade de Brasília.

———. 1957 [1894]. *As Raças Humanas e a Responsibilidade Penal no Brasil*. Salvador, Brazil: Livraria Progesso.

———. 1935 [1900/1896]. *O Animismo Fetishista dos Negros Bahianos*. Rio: Civilização Brasileira.

———. 1897. "Illusões de Catechese no Brasil." *Revista Brazileira* 3 (9): 321–22.

Rosenburg, D. 1999. "Carlinhos Brown: The Naked Drum: A Brazilian Superstar Lets It All Hang Out." *Global Rhythm* 8: 28–29.

Rowe, William, and Vivian Schelling, eds. 1991. "From Slavery to Samba." In *Memory and Modernity: Popular Culture in Latin America*. 122–27. London and New York: Verso.

Salman, Ton, and Anke van Dam. 1996. *The Legacy of the Disinherited Popular Culture in Latin America: Modernity, Globalization, Hybridity, and Authenticity*. Amsterdam: CEDLA.

Sansone, Livio. 2001. "The Localization of Global Funk in Bahia and in Rio." In *Brazilian Popular Music and Globalization*, ed. Charles A. Perrone and Christopher Dunn. 136–60. Gainesville: University Press of Florida.

———. 1997. "The New Blacks from Bahia: Local and Global in Afro-Bahia." *Identities* 3 (4): 457–92.

———. 1996. "The Local and the Global in Today's Afro-Bahia." In *The Legacy of the Disinherited Popular Culture in Latin America: Modernity, Globalization, Hybridity, and Authenticity*, ed. Ton Salman and Anke van Dam. 197–219. Amsterdam: CEDLA.

Sansone, Livio, and Jocélino Teles dos Santos, eds. 1997. *Ritmos em trânsito: Sócio-antropologia da música baiana*. São Paulo: Dynamis Editorial; Salvador, Brazil: Programa Cor da Bahia (UFBA) e Projeto S.A.M.B.A.

Santos, Orlando J. 1975. *O Ebó No Culto aos Orixás*. Rio de Janeiro: Sindicato Nacional dos Editores des Livros.

Santos, Sonia. 1998, 1999, and 2002. Personal interviews with the author.

Santos, Jocélio Teles dos. 1995. *O Caboclo nos Candomblés da Bahia*. Salvador, Brazil: Sarah Letras.

Santos, Juana Elbein dos. 1976. *Os Nagô e a morte. Padê, Pàdè, Àsèsè e o culto Egun na Bahia*. Petrópolis, Brazil: Vozes.

Santos, Paulo dos. 1998. Personal interview with the author.

Schaeber, Petra. 1997. "Musica negra nos tempos de globalização: produção musical e management da indentidade étnica—o caso do Olodum." In *Ritmos em trânsito: sócio-antropologia da música baiana*, ed. Livio Sansone and Jocélino Teles dos Santos. 145–60. São Paulo: Dynamics Editorial; Salvador, Brazil: Programa Cor da Bahia (UFBA) e Projeto S.A.M.B.A.

Schechter, John M. 1999. *Music in Latin American Culture Regional Traditions*. New York: Schirmer.

Shapiro, Dolores J. 1995. "Blood, Oil, Honey, and Water: Symbolism in Spirit Possession Sects in Northeastern Brazil." *American Ethnologist* 22 (4): 828–47.

Silva, Vagner Gonçalves da. 1995. *Orixás da metrópole*. Petrópolis, Brazil: Vozes.

Silva, Edna Portela Oliveria. 1998. Personal interview with the author.

Silva, Vanda Machado da. 2000. Ilê Axé: vivência e Invenção pedagógica as crianças do Opô Afonjá. Salvador, Brazil: EDUFBA.

Silverstein, Leni. 1995. "The Celebration of Our Lord of the Good End: Changing State, Church, and Afro-Brazilian Relations in Bahia." In *The Brazilian Puzzle: Culture on the Borderlands of the Western World*, ed. David J. Hess and Roberto A. Da Matta. 134–51. New York: Columbia University Press.

Simmons, Victoria. 1999. "The Voice of Ginen: Drums in Haitian Religion, History, and Identity." In *Turn Up the Volume! A Celebration of African Music*, ed. Jacqueline Cogdell DjeDje. 158–69. Los Angeles: UCLA Fowler Museum of Cultural History.

Simpson, George E. 1980. *Yoruba Religion and Medicine in Ibadan*. Ibadan, Nigeria: Ibadan University Press.

Skidmore, Thomas E. 1994. *Black and White: Race and Nationality in Brazilian Thought*. 2nd ed. Durham, NC: Duke University Press.

———. 1985. "Race and Class in Brazil: Historical Perspectives." In *Race, Class and Power in Brazil*, ed. Pierre-Michel Fontaine. 11–24. Los Angeles: UCLA Center for Afro-American Studies.

Small, Christopher. 1987. *Music of the Common Tongue: Survival and Celebration in African-American Music*. Hanover and London: Wesleyan University Press.

Smith, Robert. 1976. *Kingdoms of the Yorubas*. London: Methuen.

Southern, Eileen. 1997. *The Music of Black Americans: A History*. 3rd ed. New York. W. W. Norton.

Spencer, Jon Michael. 1993. *Blues and Evil*. Knoxville: University of Tennessee Press.

———. 1989. "Philosophical Prolegomena to Theomusicological Thematizing of the Nonsacred." In *Black Sacred Music: A Journal of Theomusicology*. Special issue of *The Theology of American Popular Music* 3 (2): 1–16.

Spitzer, Nicholas Randolph. 1986. *Zydeco and Mardi Gras: Creole Identity and Performance Genres in Rural French Louisiana*. Ph.D. dissertation, University of Texas at Austin.

Stearns, Marshall W. 1958. *The Story of Jazz*. 2nd ed. New York and London: Oxford University Press.

Stephens, Robert W. 1984. "Soul: A Historical Reconstruction of Continuity and Change in Black Popular Music." *Black Perspectives in Music* 12 (1): 23–45.

Stewart, Gary. 1992. *Breakout Profiles in African Rhythm*. Chicago: University of Chicago Press.

Straw, William, et al., eds. 1995. *Popular Music Style and Identity*. Montreal: International Association for the Study of Popular Music.

Stokes, Martin. 1994. *Ethnicity, Identity, and Music: The Musical Construction of Place*. Oxford: Berg.

Stuckey, Sterling. 1987. *Slave Culture: Nationalist Theory and the Foundations of Black America*. New York: Oxford University Press.

Sulsbruck, Birger. 1982. *Latin-American Percussion: Rhythms and Rhythm Instruments from Cuba and Brazil*. Copenhagen: Den Rytmiske Aftenskoles Forlag/Edition Wilhem Hansen.

Sweet, James E. 2003. *Recreating African Culture, Kinship, and Religion in the Afro-Portuguese World 1441–1770*. Chapel Hill: University of North Carolina Press.

Tarasti, Eero. 1995. *Heitor Villa-Lobos: The Life and Works 1887–1959*. Jefferson, NC, and London: McFarland.

Telles, Edward. 2004. *Race in Another America: The Significance of Skin Color in Brazil*. Princeton: Princeton University Press.

Tenaille, Frank. 2002. *Music Is the Weapon of the Future: Fifty Years of African Phenomenon*. Chicago: Lawrence Hill.

Tenser, Michael. 2003. "José Maceda and the Paradoxes of Modern Composition." *Ethnomusicology* 47 (1): 93–120.

Terrell, Tom. 2004. "Carlinhos Brown and the Gift of the Drum." *Global Rhythm* 13: 28–29.

Terry, Richard. 1934. *Voodooism in Music*. London: Terry.

Thieme, Darius. 1969. *A Descriptive Catalog of Yoruba Musical Instruments*. Ph.D. dissertation, Catholic University of America.

———. 1940. "A Summary of African Music." *Africa* 40 (4): 359–62.

Thomas, Solomon. 2000. "Dueling Landscapes: Singing Places and Identities in Highland Bolivia." *Ethnomusicology* 44 (2): 257–80.

Thornton, John. 1998. *Africa and Africans in the Making of the Atlantic World, 1440–1800*. 2nd ed. Cambridge: Cambridge University Press.

Tirro, Frank. 1993. *Jazz: A History*. 2nd ed. New York and London: W. W. Norton.

Tinhorão, José Ramos. 1991. *Pequena História da música Popular: Da modinha à lambada*. 6th ed. São Paulo: Art Editora.

Trindade, Diamantino Fernandes. 1991. *Umbanda e sua história*. São Paulo: Icone Editora.

Turner, Lorenzo D. 1942. "Some Contacts of Brazilian Ex-Slaves with Nigeria West Africa." *Journal of Negro History* 27: 55–67.

Turner, Victor, and Edith Turner. 1982. "Religious Celebrations." In *Celebration Studies in Festivity and Ritual*, ed. Victor Turner, 201–19. Washington: Smithsonian Institution Press.

Valde, Elene. 1998. Personal interview with the author.

Vansina, Jan. 1962. "Long Distance Trade-Route in Central Africa." *Journal of African History* 3 (3): 369–90.

Vásquez, Manuel A., and Marie Friedman Marquardt. 2003. *Globalizing the Sacred: Religion across the Americas*. New Brunswick, NJ: Rutgers University Press.

Vega, Marta Moreno. 1999. "The Ancestral Sacred Creative Impulse of Africa and the African Diaspora: Àsé, the Nexus of the Black Global Aesthetic." *Lenox Avenue* 5: 45–57.

Veiga, Ericivaldo. 1996. "Rastafari e cultura em Salvador." In *Olodum, Estrada da paixão*, ed. João J. S. Rodrigues. 88–92. Salvador, Brazil: Fundação Casa de Jorge Amado.

Vélez, María Teresa. 2000. *Drumming for the Gods: The Life and Times of Felipe García Villamil, Santero, Palero, and Abakuá*. Philadelphia: Temple University Press.

Verger, Pierre. 2002 [1981]. *Orixás Deuses Iorubás na África e no novo Mundo*. Salvador, Brazil: Corrupio.

———. 1957. *Notes sur le culte des Orisa et Voduns* (Memoire, 51). Dakar: Institut Français d'Afrique Noire.

Vianna, Hermano. 1995. *O mistério do samba*. Rio de Janeiro: Editora UFRJ.

———. 1988. *O mundo funk carioca*. Rio de Janeiro: Jorge Zahar Editor.

Vidigal, Leo. 1996. "Bob Marley no Brasil." *Massive Reggae* 6: 12–15.

Vincente, Raymundo. 2002. Personal interview with the author.

Voeks, Robert A. 1997. *Sacred Leaves of Candomblé: African Magic, Medicine, and Religion in Brazil*. Austin: University of Texas Press.

Wafer, Jim. 1991. *The Taste of Blood: Spirit Possession in Brazilian Candomblé*. Philadelphia: University of Pennsylvania Press.

Walker, Shelia S. 1990. "Everyday and Esoteric Reality in Afro-Brazilian Candomblé." *History of Religion* 30 (2): 108–11.

Waterman, Richard A. 1952. "African Influence on the Music of the Americas." In *Acculturation in the Americas*, ed. Sol Tax. 207–18. Chicago: University of Chicago Press.

Waterman, Christopher A. 2000. "Yoruba Popular Music." In *The Garland Handbook of African Music*, ed. Ruth M. Stone, 169–85. New York: Garland.

———. 1992. *JùJú: A Social History and Ethnography of an African Popular Music*. Chicago: University of Chicago Press.

———. 1990. "Our Tradition Is a Very Modern Tradition: Popular Music and the Construction of Pan-Yoruba Identity." *Ethnomusicology* 34 (3): 367–79.

Weinoldt, Kristen. 1998. "Beauty and the Beat." *Brazzil* [June]: 45–47.

Wilcken, Lois, and Frizner Augustin. 1992. *The Drums of Vodou*. Tempe, AZ: White Cliffs Media.

Wilder, Amos Niven. 1976. *Theopoetic: Theology and the Religious Imagination*. Philadelphia: Fortress.

Williams, Patrick, and Laura Chrisman, eds. 1993. *Colonial Discourse and Post-Colonial Theory: A Reader*. Hemel Hempstead, UK: Harvester Wheatsheaf.

Wimberly, Fayette. 1998. "The Expansion of Afro-Bahian Religious Practices in Nineteenth–Century Cachoeira." In *Afro-Brazilian Culture and Politics, 1970 to 1990s*, ed. Hendrik Kraay. 74–87. New York: M. E. Sharpe.

Wright, Simon. 1992. *Villa-Lobos*. Oxford and New York: Oxford University Press.

Woodard, Josef. 2000. "Spheres." *JazzTimes* 30 (7): 87–88.

Yúdice, George. 1997. A Funkificação do Rio." In *Abalando os anos 90: Funk e hip–hop, Globalização, violência e estilo cultural*, ed. Micael Herschmann. 24–29. Rio de Janeiro: Rocco.

Index